The
BALERNO BRANCH
and
THE CALEY IN EDINBURGH

by
Donald Shaw

THE OAKWOOD PRESS

© Oakwood Press and D. Shaw, 1989

ISBN 0 85361 366 4

Printed by Nuffield Press, Cowley, Oxford
Typesetting by Gem Publishing Company, Brightwell, Wallingford, Oxon

In memory of my father.

Published by
The OAKWOOD PRESS
P.O.Box 122, Headington, Oxford.

Contents

Introduction

Today, when the heyday of the railways is receding further and further into the past, a generation has grown up without any recollection of what it was like to have a branch railway on one's doorstep. In the 1960s many lines, including the Balerno branch, were closed even to goods traffic.

Many more people cannot remember the time before 1943 when a regular passenger service was still operated on the line; and only a few can hark back to the age before 1923 when the Balerno branch was worked by the Caledonian Railway Company, one of the five major companies which had managed the Scottish railway system since the mid-19th century. It was the Caledonian company which built the line in the early 1870s, opening it to public traffic on 1st August, 1874.

It is hoped that this text can serve as a reminder of the Balerno branch both in its Caledonian days and under the later management of the London Midland and Scottish Railway Company (the LMS) and finally British Railways. It will, I hope, awaken nostalgia in older people while also interesting those of a newer vintage – even those who never knew the line in operation.

The branch was an unusually interesting one. It had a charm peculiar to those once-numerous branch lines tucked away in rural surroundings, far from the madding crowd, offering traveller and onlooker alike a succession of attractive sights (and sounds) in great variety. Yet it twisted and turned through its narrow valley for just six miles.

The text also recalls the Caledonian network in and around Edinburgh apart from the Balerno branch. The main line pre-dated the Balerno branch by 26 years; while the branches to Granton, Leith, Barnton and south Leith completed the system.

Donald Shaw
December 1988

Chapter One
The Railway in the Valley

The branch railway to Balerno, a village nestling on the fringes of the Pentland hills seven miles south-west of Edinburgh, was a picturesque and unusual line. In its six mile course – mostly along the winding valley of the Water of Leith – were to be found some of the most demanding operating conditions on any railway in the country. "A single line of bad curves and gradients" was the description of a Board of Trade officer investigating an accident in 1880.

The railway was built and initially operated by the Caledonian Railway Company. Opened in 1874, it was intended mainly to convey goods traffic to and from the many mills – notably the paper mills – which formerly lined the upper Water of Leith, but passenger train services were also provided from the very outset.

The branch was in fact a loop line, since a spur ran west from Balerno to rejoin the Caledonian main line, which opened in 1848 and ran between Edinburgh, Carlisle and Glasgow; and in its early years the whole length of the branch was traversed by trains giving a through service between Edinburgh and Midcalder station. By the 1880s, however, most trains were terminating at Balerno, 4¾ miles up the line – although they still had to run on empty to the main line junction 1¼ miles further west simply to turn round! (In 1899 a passing loop for engines was finally provided at Balerno station.)

The Balerno branch was the first of the Caledonian Railway Company's local lines in the Edinburgh area to carry passenger traffic, though it was not the first to be built; the Leith branch opened in 1864 but handled only goods traffic until 1879, and an earlier line to Granton (opened in 1861) never carried regular passenger traffic. A third passenger branch, to Barnton, opened in 1894.

The "Caley", as it was known, played a secondary role in Edinburgh's rail network, behind the North British Railway Company, whose main terminus was Waverley station. The Caley terminus was Princes Street station. Both companies operated lines throughout Scotland until 1923; in the west it was the Caley who held the stronger hand. Today, however, both are long gone, their existence in Edinburgh being commemorated only by the two great hotels which stand at each end of Princes Street; the Caledonian Hotel opened in 1903 above Princes Street station – now sadly no more – while the North British Hotel rises over Waverley station.

For such a short railway – and only a tiny part of a large company's network of lines – the Balerno branch achieved a rare distinction, of giving rise to two special classes of engine built specifically to operate over its demanding gradients and curves, first in the 1870s and then in 1899. A set of special carriages was also built for the branch.

Near Balerno there was a sub-branch running south-west for a quarter of a mile into a goods yard close under the village by Balerno bridge. This caused some controversy late last century when local residents began to resent the preferential treatment given to goods traffic while they had to walk round the yard to reach the inconveniently placed passenger station at Newmills. This was situated on the Balerno–Ravelrig section, a legacy of earlier years when nearly all trains travelled along this section to and from Midcalder. When services began mostly terminating at Balerno from the 1880s on, residents understandably hoped that trains might be run into the handier goods station. However, their appeals, noted in 1888, 1891 and 1895, were rejected by the Caley!

The Balerno branch left the main line a quarter of a mile west of Slateford station at Balerno Junction and just 2½ miles from Princes Street station. There were four stations along the branch, at Colinton after 1¼ miles, Juniper Green (2¼ miles), Currie (3½ miles), and Balerno (4¾ miles). The line climbed steadily all the way from Slateford with gradients of 1 in 50 common. On the section west of Balerno there was a ruling gradient of 1 in 70.

Passenger traffic on the branch lasted for 69 years until in 1943 local bus services were deemed to have made the line redundant. It remained open to goods traffic for a further 24 years, serving the surviving mills along the way before being completely closed in 1967. Since it was for the mills that the branch was originally built – indeed it was independently planned by the local mill-owners in 1864 before the Caley offered to assume full responsibility for it – it was perhaps appropriate that its last years were devoted to freight-only transport.

Today nearly all the mills have gone. The four villages have become, in effect, dormitory suburbs of Edinburgh; Colinton and Juniper Green were officially absorbed by the city in 1920 and Currie and Balerno in 1975 under regional reorganisation. All four, however, still preserve a sense of independence.

So prosperous are the villages of today that it is hard to believe the comments of a local laird, Sir William Gibson-Craig of Riccarton, who criticised the proposed Balerno railway in 1870 on the grounds that such "small and poor villages" could not provide any worthwhile traffic!

Much of the old railway track has now been incorporated into a pleasant footpath, the Water of Leith walkway, which looks and feels more like a traditional byway than a railway of recent use over which passed thousands upon thousands of wagons full of paper, coal, esparto and lime, and carriages well-laden with commuters and trippers. Gone too is that thriving world of mills making paper, grain, snuff and cloth, for the benefit of which the branch was built in the 1870s. There were so many of them that in places the railway could barely squeeze past; indeed several buildings had to be demolished.

Though one or two mills still survive, many more are ruinous or have disappeared without trace. Once, if you had stood in Colinton Dell where the walkway overlooks the remains of Redhall mill, you could have seen beside it Kates paper mill, a sprawling complex of buildings which in the 1880s was one of the biggest mills in the country; over 200 men, women and children worked there. It burnt down in 1890. Today the only clues to its existence are a cobbled track which leads down towards the river from the walkway – along which carts travelled between the mill and the special siding opened from the Balerno branch in 1879 – and also, across the river, the mill-lade where the water that drove the wheels of the mill once flowed. Redhall barley mill was served by the same lade.

That mill-lade, like another still to be seen at Kinleith, is a reminder of the debt local industry once owed to water-power and the unpretentious Water of Leith which provided it. It was with the river, indeed, and with the mills it served, that the story of the Balerno branch railway really begins.

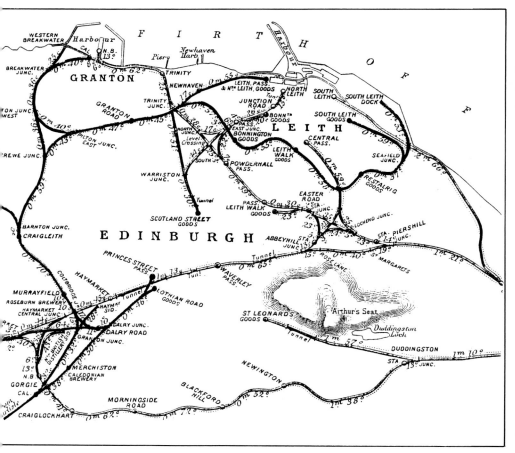

The 1917 Junction Diagram map of the area around Edinburgh.

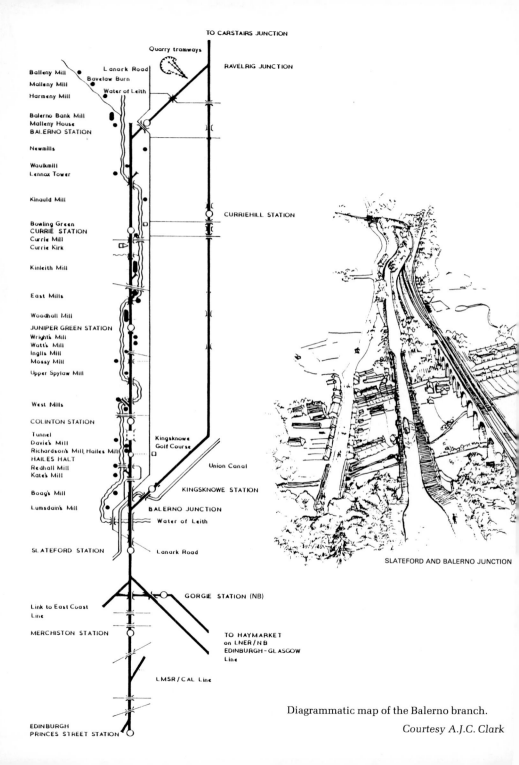

TO CARSTAIRS JUNCTION

Quarry tramways

RAVELRIG JUNCTION

Lanark Road
Balleny Mill
Malleny Mill
Bavelaw Burn
Harmeny Mill
Water of Leith

Balerno Bank Mill
Malleny House
BALERNO STATION

Newmills

Waulkmill
Lennox Tower

Kinauld Mill

Bowling Green
CURRIE STATION
Currie Mill
Currie Kirk

CURRIEHILL STATION

Kinleith Mill

East Mills

Woodhall Mill

JUNIPER GREEN STATION
Wright's Mill
Watt's Mill
Inglis Mill
Mossy Mill

Upper Spylaw Mill

West Mills

COLINTON STATION

Tunnel
Davie's Mill
Richardson's Mill, Hailes Mill
HAILES HALT
Redhall Mill
Kate's Mill

Kingsknowe
Golf Course

Union Canal

KINGSKNOWE STATION

Boag's Mill

Lumsdain's Mill
BALERNO JUNCTION
Water of Leith

SLATEFORD STATION
Lanark Road

GORGIE STATION (NB)

Link to East Coast
Line

MERCHISTON STATION

TO HAYMARKET
on LNER/NB
EDINBURGH-GLASGOW
Line

LMSR/CAL Line

EDINBURGH
PRINCES STREET STATION

SLATEFORD AND BALERNO JUNCTION

Diagrammatic map of the Balerno branch.

Courtesy A.J.C. Clark

Chapter Two

The Locality

The Water of Leith

The Water of Leith, despite being a modest river, not much wider than a stream in places, once turned the wheels of seventy mills in its course of a little over twenty miles.

In its lower reaches the Water of Leith is Edinburgh's river. Historic communities like the Dean village (formerly the Water of Leith village) grew up along its banks. At Canonmills the Scottish King David I gave the canons-regular of Holyrood Abbey permission to grind their corn in the 12th century.

"The Water of Leith is a most serviceable drudge, and is by no means spared," wrote the minister of Colinton parish, Lewis Balfour, in 1838. He also remarked that the usually placid stream was not always so peaceful, and that in 1832 three successive days of flooding had caused the bridge at Slateford to be swept away after standing for seventy years.

One of Lewis Balfour's grandchildren was Robert Louis Stevenson, who spent many childhood holidays at the manse in Colinton during the 1850s. The river flows past the manse, and one of Stevenson's earliest memories was of being carried across the garden one evening by his father to see it in a sudden flood.

But more often than not it was the lack of water in the river during dry spells that caused problems, for then there was insufficient power to turn the wheels of the numerous mills. In the 1840s and 1850s several compensation reservoirs were constructed to the south and west of Balerno in order to guarantee a regular flow of water.

The Water of Leith takes its place in Scottish law. In 1618, at a ceremony held in Edinburgh to define various standard weights and measures, a jug which by tradition held the widely-quoted "Linlithgow measure" was filled with water taken from the river; after the volume of the contents had been measured as 21 pints and a mutchkin, they were weighed and declared to be "Thrie punds and seaven unces of french Troys weght of clear runing water of the water of Leith."

"Clear running water" would have been hard to associate with the river until a few years ago, for it was notoriously polluted by paper mills and other works. In the late 19th century a special commission set about the task of cleaning up the river. As late as the 1960s, though, it remained a traditional dirty brown colour before, in recent years, returning to a clear stream in which the stock of trout with which it is annually supplied can flourish.

The source of the Water of Leith is over 1,300 ft high in the Pentland hills to the west of Balerno. As it passes Balerno the Bavelaw Burn tumbles in, and thereafter the river meanders along past Currie and Juniper Green towards Colinton, keeping close under the ridge of the Lanark Road and with the old track of the Balerno railway for company as well. Near Colinton the Water of Leith makes a sweeping curve to the south-east, running now under steeply wooded banks. A second curve encloses Colinton Kirk and the manse; here the river bank proved too steep for the railway to traverse and it dived through the only tunnel on the line.

Below Colinton is the dell, a beautiful secluded valley where it is hard to believe that the heart of Edinburgh is only three miles away. The railway ran high above the river on the northern bank, with trains entering and leaving the dell opposite Redhall House. Further on, one more broad curve brings the river round to Slateford where it emerges in flat terrain, to be crossed in quick succession by a road bridge, a canal aqueduct and a railway viaduct over which Balerno-bound trains ran just before leaving the main line for the branch at Balerno Junction.

The Water of Leith left a lasting impression on Robert Louis Stevenson, who later recalled happy childhood days spent beside it in his essay "The Manse":

> I have named, among many rivers that make music in my memory, that dirty Water of Leith. Often and often I desire to look upon it again; and the choice of a point of view is easy to me. It should be at a certain water-door, embowered in shrubbery. The river is there dammed back for the service of the flour-mill just below, so that it lies deep and darkling, and the sand slopes into brown obscurity with a glint of gold; and it has but newly been recruited by the borrowings of the snuff-mill just above, and these, tumbling merrily in, shake the pool to its black heart, fill it with drowsy eddies, and set the curded froth of many other mills solemnly steering to and fro upon the surface.

Mills

The mills to which Stevenson was referring were Richardson's snuff mill by Colinton bridge and William Walker's flour mill a little to the west, known from ancient days as Hailes mill or Hole mill. It was owned for a time by the Caledonian Railway Company who bought it in 1866 in connection with purchasing land for the Balerno branch railway.

Grain mills and snuff mills were common along the upper Water of Leith but it was particularly the numerous paper mills for which the district became famous and which gave the impetus to the making of the railway.

The first mills were recorded at Colinton and further up the river in mediaeval times. In 1226 the owner of a mill close to the church of "Halis" – Hailes being the ancient name for Colinton (the parish was known in the 18th century as "Hailes alias Collintone") – argued with the church rector about the mill's boundaries.

In 1376 a fulling mill (where cloth was scoured clean using fuller's earth) was recorded at "Ballernoch" (Balerno). The ruin of a 15th century grain mill is still visible at the north end of Currie bridge. Such grain mills, until about the 18th century, and often later, were the property of estate-owners who rented them out to a tenant who thereby acquired the right to grind the corn of all the inhabitants on the estate and deduct a portion of grain in payment. Moreover, local people were invariably obliged to repair the miller's dam and mill stream and to supply millstones as required. Consequently millers were not always the most popular of local characters!

In 1870 when the Balerno branch railway was finally authorised there were still ten water-driven grain mills scattered along the Water of Leith from Boag's mill (an ancient mill near where the railway was to enter the valley) to Leith-head west of Balerno. Already, though, their numbers were falling as steam power became more widely used. Most survived until this century but by 1925 only two were open, West mill at Colinton making porridge oats and employing steam power, and Inglis' grain mill at Juniper Green. The latter is still open though only for grain-drying.

The first paper mill to be recorded in the district was at Spylaw, between Colinton and Juniper Green, in 1682. It was the first of many as paper-making grew to be the main activity in the valley. By the mid-19th century there were seven well-established paper mills; as recently as the 1960s there were still four, employing several hundred workers.

In 1700 there were five paper mills on the whole river – two at Canon-mills, two at Dalry, and the Spylaw mill. During the 18th century others were gradually set up around Colinton, Woodhall and Balerno; Boag's mill was converted to make paper in 1717 and produced special paper for Bank of Scotland currency from 1735 on when required.

About 1790 two large new mills were erected near Currie. The Balerno paper mill (in fact it was nearer Currie than Balerno, at Kinauld) was opened by Nisbet and Macniven in 1788 while Kinleith paper mill was opened in 1792 by Robert Walker and Company.

A revealing account of the Balerno paper mill was given by the Minister of Currie in 1791. It was, he reported,

> ... perhaps the most extensive of any at present in the island; and, since its erection, it has increased the population of the parish about 200 souls. While the advantages of manufactures in Scotland cannot be too strongly inculcated, those, in particular, that employ the very young and the aged, ought to meet with every encouragement. The paper trade employs children from 10 or 12 years of age, a period when they can do nothing very laborious, and when their morals, from idleness and neglect, are very apt to be corrupted. It employs also, in some departments, people who are a good deal advanced in life, and after they can no longer work at those occupations without doors that require much exertion.

Paper was always made by hand, a laborious process, until the 1830s or so when steam-driven machines began to be installed.

In 1845 when the main Caledonian Railway was authorised there were seven paper mills operating along the river from Kates mill below Colinton to Balerno Bank mill on the Bavelaw Burn above Balerno. In between were the West mill at Colinton; Mossy mill a little further upstream; Woodhall mill at Juniper Green; Kinleith mill; and the Balerno mill at Kinauld.

Working conditions were still hard; the Currie minister noted in 1845 that among 150 people working at the three paper mills in his parish, and also at the yarn and sail-cloth factory on the Bavelaw, were "a good many women, and children under 14 years of age, who are employed in picking rags, finishing paper etc., and earn from 3s. 6d. to 6s. per week." The working week then was 60 hours and more.

At Kates mill, where 238 tons of paper were made in 1845 and fetched £16,750 or £70 a ton, there was a school room complete with a pair of thongs! Here the many children employed at the mill were expected to attend lessons after their hard day's toil; this was a common practice.

Among the costs of running Kates mill in 1845 were the sum of £6,260 spent on rags, the main raw material until esparto grass became widely used, and £3,249 in excise duty (until 1861 paper was liable to duty; its removal gave a great boost to the expansion of the industry). The owners of Kates mill, James Cowan and Co. of Penicuik, still paid rent to the Redhall estate in money and paper – £13 annually plus one ream!

Twenty years later, in 1865, when the Balerno branch railway was authorised to be built along the valley, primarily to serve the paper mills, there had been great expansion. Kates mill was the 20th-biggest in Scotland, making double its 1845 output; but Kinleith mill was easily the biggest of the local mills, and 5th-biggest in the country, with an output of 1300 tons a year.

A decade later, in 1876, thanks largely to the coming of the Balerno branch railway, Kinleith had developed again: 2000 tons of paper were produced, and fetched £88,000 or £44 a ton, being made by a workforce of nearly 300 who received from 6s. 8d. a day or £2 a week (for a millwright – a skilled man) to as little as 8d. a day or 4s. a week for assistant cutters and calenders. The 88 rag and esparto sorters, mostly women, were paid 1s. 4s. a day or 8s. a week, the week being 60 hours.

Three local mills closed about the turn of the century, but three of the others survived until recently, the first to go being Kinleith mill in 1966 – a closure which effectively killed off the goods service on the Balerno branch – followed by Mossy mill in 1972 and Woodhall mill in 1984.

Balerno Bank paper mill is still open today, however, under the ownership of DRG Transcript, a major nationwide producer. Known now as Balerno paper mill, it is the last representative of an industry to which the local area has owed so much of its development.

When the Balerno branch railway was originally promoted in 1864, it had the support of the owners of the twenty-two mills which lined the banks of the Water of Leith above Slateford.

Of those twenty-two mills no fewer than five were snuff mills. Boag's mill, where paper-making had been abandoned, was at the eastern end of the planned line near Slateford; Richardson's mill, familiar to Robert Louis Stevenson, stood by Colinton brig below the kirk; Upper Spylaw mill was hidden away between Colinton and Juniper Green across the river from Mossy mill; the two snuff mills highest up the river were Woodhall Bank mill at Juniper Green and, a little to the west, East Mills snuff mill, both run by members of the Watt family.

By the time the railway opened in 1874 however only the last three were still producing snuff. Boag's mill had switched products yet again after a fire in 1867; the mill was rebuilt to make meal and spices. Richardson's mill at Colinton was replaced in 1870 by another paper mill.

The first snuff mill in the district was set up in 1749 at East Mills at a time when the taking of snuff was increasing in popularity. Even the queen of George III took it, acquiring for herself the nickname "Snuffy Charlotte"! In the mid-18th century tobacco stalks – from which snuff is ground – were a major smuggling item along with tea and spirits.

The last snuff mill to survive on the Water of Leith (and in Scotland) was the Juniper Green mill, which closed only in 1940. There are only a handful of mills still turning out snuff today in Britain, thanks to the decline in the popularity of this once-common habit.

Over the years there have been other sorts of mills working by the riverside. The flax mill at Malleny Mills on the Bavelaw Burn employed a hundred or so flax dressers and yarn bleachers in the 19th century. Woodflour was produced at Redhall mill in Colinton Dell to make linoleum and other products between 1905 and 1967; this was formerly a barley mill. Other old mills were similarly converted to new purposes, such as the one-time Byrnie paper mill on the Bavelaw Burn which was until quite recently a saw mill.

But nearly all the once-numerous mills of the district have now disappeared. Many were destroyed by fire, not surprisingly, considering what dusty places they were. The cost of rebuilding them became increasingly prohibitive from the late 19th century on, as the advent of alternative sources of power – first steam, then electricity – meant that the old waterside sites, often awkwardly placed, were no longer desirable or needed.

The Villages

In the 1870s, when the Balerno branch railway opened, some 3600 people lived along its course from Boag's mill and Redhall quarry in the east to the farm communities west of Balerno.

The biggest of the villages was Juniper Green with over 700 residents. That was a remarkable total because until the late 18th century Juniper Green had been nothing more than a farm set in the middle of moorland known as Currie Muir. The Statistical Account of 1791 contained the following explanation of its name written by the minister of Colinton Parish:

> The lands belonging to the farm called Juniper Green were, formerly, moorish grounds covered with juniper. They are now inclosed and cultivated, nor is there a plant of juniper to be seen.

The minister, Dr John Walker, was also the Professor of Natural History at Edinburgh University so he no doubt knew his facts!

Juniper Green blossomed as a village in the 19th century for several reasons. One or two mills were set up, though in fact these were not large affairs: Woodhall grain mill and Woodhall paper mill were to east and west with Wright's meal mill and Woodhall Bank snuff mill in between. The paper mill dated from the 18th century. But more importantly Juniper Green became a popular resort with visitors, some of whom built cottages and villas. A good road transport service helped to attract them.

By 1831 there were 338 inhabitants and this total rose to 716 in 1871. The opening of the Balerno branch railway encouraged even more growth after 1874; by 1901 Juniper Green had a population of 1607.

In the 1870s the next-biggest village after Juniper Green was Balerno with a population of 500, followed by Currie with 250 and Colinton with 200. The latter was soon to develop rapidly, growing to a population of 782 in 1901 due in large part to the railway which allowed commuters to travel easily in and out of Edinburgh every day.

But before the advent of the railway Colinton was very much the smallest of the villages, being little more than a cluster of cottages around the ancient brig over the Water of Leith. The church and the manse stood across the river, with Hailes mill and the snuff mill (until 1870) to each side of the manse. The little village was tucked away from the world with steep banks on all sides. Above, to the east, was Colinton House with the ruins of Colinton Castle, the home of the Foulis family from 1519 to 1800. The Foulises had at one time been by far the biggest landowners in the area with estates stretching from Craiglockhart east of Colinton to Pilmuir and Baads west of Balerno. By the 1870s they retained only Woodhall at Juniper Green.

Colinton church was the centre of an ancient parish which, until the beginning of the present century, also took in Juniper Green and Slateford. Juniper Green did not have its own Church of Scotland until 1892 despite being so much bigger than Colinton, though it did have a Free Church from the 1840s. The original kirk at Colinton was dedicated as long ago as 1243 when the parish was known as "Halis", which later evolved to Hailes.

A century ago other sizeable communities existed locally which were then considered quite separate from the four main villages but would nowadays be included in one or other. There being little more than a mile between each village, they all today run into each other thanks to the spread of housing. But in the late 19th century a mile was a long way. For example, at the junction of the present Gillespie Road with Lanark Road, between Colinton and Juniper Green, was for many years the separate hamlet of Curriemuirend which in 1871 was listed as having a population of 84.

Other communities had grown up round mills. In 1871, 77 people lived at Kates mill in Colinton Dell, only a stone's throw downstream from Colinton but independent of it. There were more communities of mill-workers and their families at West Mills, Kinleith paper mill, Balerno mill between Currie and Balerno, where workers lived in houses known as Red Row and Old Distillery and also at Malleny Mills above Balerno.

Currie village, like Colinton, was for many years a mere scattering of cottages round a church and a bridge. But, unlike Colinton, Currie enjoys a lofty and exposed situation, with views over the Forth to distant Fife and beyond.

Currie's population in 1871 was 249. There was a small knot of cottages to the immediate west of the church, manse and school, while to the north of the river was the other half of the village bordering the Lanark Road. As well as the toll house and Society Hall, built in 1823 by the local Friendly Society, this part of the village comprised chiefly the three old farmhouses of Easter, Mid and Wester Currie, all close together. Wester Currie became the Riccarton Arms Hotel in 1874 while Mid and Easter Currie remained farms until recently.

Currie parish formerly took in the village of Balerno as well as Currie. Its church was originally dedicated in 1296, not long after Colinton's, though the present building is of course much more recent and dates from 1785 – shortly after the present kirk at Colinton was erected in 1771, though both have since been altered. Currie parish was originally known as Keldeleth, which later evolved into Killeith and (today) Kinleith.

Since the late 18th century Currie village has had no mills in its immediate vicinity, though until then an ancient grain mill – the "mylne of Currie" – stood at the north end of the bridge (its ruin is still visible). By the 19th century the only mills near Currie were half a mile distant to east and west – Kinleith paper mill and Balerno paper mill respectively.

The village of Balerno, however, was very much a mill village, hardly surprising in view of its situation in the angle of the Water of Leith and its tributary the Bavelaw Burn. By the 18th century there were several paper mills established locally (the Royal mill at Larch Grove, Helen Logan's mill at Harmeny) and more employment was created with the opening in 1805 of Balerno Bank mill, and about the same time a flax mill and spinning mill – all of these mills except the Royal being established on the Bavelaw Burn.

Quarrying was another local industry. In the 1840s work on the new reservoirs at Bavelaw above Balerno also boosted the population; for some of the men (mostly Irish) who worked on the scheme settled in the district afterwards, marrying local girls.

Curiously, the estate of Bavelaw, where the reservoirs were built, belonged to Penicuik parish and not Currie parish – the parent church being some miles away to the south, on the other side of the Pentland hills.

Midway between Currie and Balerno, overlooking the track of the Balerno branch from its southern side, stands the ruin of Lennox Tower. Though mystery surrounds its origin, the Earl of Lennox did own land hereabouts in the 16th century. By tradition the tower was an occasional residence of Mary, Queen of Scots, in the 1560s – and was held by the Queen's Party during the civil war of 1572 at the same time as Curriehill Castle nearby was held by the King's Party, the supporters of the claim of the infant James VI.

A major factor in the evolution of the whole district between Balerno and Colinton in the last 200 years has been the development of transport. Vital to the trade of the mills and quarries and farms, the opening of the Lanark–Edinburgh road in 1790, the Union Canal in 1822, the Caledonian Railway in 1848 (providing Currie with a station) and the Balerno branch railway in 1874 (giving each village a station) were important breakthroughs in turn. From about the middle of the 19th century improved means of communication encouraged not just commercial traffic but residential traffic also; commuters were drawn to the area.

However, not every section of the district prospered during these years. A drift from the land due to the improvement in farming methods and the enclosures of the 18th century resulted in some well-established communities disappearing. Caldhame hamlet, south of Currie, was one; while the ancient farming and milling community of Bonaly above Colinton was cleared away in 1810 by Henry (later Lord) Cockburn as part of his plans for a new estate, including Bonaly Tower.

The 19th century also witnessed a reduction in the power and extent of the great estates. Redhall, Colinton, Spylaw, Woodhall and Malleny lay to the south of the river while Hailes, Baberton, Riccarton, Curriehill and Ravelrig were to the north. These estates had for centuries accounted for nearly all the land in and around the villages.

Among local figures who have achieved national prominence mainly in political, legal and military life were the Foulises, many of whom were both

MPs and judges between the 16th and 18th centuries, and the Gibson-Craigs of Riccarton, prominent Whigs in the 19th century. The military tradition was at its peak in the early 1800s when local lairds included General Scott of Malleny, Admiral Christie of Baberton and Admiral Inglis of Redhall.

The Hills

The Pentland Hills form an imposing southern backdrop to the Water of Leith valley from Colinton to the west. They extend altogether for some twenty miles from the easternmost tops, Caerketton and Allermuir (a little to the east of Colinton), into Lanarkshire. The highest point is Scald Law to the south of Currie (but hidden from it by Black Hill) at 1,898 ft.

Allermuir Hill is so close to Edinburgh that it forms part of the city boundary, 1,617 ft high. Below it to the north is Swanston village, part of Colinton parish, where Robert Louis Stevenson spent many days in his youth after 1867 when the family first rented Swanston cottage. The Pentlands were Stevenson's "hills of home" which he loved to explore, often in the company of John Todd the shepherd.

Access to the hills is easy from Colinton, Currie and Balerno, a circumstance which used to make the trains running along the Balerno branch railway especially popular at weekends.

One of the most pleasant approaches to the Pentlands is from Colinton by Bonaly Tower. This handsome building was erected by another famous Colinton resident, Lord Cockburn, who was both a judge and an author.

The Pentland hills remain today largely as they were created; no road, other than one or two ancient drove-roads, has ever crossed them. One of those tracks formerly used by drovers taking their cattle between Scotland and England was the Cauldstane Slap, running from Little Vantage west of Balerno to West Linton to the south. It passes high between the West and East Cairn Hills, in countryside close by the source of the Water of the Leith, where the terrain is bleak, heathery moorland and the only residents grouse and whaup. But there is real peace and beauty in this remote setting.

It was here, in the 17th century, that the persecuted presbyterians known as the Covenanters came to worship in open-air meetings or conventicles. Several miles west is the Covenanter's Grave, marking the resting-place of a fugitive from the battle of Rullion Green on 28th September, 1666; the battle ended the Pentland Rising, as it became known, during which presbyterians marched to Edinburgh from the south-west of Scotland, looking for support for their cause. Finding none, they turned back at Colinton but got only as far as Rullion Green to the south of the hills beyond Swanston when they were intercepted by a government army under James Dalyell; he had cut across from Currie to bar the way. Those of the "rebels" who were not killed were later harshly dealt with.

Near the north end of the Cauldstane Slap is Temple House, a legacy of the days when the ancient orders of Knights Templars and Hospitallers had land in the district. The Hospitaller knights were based at Torphichen, a little north-west, and the Templars at the present-day village of Temple, south-east across the hills. Late last century Templar relics were unearthed in Currie church-yard; they are today preserved within the church.

Chapter Three

Early Transport

Roads

Until the Balerno branch railway opened in 1874 most transport, both of people and of goods, was by road. Before 1822 it was exclusively by road, but that year the Union Canal opened, passing by the district a mile and a half to the north, and began to attract some of the traffic to and from local mills. From 1848 the main Caledonian Railway also ran nearby, but still a mile or so away, so the intervening distance had to be covered by road.

Two main highways have traditionally served the four local villages. The Lanark Road is the link between Juniper Green, Currie and Balerno and Edinburgh (though Balerno used to be a little detached from it) while the Colinton Road has always been a separate thoroughfare. Nearer Edinburgh the Lanark Road is known as the Slateford Road.

In the second half of the 18th century the Lanark Road was progressively built up from a mere track to a proper road. Thus in 1758 a Slateford man was appointed to maintain it from Fountainbridge (then a village to the immediate west of Edinburgh) as far as "that part of the road called Juniper Green opposite to Woodhall where the new made road ends."

A bridge was built at Slateford in 1764. By 1790 the whole Lanark Road had been completed and for the next fifty years it was a busy through route connecting the capital with the cotton mills of New Lanark. However, the opening of the Caledonian Railway in 1848 effectively turned the road west of Balerno into a backwater. This is the 20 mile section known as the "Lang Whang" which runs across high, bleak moorland to Carnwath.

Between the mid-18th century and the 1880s the Lanark Road, Colinton Road and other main roads were the responsibility of "Turnpike Trusts", committees of landowners who were authorised to set up toll-bars and rent them out to independent toll-collectors, using the rent received to maintain the roads. An Act of 1751 designated eight district trusts around Edinburgh, one being the Slateford trust who were to manage the Lanark Road. The trustees quickly set up a toll-bar at Tynecastle Braehead at the top of what is now Ardmillan Terrace.

Travellers in the 18th century reached Edinburgh from the Lanark/Slateford Road by continuing along the present Dundee Street and through Fountainbridge, the West Port and the Grassmarket. Users of the Calder/Gorgie Road further north joined the Slateford Road at the top of Henderson Terrace. The more common route to town today is by Ardmillan Terrace and Dalry Road, but these were built only in 1806.

But in those days of course, Edinburgh was still the "old town" and Princes Street nothing more than a track known as the Lang Dykes. The building of the new town in the late 18th century changed all that.

In 1773 Slateford Trust erected a second toll-bar on the Lanark Road near Whelpside west of Balerno, known as either Craigmill or Ravelrig Toll.

In 1791 the minister of Currie parish wrote in glowing terms of the now-complete Lanark Road. He remarked that, thanks to its improvement, it was

Tolls, commencing 25th August 1809.

I. Stage Coach, Long Coach, &c. drawn by Two Horses, and licensed or employed as under.

	s	d
1. Six Inside passengers, or any smaller number, & no outside passengers	1	
2. With any outside Passengers	1	8
3. Each additional Inside passenger		2
4. Each Outside passenger (exclusive of Coachman & Guard) over and above the preceding rates		1

II. Stage Coach, Long Coach &c. drawn by Three or More horses, and licensed or employed as under.

	s	d
1. Four Inside and Two Outside passengers or any smaller number	2	
2. Four Inside, and not exceeding five outside passengers	3	
3. Four Inside, and above five outside passengers	5	
4. Six Inside, and not more than two Outside passengers	2	4
5. Six Inside, and not exceeding five outside passengers	3	8
6. Six Inside, and above five outside passengers	6	
7. Eight Inside, and not exceeding two outside passengers	3	8
8. Eight Inside, and not exceeding five outside passengers	4	4
9. Eight Inside, and above five outside passengers	7	
10. Ten Inside, & not exceeding two outside passengers	4	
11. Ten Inside, and not exceeding five outside passengers	5	
12. Ten Inside, and above five outside passengers	8	
13. Above Ten Inside, and not exceeding two outside passengers	4	8
14. Above Ten Inside, & not exceeding five outside passengers	5	4
15. Above Ten Inside, and above five outside passengers	9	
16. Each Outside passenger (exclusive of Coachman and Guard) over and above the preceding rates		1

Note— If any person be convicted of having concealed the number of Inside or Outside passengers, he shall on each conviction, be adjudged to pay the highest Rate of Toll on such carriage for one Week backwards from the date of the default.

The table of tolls fixed by the Slateford Turnpike Trust for 1809–10.

III. Coach, Chaise &c with 1. Horse &c _____ 4

                                2. Horses &c _____ 9

                                3. _____ 1 3

                                4 or 5 _____ 1 6

                                6 or more _____ 2 3

IV. Waggons &c with More than Two Wheels

	Manure	Stones	Other articles
Drawn by 1. Horse &c	1	6	3½
2. Horses &c	1½	8	4
3	6	3	1 10½
4	8	4	2 6
5	1 9	6	3 9
6 or more	2	8	5 -
If on broad wheels	One half	One half	One half
Manure not for Sale or bought &c	No Toll		

V. Cart &c with Two Wheels

	Manure	Stones	Other
1st For 26 Cwt & under. { 1st 1 Horse &c	1	6	3½
{ 2d 2 or more Horses	1½	8	5
2 Above 26 Cwt & under 34 Cwt	2¼	1	7½
3 For 34 Cwt & upwards	3	1 4	10
4 If on broad wheels	One half	One half	One half
5 Cart No. 2 with Manure on broad wheels is chargeable with	1½		
6 Manure not bought or for Sale &c	No Toll		

VI. Saddled horse _____ 2

VII. Horse not Drawing _____ 1

VIII. Ass _____ ½

IX. Oxen or Neat Cattle per Score, & so proportionally.

    1. From 1st February to 1st October _____ 1 -

    2. From 1 October to 1st February _____ 1 3

X. Calves, Hogs, Sheep, Lambs, Goats per Score & so proportionally _____ ½

XI. The Trustees may diminish all or any of these Rates and for any period. Whenever that power is exercised it will be indicated by rectified Tables at the bars where it is to operate.

Courtesy, Keeper of the Records of
Scotland (Ref. CO2/4/7)

now possible for a single cart to carry 150 stones of hay in the charge of two horses and one man, where forty years earlier fifteen horses and seven men had been needed to transport the same load, as carts became bogged down in the mud if too heavily laden.

Clearly the road was of great importance to farming and industry. It also permitted a passenger service to be operated. The minister reported that two stage coaches now ran twice a week between Edinburgh and Lanark.

But the road evidently also encouraged the growth of trade in some items against which the minister warned:

> Till within these few years the people of this parish were sober, industrious and economical. The vices of the capital, however, are beginning to spread fast among them, and the introduction of those baneful articles to the poor, tea and whisky, will soon produce that corruption of morals and debility of constitution which are already so severely felt in many parishes, and which must soon materially injure the real strength and population of Scotland.

Colinton village was linked to Edinburgh by its own road, which followed the same route as today, merging with the road to Fairmilehead and Biggar near Boroughmuirhead. From 1751 on, Colinton Road was managed by the Wrights Houses Turnpike Trust whose major concern was in fact the Biggar Road. Travellers to and from Colinton paid their toll dues at the toll-bar set up near Tollcross close to Edinburgh and known as Wrights Houses bar (from the old mansion nearby, Wrychtishousis).

Colinton Road was deemed by the new Trust a "cross road", a status less important than a full turnpike road. It was then evidently badly neglected, for local residents along the way complained frequently over the next fifty years about its state. They were angered because, before 1751, Colinton Road had been known as a "radical road" and was allocated a grant from customs revenue for its upkeep, whereas now the Wrights Houses trustees were ignoring it in favour of the Biggar Road.

Protests came to a head in 1783 when various Colinton residents including Sir James Foulis lobbied the Midlothian Turnpike Trust – an overall supervisory body – to bring the Wrights Houses trustees to heel. Sir James emphasised the importance of Colinton Road by recalling that it "had existed for at least one hundred years previous to building Slateford bridge as the principal line of communication between the metropolis and those parts of the west country that now chiefly travel the Slateford Road."

The upshot was that an annual grant of £36 was ordered to be paid by the Wrights Houses trust to the users of Colinton Road to maintain it.

But even after this there were protests. In 1801 local residents complained that the annual grant, which had meantime been raised to £50, should be further increased to £90; Wrights Houses Trust could easily afford this thanks to the extra tolls they were receiving due to "the number of mills that have been erected and set agoing in the Colinton road district within the last three years."

The Trust reacted testily by refusing a bigger grant and by taking back full control of Colinton Road themselves! Thereafter they looked after it (or not, as the case may be!) until the end of the turnpike system in 1882.

Turnpike toll dues varied in amount according to the type of transport involved – carts, coaches and so on – and the size and nature of their load, whether human or freight. (See *table, pages 18–19.*)

Some traffic was exempt. For instance, until 1790 carts carrying stone from quarries paid no dues. But, for those carters or coach operators not so exempted, there were stiff penalties for any who tried to evade paying dues by slipping through fields or along side roads. To stop such evasions, additional toll-bars known as check-bars were often erected on these side roads.

There was a third main highway serving the district around Colinton in the old days. This was the road from Colinton to Fairmilehead, two miles south-east, along which coal was brought from collieries at Loanhead, Polton and Carlops. Known in fact as the "Great Coal Road", it was elevated from a parish road to a full turnpike road under the care of the Wrights Houses Trust in 1811, when a toll-bar was erected at Fairmilehead.

The Union Canal

It was partly in order to secure a cheap supply of coal to Edinburgh that the Union Canal between there and Falkirk was promoted in 1814, 1815 and (successfully) in 1817. The canal was to link with the Forth and Clyde Canal which was already in operation between Falkirk and Glasgow, having opened in 1787.

The new canal was, however, roundly opposed by the various Turnpike Trusts around Edinburgh, who feared a resultant loss of road traffic and toll revenue. This was a serious personal threat to many trustees who had borrowed money on the security of tolls for use in road maintenance.

In late 1816, when the Union Canal Bill was submitted to Parliament for a third time, the Midlothian Road Trust was moved to declare:

> If the subscribers to the Union Canal succeed in their intended application, other canals will spring up in every direction, and thus, while the public are amused with the speculation of the immense advantages – public and private – that are to arise from these canals, the roads through the country which form the radical source of all improvement will be neglected and the greatest mischief will be done.

Their protests were unavailing, however. The Union Canal was authorised in June 1817 and work began on constructing it at the Edinburgh terminus just off Lothian Road (where the ABC cinema now stands) in March 1818.

In fact the canal was one of the last to be built, for the first railways were by now just round the corner.

During the making of the canal (which proceeded from east to west) a special quarry was opened at Balerno, to the east of the Harlaw Road, from which stone was taken for use in the masonry of canal bridges. The Slateford road trustees were alerted to the possibility of stone-carts slipping through their net and set up a temporary toll-bar at Malleny to catch the dues from these carts!

Meanwhile, pending the opening of the canal, all passenger and goods traffic continued to be confined to the roads. On the Lanark Road there were still, in 1816, two stages running each way twice a week; one firm ran a coach from the Grassmarket in Edinburgh to Lanark on Tuesdays and Fridays, leaving at 7 am to return the following day, while another firm also operated a coach on these days but leaving from the High Street at 10 am. Thus residents of Juniper Green, Currie and Balerno could travel to town on these coaches on Wednesdays and Saturdays.

Coach services were operated by private individuals, often inn-keepers. On longer routes they would co-ordinate with other operators, each handling a section of route; horses would be changed at each stopover – hence inns were also known as change-houses. On Lanark Road there were such inns at Currie (at the brig-end), Boll o'bere, House o'Muir and Cairns castle, (the latter after 1823).

The Union Canal opened on 4th May, 1822. It ran at a steady height of 242 ft for 31½ miles from the Edinburgh terminus at Port Hopetoun to Falkirk where a series of locks connected it to the Forth and Clyde Canal. The final cost, £462,000, was nearly twice the original budget, as a result of which the canal shareholders found themselves heavily in debt.

Though passing over a mile to the north of Colinton, Juniper Green, Currie and Balerno, the Union Canal was still of great importance to the mills of the district. At Stoneyport, a loading area to the west of Slateford, paper from Kates mill was dispatched and raw materials and coal imported. As the name suggests, the largest traffic here was in stone brought from the nearby Redhall Quarry. A little further west, Hailes Quarry also had its own loading stage.

When Balerno paper mill was advertised for sale in 1826 it was stated that the mill was "conveniently situated on the Water of Leith, six miles from Edinburgh, and one and a half from the Union Canal."

The Advent of the Railway

The Union Canal's opening duly removed some of the traffic from the roads west of Edinburgh; and no sooner had it done so than a new threat to road transport loomed in the shape of the first railways. In November 1824 newspaper advertisements invited subscriptions for a "rail-way" between Edinburgh and Dalkeith. The line was authorised in 1826, opened in 1831 and carried its first passengers in 1832, all trains being horse-drawn.

The first locomotive-hauled trains in Scotland ran on the Glasgow and Garnkirk Railway in 1831. Thereafter further lines were gradually planned and opened although the establishment of a real network of railways happened only during the 1840s.

On the roads too there were innovations, albeit short-lived; steam-coaches were tried out in a number of locations in the 1820s and 1830s including the Calder Road north of Currie. On 27th March, 1834 William Gibson-Craig of Riccarton protested that these coaches had been endangering lives by inducing panic in passing horses! In fact they were soon withdrawn everywhere, after being opposed on the grounds of their perceived danger, and also because they were handicapped by being restricted in speed for the same reason.

In 1831 the Slateford District Turnpike Trust opened two new toll-bars at Currie and at Little Vantage six miles further west; the toll-bar at Ravelrig was now closed. The Trust's intention was simply to increase their revenue by having three toll-bars instead of two. The Currie toll-house was only quite recently demolished.

The Union Canal experienced its heyday between the mid-1830s and 1841 when first of all a service of "swift passenger boats" attracted many customers (over 127,000 in 1835, when six boats plied daily all the way between Edinburgh and Glasgow at through fares of 2s. 6d. or 3s. 6d.) and then in 1841 a joint service was operated with railways. This involved passengers travelling by train between Glasgow and Causewayend Basin on the canal west of Linlithgow along three different railways with end-on connections, including the recently-opened Slamannan Railway; canal barges operated over the remaining distance between Causewayend and Edinburgh.

But the opening in 1842 of the Edinburgh and Glasgow Railway dealt a major blow both to canal transport and road transport. The Slamannan Railway was extended to link with it; and the Union Canal, thus left in the lurch, joined forces with the Forth and Clyde Canal to fight a desperate battle for a share of traffic.

For most of the 1840s in fact a three-cornered fight between the rival road, canal and railway interests went on, affecting the profits of all of them. Many stage coach operators protested about the size of the toll dues they were forced to pay and were given reductions to allow them to stay in business.

Thus on 7th March, 1843 John Croall and Company, who ran numerous services in the Edinburgh area, were granted reduced toll rates for their coaches running between Edinburgh and Lanark via Currie and also for coaches on a new route which they planned to operate between Balerno and Edinburgh.

There was another coach operator providing a service along the Lanark Road at this time between Edinburgh and his inn at Little Vantage; James Waterston had run his coach three times a week in summer and once a week in winter since the late 1830s and in May 1844 began operating a daily service. His request for reduced rates of toll was granted in November.

But Waterston and Croall received bad news in December 1844 when it was announced that the Caledonian Railway was to be built nearby. Nor were the local turnpike trustees best pleased, and on 17th February, 1845 they formally opposed the project, but without success; the line was authorised in July.

In 1847 James Waterston was struggling to maintain his stage coach service. He reported that the coach had in fact been off the road for six months due to the high cost of feeding his horses, but that if the road trustees would further cut his rates of toll from 6d. to 4½d. per horse he might restart it.

The Caledonian Railway opened on 15th February, 1848. Its arrival, though a significant transport development, still did not fully satisfy the requirements of the villagers between Colinton and Balerno, for the nearest stations (Currie and Kingsknowe) were some way off. Yet the railway could not fail to damage road transport business; coach services ceased shortly afterwards.

Before the railway opened, the local road trustees erected check-bars on the roads approaching Currie and Kingsknowe stations, thus ensuring that customers of the railway also supported their roads! The trustees even tried, without luck, to persuade the Caley to foot the bill for these check-bars!

On the Union Canal passenger services were withdrawn after the Caledonian Railway opened, though for a short time a local firm operated boats between Edinburgh and Broxburn. The canal was purchased in 1849 by its erstwhile competitor the Edinburgh and Glasgow Railway, who thereafter attempted to attract goods traffic to it as best they could. The North British Railway Company became the canal's owners in 1865 after merging with the E&GR.

The canal remained open to commercial traffic until well into this century, still dealing with 117,735 tons of goods in 1907, but finally ceased operations in 1933. Before that, in 1921, the Edinburgh basins, Port Hopetoun and Port Hamilton had been filled in. But the great aqueduct at Slateford remains as a monument to a time not so long ago when inland waterways were the most efficient means of transport known. It adds to one's appreciation of the aqueduct, with its eight handsome arches and a span of 500 ft, to reflect that, like the neighbouring railway viaduct, it was built entirely by hand.

Chapter Four
The Caledonian Railway

The Caledonian Railway which ran from Carlisle to Edinburgh and Glasgow was the trunk line from which the Balerno branch, as it were, later grew. It opened throughout on 15th February, 1848, having originally been conceived in 1836.

That year the Directors of the Grand Junction Railway, which had just opened between Birmingham and Lancashire, turned their thoughts to wondering whether a through railway between London and Glasgow might be feasible. They appointed an engineer, Joseph Locke, to go and survey possible routes for such a line in Scotland.

Locke looked at two lines, one running through Annandale and involving a daunting gradient north of Beattock village, the other through Nithsdale further to the west. He opted for the latter. He estimated that a railway 417 miles long between London and Glasgow was feasible, over which trains could travel in about 21 hours. ("The mail", he noted, "now occupies more than double, and the ordinary stages nearly treble that time.")

Locke also had an eye to the value of traffic to and from Edinburgh. Travel between there and England, he proposed, would be via Glasgow and would make use of the planned Edinburgh and Glasgow Railway (which opened in 1842).

The choice of a route seemed all-important in the 1830s, for it was then assumed that one line and only one would be viable. "Two great lines from Scotland to England cannot pay," remarked Locke. In 1837 he was asked for a second report; this time he re-surveyed Annandale and decided it was after all a realistic route – and he also for the first time explored a possible line to Edinburgh. This would leave the Glasgow line at Symington and run round the south side of the Pentland hills to reach the capital via Liberton.

In Scotland a committee of supporters of the Annandale scheme was set up. They saw the railway as a passenger line only, goods traffic being already catered for by "the ease and perfection of steam navigation from the Clyde to Liverpool on one hand and from Leith, Dundee etc on the other"!

A new route for a line to Edinburgh was surveyed in 1840. This would run round the northern side of the Pentland hills and reach Edinburgh from the west. The surveyor, Mr McCallum, observed that a railway along this route would involve easier gradients than the southern alternative, although it would be two or three miles longer.

In 1841 a government commision adjudicated as to the best route for the Anglo–Scottish railway and gave their support to the Annandale line. The way was now clear for a company to be formed to promote the railway and come to Parliament for authorisation to build it. Every new railway had to be authorised in this way.

It was not until early in 1844 that the first meeting of the Caledonian Railway Company was held, in London, at which nine interested people – "favourable to the construction of the Scottish Line of Railway recommended by the Government Commissioners in their report dated 15th March, 1841" – assembled. They appointed Joseph Locke and John Errington as Engineers of the line, and resolved to seek support from various landowners.

Planning the "Edinburgh Branch"

On 5th August, 1844 the Caledonian Directors received a final report in person from Joseph Locke as to the merits of the two proposed routes for a line to Edinburgh. The Board resolved beforehand to accept his recommendation.

Locke found that the southern route would be more expensive. Major works would be involved, including the making of the terminus near Watson's Hospital at the Meadows. The hospital itself (actually a school) would have to be purchased.

The terminus of the northern route, which was to be either at Gillespie's Hospital or the Lochrin Distillery, both in the Tollcross area, would be less convenient; but the route would be cheaper overall and have other advantages. It would allow of a junction being made with the Edinburgh and Glasgow Railway by means of which access could be gained to the city centre and also to Leith and Granton via another existing line. The route would also encourage traffic between Edinburgh and Lanarkshire.

The route running to the north of the Pentlands was recommended and duly approved by the Board. In November 1844 a new proposed site for the Edinburgh terminus, beside Lothian Road, was inspected and approved.

Negotiations for the purchase of land required for the "Edinburgh branch" now proceeded. The line was to fork with the "Glasgow branch" at Carstairs Junction, the section to Edinburgh being 27½ miles long.

A number of landowners in the area lying between Balerno and Slateford had to be settled with, among whom two evidently opposed the planned railway. A company minute of 5th February, 1845 noted that £1500 was to be offered to Sir James Gibson-Craig of Riccarton and 5000 guineas to the Earl of Morton "if by so doing their hostility to the Edinburgh branch would be removed and their assent secured." The Caledonian authorised their agents to go as high as £2000 in the case of Sir James "rather than not conclude an arrangement with him."

There are various possible reasons for such opposition. Sir James, who was 80 years old and a prominent Whig (he had been created first Baronet of Riccarton in 1831 by the Prime Minister Earl Grey) may have simply disliked the prospect of a railway intruding on his land, though equally he may have been negotiating tactically to secure a better final deal. Indeed it is unlikely he opposed the railway out of principle for he had been the chairman of the subscribers to the first proposed railway between Edinburgh and Glasgow in 1826.

By the time an Act was secured for the Caledonian Railway on 31st July, 1845 the company had concluded agreements with seven local landowners. As well as Sir James Gibson-Craig and the Earl of Morton, Mr Inglis of Redhall, Sir Thomas Gibson-Carmichael of Hailes, Mr Christie of Baberton, Mr Marshall of Curriehill and Mr Davidson of Ravelrig had come to terms. A deal had also been done with the Union Canal company (the canal was to be crossed by the railway at Kingsknowe) whereby a short branch was to link the canal and the railway nearby, 200 yds long and "expected to command a considerable traffic". In fact it was never built.

Construction of the railway was begun at the Beattock summit cutting on 11th August, 1845. John Stephenson and Company had obtained the contract for the works at a price of £1,275,000. (Stephenson was a relation of George Stephenson, who built the famous *Locomotion* and *Rocket*.)

The construction of the railway was to occupy the next two and a half years.

Edinburgh's Railways — and Lord Cockburn of Bonaly

The Edinburgh Branch of the Caledonian Railway was not the first line to be built to the capital. In 1842 the Edinburgh and Glasgow Railway opened, giving the city its first major, locomotive-hauled services; but long before that, in 1832, the first passengers had been carried on the horse-drawn trains of the Edinburgh and Dalkeith Railway.

This line opened in 1831 for goods traffic, its Edinburgh terminus being at St Leonard's off the Pleasance (near the present Commonwealth Pool). During the 1830s new branches were built from the line, to Musselburgh and Leith, both of which carried passengers.

The opening of the Edinburgh and Glasgow Railway on 22nd February, 1842 to a station at Haymarket, with intermediate stations further west at Gogar and Ratho, was followed in August by the opening of the first section of another local railway. This was the Edinburgh, Leith and Granton Railway, which was eventually opened throughout in 1847; it ran from a station beside Princes Street, on the site of the present Waverley Market, down a long steep tunnel under St Andrew Square and Dublin Street to Scotland Street (trains ran down by gravity and were hauled up by rope), where the tunnel ended and locomotives took over. Beyond, the line divided into two sections, one running to Leith and one to Granton.

The section which opened in August 1842 was between Canonmills at the foot of the tunnel and Trinity. The tunnel itself only opened in 1847.

In 1846 the Edinburgh and Glasgow Railway was extended from Haymarket via a tunnel into Princes Street Gardens and what is now Waverley Station. This backed on to another new station, that of the North British Railway which had opened six weeks earlier on 18th June, running between Edinburgh and Berwick with a branch to Haddington. The North British company were later to dominate the Edinburgh scene. By 1846 they had also acquired the Dalkeith Railway (horse-operated until that year) and were constructing a line to Hawick. Meantime work was also progressing on the other side of Edinburgh on the Caledonian line.

Indeed, between 1844 and 1846 an astonishing number of railways were promoted all over Britain in what is referred to as the Railway Mania. Many never got off the ground and many more failed through want of funds.

A prominent Colinton resident took great exception to all this activity. Lord Cockburn of Bonaly Tower had long been disturbed by the effects of railways on land, people and their way of life. During an earlier rush of railway promotions he had accurately predicted (in April 1836):

> Many will be ruined; but ultimately the country will be pierced in every direction ... In twenty years London will probably be within fifteen hours by land of Edinburgh, and every other place will be shaking hands, without making a long arm, with its neighbour of only a county or two off.

He was even more disturbed by the mania of the mid-1840s. In November 1845 he wrote:

> Britain is at present an island of lunatics, all railway mad. The patients are raving even in the wildest recesses of the Highlands.

The building of the Edinburgh and Glasgow Railway through Princes Street Gardens appalled him. He deplored the disregard of speculators for those whose land was affected and the preponderance of Members of Parliament who had a vested interest in railways; for it was Parliament which had the final say on whether any given line should be built.

On the other hand Cockburn could see the potential benefits of railways and was himself a pioneer traveller. He could even claim to be one of the first commuters. In September 1842, during a fortnight's stint as a circuit judge in Glasgow, he had what was then an innovative idea:

> One of our days was a Sunday, a very serious thing in Glasgow. To avoid its horrors, Lord MacKenzie spent the day at Possil. But I rather think I fell upon a better scheme. Because the Court having risen at six on the Saturday evening, I got into the seven o'clock train and found myself here at tea and an egg, before ten.

'Here' was Bonaly tower; Cockburn returned safely to Glasgow on the Monday morning.

In 1845, as work began on building the Caledonian Railway, it was apparent that railways were about to eclipse road and canal traffic. Yet, for the time being, all three modes of transport were almost equally important to Edinburgh.

No fewer than 90 mail-coaches and stage-coaches still left the city daily in 1845, while 200 omnibuses, cabs and hackney-coaches plied within it. The Union Canal still conveyed over a third of Edinburgh's coal (83,081 tons); more than the Edinburgh and Glasgow Railway (36,288 tons) although rather less than the Dalkeith Railway (100,222 tons). The rest (23,000 tons) came by road.*

Railways were still young enough not to have been universally accepted in the community. Many shared Henry Cockburn's resentment of them. One recurring complaint involved the immorality of those companies which ran trains on Sundays; in May 1841, for example, the minister of Colinton parish, Lewis Balfour, was invited to join a proposed union of kirk sessions to campaign against the "railway desecration of the Lord's Day" by the Edinburgh and Glasgow company! The E & G in fact initially ran two trains on Sundays but subsequently bowed to Sabbatarian pressure and removed them.

Construction of the Edinburgh Branch

Around Edinburgh, the contractors building the Caledonian Railway encountered several major problems.

Before starting on the main station they had first to demolish a coach works and a printing works and then excavate the site — and this excavation

---

* Figures from the 1846 Statistical Account of Scotland

proved extremely difficult and costly. Eventually, though, the Caley felt able to arrange a ceremony to lay the station's foundation-stone and on 9th April, 1847 a large crowd assembled to hear the Duke of Athole enthuse over the railway and the handsome, Italianate station building which was to rise here.

Unfortunately it was never built! The Caley were about to become enmeshed in a financial crisis which led to them erecting a "temporary" wooden structure (it lasted until 1870) as and when funds permitted.

To the west of the station site the contractors faced another challenge. The railway was to pass below the junction of Morrison Street with Gardner's Crescent, through a massive archway – under which the Western Approach Road now runs. The problem was that the top of the archway was due to come within feet of nearby houses; at first it was thought it would be necessary to demolish part of Gardner's Crescent for safety. However, the street eventually remained intact. As late as the autumn of 1847, when the line between Carlisle and Beattock was already open, The Scotsman reported that an "immense" number of men were still working here.

At Slateford a massive 14-arch viaduct was built over the Water of Leith, parallel to the nearby canal aqueduct but a little lower than it. The Caley in fact made use of the canal to transport stone for the viaduct from Hailes quarry just a few hundred yards to the west. The canal Directors allowed a special landing-stage to be built at the west end of the aqueduct, complete with a crane for unloading stone and timber.

Work went on throughout 1846. In March 1847 The Scotsman reported:

> The piers and several niches of the viaduct over the Water of the Leith at Slateford have been already completed. The masonry has been constructed almost entirely from stone from Hailes Quarry, the immediate vicinity of which to the line of railway has afforded great facilities.

Provisional plans for the intermediate stations along the Edinburgh branch were drawn up in 1846 and 1847. At first the list (from east to west) comprised Slateford, Currie, Kirknewton Hill House, Midcalder, West Calder, Auchengray and Carnwath; but in May 1847 Kirknewton Hill House was withdrawn and West Calder re-designated "Torphin".

All the stations except Midcalder were to be "second class". Four of the six intermediate stations were to have just one employee, a "station keeper", at a wage of £1 per week; these were Slateford, Torphin, Auchengray and Carnwath. Currie station was to have a station keeper at a wage of 30s. per week and in additon a porter at 18s. per week. These wages were in fact fairly generous in relation to the average then prevailing.

At the first class station of Midcalder there were to be three staff: a station keeper, a porter and a night keeper for the level crossing.

The Lothian Road station, like the Glasgow terminus, was to be staffed by 15 men. The superintendent was to be paid £300 per annum. Under him would be seven clerks and seven porters; the clerks receiving from £30 to £120 a year (12s. to 48s. weekly), the porters from 15s. to 30s. a week.

Some stations were so incomplete when the railway finally opened that they were omitted from timetables. Slateford station, then on the site of today's Kingsknowe station, was actually included in the first month's timetable but then dropped for several months. Other stations were no more than stop-gap affairs.

In 1846 the Caley applied for Parliamentary powers to build a branch from Slateford to Granton with the aim of securing some of the lucrative goods traffic to and from the port; they also had their sights on Leith further east. The 1846 Bill was rejected but an Act was obtained in 1847. However, a stubborn landowner then refused to allow the line to be made.

Later, in the early 1850s, the Caley attempted to reach the ports by building a short line from Slateford to the Edinburgh and Glasgow Railway at Haymarket, from where their trains might run along the E&G to Waverley and thence, by a connecting line, on to the Edinburgh, Leith and Granton Railway (by then part of the Edinburgh, Perth and Dundee Railway). The Haymarket branch opened in 1853; but the whole scheme was abandoned when the E&G unexpectedly became awkward and refused the Caley access to their line. It was not until 1861 that the Caley finally got to Granton with a branch of their own.

Navvy Troubles

The huge numbers of navvies employed in building the Caledonian Railway were a source of constant trouble.

Navvies were notoriously hard men, often strong-drinking and quick-tempered, particularly the Irish, of whom there were thousands on the line, and those from the Highlands. The navvies, who led strange, nomadic lives building one railway after another, generally staying with the same contractor, were accommodated in communities of very basic huts at intervals along the line. Conditions in such huts could be primitive; Benjamin Hall Blyth, an engineer in the firm which planned the Balerno branch, later recalled a typical example:

> In some of my old specifications, after stating the sizes of the houses and the number of cubic feet, etc, to be provided in workmen's houses, the following clause occurs: "Each bed to contain not more than two men, and to be at least six feet long and four feet wide inside." That specification was in use for many years, and, as far as I can make out, up to 1874. I am afraid the navvies in those days must have been of a smaller size than many we see about us now.

Tensions among the navvies were created by the notorious "truck" system under which they were compelled to spend their wages at special "tommy shops" run by the contractors or their agents. Goods in the shops were sold at extortionate prices and were of low quality. Wages being paid only monthly, navvies had problems getting by without asking for "subs" or "lines" to tide them over; and the subs had to be spent in the tommy shops. Any navvy who tried to take his money elsewhere was in trouble, for subs would then be withheld and he would find it impossible to keep going.

Spirits were sold in the shops as part of a policy to encourage the men to waste their wages and remain in debt to the contractors.

There was a tommy shop in Juniper Green when the Caledonian main line was under construction in the district. It featured in an outbreak of trouble

CALEDONIAN RAILWAY.
ALTERATION OF TRAINS.
TIME TABLE.
On and After 1st APRIL, 1848, and until further Notice.

EDINBURGH AND GLASGOW TO CARLISLE, &c.
UP TRAINS.

	Mixed Train. Class 1 2 & 3 To London 1st only.	Mail Train. Class 1 & 2	Parlm. Train. Class 1 2 & 3	Mail Train. Class 1 & 2 From Carl. 1st only	SUNDAY TRAINS Mail 1 2 & 3	Mail 1 2 & 3 From Carlisle 1st only
Trains Leave	A.M.	A.M.	P.M.	P.M.	A.M.	P.M.
Edinburgh...	6.50	11.15	5.0	9.15	11.15	9.15
Glasgow.....	6.30	11.5	4.50	9.5	11.5	9.5
Arrives at		P.M.		A.M.	P.M.	A.M.
Carlisle......	11.30	3.48	10.50	1.29	3.48	1.29
	P.M.					
Newcastle...	3.40	7.30	...	...	8.15	...
Preston	3.55	8.3	...	5.39	8.3	5.39
Manchester	5.40	9.40	...	6.50	9.40	6.50
Liverpool ...	5.50	10.0	...	7.0	10.0	7.0
		A.M.		A.M.	A.M.	
Birmingham	8.10	1.10	...	9.55	1.10	9.55
				P.M.		P.M.
London........	10.30	4.45	...	1.0	4.45	1.0

CARLISLE, &c., TO EDINBURGH AND GLASGOW.
DOWN TRAINS.

	Mail Train. Class 1 & 2	Parlm. Train. Class 1 2 & 3	Mixed Train. Class 1 & 2	Mail Train. Class 1 & 2	SUNDAY TRAINS Mail 1 2 & 3	Mail 1 2 & 3 (1 & 2 only to Carl.)
Trains Leave	P.M.	A.M.	A.M.	P.M.	P.M.	A.M.
London	8.45	...	{ *8.30 / 10.0 }	8.45	8.45	10.0
	A.M.			P.M.	A.M.	P.M.
Birmingham	12.30	...	6.0	1.0 / 1.45	12.30	1.45
Liverpool....	...	7.45	10.40	3.25	...	...
Manchester.	3.23	7.55	10.50	3.35	3.23	...
			P.M.			
Preston	5.15	9.50	12.30	5.16	5.15	5.16
Newcastle...	5 30	11.0	1.45	4.0	...	5.0
		P.M.	P.M.			
Carlisle......	9.16	2.15	5.0	9.16	9.16	9.16
Arrives at	P.M.			A.M.	P.M.	A.M.
Edinburgh...	1.45	8.0	9.40	1.30	1.45	1.30
Glasgow.....	1.55	8.15	10.0	1.40	1.55	1.40

* The 8.30 A.M. Train from London, and 1.0 P.M Train from Birmingham, is a Mixed Train, and takes Private Carriages. The 10.0 A.M. Train from London, and 1.45 P.M. from Birmingham, is First only.

N.B.—No change of carriage between London and Edinburgh and Glasgow.

EDINBURGH AND GLASGOW SECTION.

EDINBURGH TO GLASGOW.

	Local Train. Class 1 2 & 3	Mail Train. Class 1 & 2.	Local Train. Class 1 2 & 3	Parlm. Train. Class 1 2 & 3	SUNDAY TRAINS Mail. 1 2 & 3.	† Mail. 1 2 & 3.
Trains Leave	A.M.	A.M.	P.M.	P.M.	A.M.	P.M.
Edinburgh ...	6 50	11 15	1 30	5 0	11 15	9 15
Arrive at		P.M.			P.M.	A.M.
Glasgow	9 45	1 55	4 36	8 15	1 55	1 40

GLASGOW TO EDINBURGH.

	Local Train. Class 1 2 & 3.	Mail Train. Class 1 & 2.	Local Train. Class 1 2 & 3.	Parlm. Train. Class 1 2 & 3	SUNDAY TRAINS Mail. 1 2 & 3.	† Mail. 1 2 & 3.
Trains Leave	A.M.	A.M.	P.M.	P.M.	A.M.	P.M.
Glasgow........	6 30	11 5	1 20	4 50	11 5	9 30
Arrive at		P.M.			P.M.	A.M.
Edinburgh....	9 35	1 45	4 11	8 0	1 45	1 30

† Passengers going by this Train, between EDINBURGH and GLASGOW, or GLASGOW and EDINBURGH, must wait the arrival at CARSTAIRS JUNCTION of the Down Mail Train.

The Caley advertised an amended timetable in 'The Scotsman' in March 1848, just a month after the opening.

EDINBURGH TO CARLISLE, &c.

Miles.	Stations.	UP TRAINS.					SUNDAY TRAINS.		FARES.		
		Mixed Train. Class 1 2 & 3 (To London 1st only.)	Mail Train. Class 1 & 2	Local Train. Class 1 2 & 3	Parliamentary Train. Class 1 2 & 3	Mail Train. Class 1 & 2 (From Carlisle 1st Only)	Mail 1 2 & 3	Mail 1 2 & 3 (From Carlisle 1st Only)	1st	2d	3d
	TRAINS LEAVE	A. M.	A. M.	P. M.	P. M.	P. M.	A.M.	P. M.	s. d.	s. d.	s. d.
	EDINBURGH	6 50	11 15	1 30	5 0	9 15	11 15	9 15			
5	Currie	7 5	...	1 45	5 17	...	...	...	1 0	0 10	0 5
10	MIDCALDER & Kirknewton	7 20	11 40	2 0	5 35	9 40	11 40	9 40	2 0	1 8	0 10
15	West Calder & Torphin	7 35	...	...	5 50	...	...	...	3 0	2 6	1 3
20¼	Auchengray	7 50	P. M.	...	6 8	...	P. M.	...	4 3	3 6	1 8
26	Carnwath	8 5	...	2 45	6 25	...	...	...	5 6	4 4	2 2
26¼	CARSTAIRS Junction	8 15	12 30	2 56	6 35	10 30	12 30	10 30	5 6	4 4	2 2
31½	Thankerton	...	...	...	6 52	...	...	...	6 6	5 3	2 7
33½	SYMINGTON for Biggar	8 33	12 54	...	6 59	10 45	12 54	10 45	7 0	5 7	2 9
37	Lamington	...	...	...	7 12	...	...	...	8 0	6 2	3 1
42¼	ABINGTON	8 53	1 20	...	7 30	11 10	1 20	11 10	9 0	7 1	3 6
47	Elvanfoot	9 5	...	...	7 45	...	...	...	10 0	7 10	3 11
60¼	BEATTOCK for Moffat	9 53	2 10	...	8 32	12 0	2 10	12 0	12 6	10 1	5 0
65¼	Wamphray	10 5	...	...	8 50	...	...	...	13 6	10 11	5 5
71	Nethercleugh	...	...	...	9 9	A. M.	...	A. M.	15 0	11 10	5 11
74	LOCKERBIE	10 25	2 45	...	9 19	12 21	2 45	12 21	15 6	12 4	6 2
80	ECCLEFECHAN	10 40	3 0	...	9 40	12 33	3 0	12 35	16 6	13 4	6 8
83	Kirtlebridge	...	...	...	9 51	...	...	...	17 6	13 10	6 11
87	Kirkpatrick	10 57	...	...	10 5	...	...	...	18 0	14 6	7 3
91½	GRETNA	11 10	3 28	...	10 20	1 9	3 28	1 9	19 0	15 3	7 7
96	Rockcliffe	...	...	...	10 34	...	...	...	20 0	16 0	8 0
100	ARRIVAL AT CARLISLE	11 30	3 48	...	10 50	1 29	3 48	1 29	21 0	16 8	8 4
	TRAINS ARRIVE AT	P. M.									
	Newcastle	2 40	7 30	...	...	...	8 15	...			
	Preston	3 55	8 3	...	...	5 39	8 3	5 39	39 0	29 2	15 10
	Manchester	5 40	9 40	...	...	6 50	9 40	6 50	45 0	33 2	19 0
	Liverpool	5 50	10 0	...	...	7 0	10 0	7 0	45 0	38 2	19 0
			A. M.				A. M.				
	Birmingham	8 10	1 10	...	...	9 55	1 10	9 55	57 6	42 8	24 7
								P. M.			
	London	10 30	4 45	...	...	1 0	4 45	1 0	77 6	56 8	34 0

GLASGOW TO CARLISLE, &c.

Miles.	Stations.	UP TRAINS.					SUNDAY TRAINS.		FARES.		
		Mixed Train. Class 1 2 & 3 (To London 1st only.)	Mail Train. Class 1 & 2	Local Train. Class 1 2 & 3	Parliamentary Train. Class 1 2 & 3	Mail Train. Class 1 & 2 (From Carlisle 1st Only)	Mail 1 2 & 3	Mail 1 2 & 3 (From Carlisle 1st Only)	1st	2d	3d
	TRAINS LEAVE	A. M.	A. M.	P. M.	P. M.	P. M.	A. M.	P. M.	s. d.	s. d.	s. d.
	GLASGOW	6 30	11 5	1 20	4 50	9 5	11 5	9 5			
4½	Steps Road	...	...	...	5 5	...	...	...	1 0	0 9	0 4
7	Garnkirk	...	...	...	5 14	...	...	...	1 6	1 2	0 7
9¼	COATBRIDGE	6 55	11 30	1 45	5 23	9 30	11 30	9 30	2 0	1 7	0 9
13	Holytown	7 8	...	1 56	5 35	...	...	...	2 9	2 2	1 1
15	MOTHERWELL	7 16	11 45	2 2	5 42	9 45	11 45	9 45	3 0	2 6	1 3
18	Wishaw	7 27	...	2 11	5 50	...	...	...	3 9	3 0	1 6
22	CARLUKE	7 40	P. M.	2 23	6 0	...	P. M.	...	4 6	3 8	1 10
28	LANARK	7 57	12 15	2 41	6 18	10 15	12 15	10 15	5 9	4 8	2 4
30¼	CARSTAIRS Junction	8 15	12 30	2 56	6 35	10 30	12 30	10 30	6 3	5 1	2 6
35½	Thankerton	...	...	...	6 52	...	...	...	7 6	5 11	2 11
37½	SYMINGTON for Biggar	8 33	12 54	...	6 59	10 45	12 54	10 45	8 0	6 3	3 1
41	Lamington	...	...	...	7 12	...	...	...	8 6	6 10	3 5
46¼	ABINGTON	8 53	1 20	...	7 30	11 10	1 20	11 10	9 6	7 9	3 10
51	Elvanfoot	9 5	...	...	7 45	...	...	...	10 6	8 6	4 3
64¼	BEATTOCK for Moffat	9 53	2 10	...	8 32	12 0	2 10	12 0	13 6	10 9	5 4
69¼	Wamphray	10 5	...	...	8 50	...	...	...	14 6	11 7	5 9
75	Nethercleugh	...	...	...	9 9	A. M.	...	A. M.	15 6	12 6	6 3
78	LOCKERBIE	10 25	2 45	...	9 19	12 21	2 45	12 21	16 0	13 0	6 6
84	ECCLEFECHAN	10 40	3 0	...	9 40	12 35	3 0	12 35	17 0	14 0	7 0
87	Kirtlebridge	...	...	...	9 51	...	...	...	18 0	14 6	7 3
91	Kirkpatrick	10 57	...	...	10 5	...	...	...	19 0	15 2	7 7
95½	GRETNA	11 10	3 28	...	10 20	1 9	3 28	1 9	20 0	15 11	7 11
100	Rockliffe	...	...	...	10 34	...	...	...	21 0	16 8	8 4
104	ARRIVAL AT CARLISLE	11 30	3 48	...	10 50	1 29	3 48	1 29	21 0	16 8	8 4
	TRAINS ARRIVE AT	P. M.									
	Newcastle	2 40	7 30	...	...	...	8 15	...			
	Preston	3 55	8 3	...	...	5 39	8 3	5 39	39 0	29 2	15 10
	Manchester	5 40	9 40	...	...	6 50	9 40	6 50	45 0	33 2	19 0
	Liverpool	5 50	10 0	...	...	7 0	10 0	7 0	45 0	33 2	19 0
			A. M.				A. M.				
	Birmingham	8 10	1 10	...	...	9 55	1 10	9 55	57 6	42 8	24 7
								P. M.			
	London	10 30	4 45	...	...	1 0	4 45	1 0	77 6	56 8	34 0

The April 1848 timetable. *Note the omitted incomplete Kingsknowe/Slateford station.*
Scottish Record Office

Mid Calder Station

Mid-Calder station was originally the terminus for nearly all the Balerno branch trains. Opened in 1848, Balerno branch services still appeared here as late as 1939, though only a once-weekly up train was operating by then, taking farmers home from the Edinburgh market. *Lens of Sutton*

Diesel shunter D3891 arriving at Ravelrig Junction from the Balerno branch on the 17th December, 1960. *W.S. Sellar*

Ravelrig Platform was at the western end of the Balerno loop-line and actually on the main line. Opened first in 1884 (ten years after the branch) as a platform for Volunteers "craving to exercise", for many years one main-line train called daily in each direction, although at first a number of trains (including those from the Balerno branch) called. The Platform had a new lease of life in 1927 when Dalmahoy Golf course opened nearby. *Lens of Sutton*

The new Curriehill station on the first day of services in October 1987. *Author*

Curriehill station (closed 1951) looking west. Currie's main line station originally opened in 1848 and a new halt opened here in 1987. *Lens of Sutton*

0−4−4 passenger tank LMS 15261 (after running round its train of 8-wheeled bogie coaches) is seen leaving Balerno with the 4.09 pm down train for Edinburgh on the 30th October, 1943, the last day of passenger services on the branch. Note the spur to the Balerno goods yard on the right, with the Water of Leith adjacent.   *D.L.G. Hunter*

Balerno Goods Junction seen here on 22nd June, 1934. The spur to the goods yard ran off to the left, while the passenger line continued through the tunnel under the Lanark road to emerge at Balerno station. The station house is visible beyond the signal box, being on the opposite side of the Lanark Road from the box.   *Mowat Collection*

A general view of Balerno Goods station yard in 1934. *Mowat Collection*

Balerno station (from an old postcard) with the station master and porter's house on the left. *Lens of Sutton*

Balerno Bank Paper Mills, Hill Craig & Co. private owner wagon No. 6.
Historical Model Railway Society Collection

Currie station in 1934, looking west. Note the ornate station awning and the signal box on the right, under the wooden footbridge. *L.G.R.P., courtesy David and Charles*

Currie station in CR days with the station staff and crew of engine No. 252 (an elderly 0−4−2 goods engine that worked the branch) *see Chapter Twelve*. Note George Melrose, station master on the right. Mr Melrose's children are sitting on the bench, on the left. *Courtesy Mrs J. Tweedie*

An excursion train *en route* to Balerno on 30th September, 1962 (this was the second of three excursions). *W.A.C. Smith*

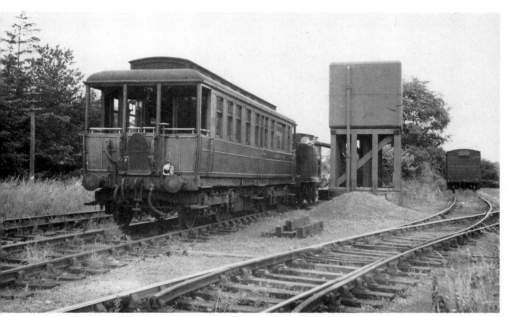

Currie station showing the water tank. This train was an officer's special in 1961 and the locomotive (hidden from view) was an 0−4−4T No. 55189, now preserved at Bo'ness as CR No. 419.   *W.S. Sellar*

A private owner wagon No. 6 for Henry Bruce and Sons of the Kinleith Paper mills at Currie. Twenty five of these wagons were built for the mill at around the turn of the century.   *Historical Model Railway Society Collection*

A fine 1912 view of Currie village showing the manse and church behind the railway line with the commencement of the station on the far right.

Courtesy Mrs J. Tweedie; Royal Commission on the Ancient and Historical Monuments of Scotland

Currie station (looking west). This was the only station with two platforms. Note the sharpness of the curve and the check-rail. *Edinburgh City Libraries*

among the navvies, recorded by J.E. Handley in *The Navvy in Scotland*:

> One Saturday evening a sub-contractor disappeared without settling. Upwards of a hundred navvies marched into Edinburgh in search of him and brought him back to Currie, where he paid a portion of what was due to them. On Sunday, a body of police had to protect him from the violence of the men. On Monday, a number who had received "lines" from him in lieu of money found when they went to the store at Juniper Green that his credit had been stopped and that no provisions would be forthcoming in his name. To prevent trouble, the principal contractors paid what was due by him and relieved him of his contract.

There was worse trouble a few miles to the west on 4th January, 1848. As *The Scotsman* reported, 300 Irish navvies who had just been discharged after completing their section of line west of West Calder,

> . . . resolved, before they departed, on wreaking their vengeance on the inhabitants of the village and on the English and Scottish labourers resident there, in consequence of the ready aid which they had always rendered to the police in the repressions of the disturbances which were of so frequent occurrence among the Irish labourers, and in the apprehensions of the offenders.

The navvies therefore marched on West Calder, to be confronted in a fierce fight by the local population, who drove them off. One navvy who stole a gun was arrested. But the men threatened to return in the evening with reinforcements and when news of this threat reached the authorities in Edinburgh later that day, they called out the army. Fifty men of the Third Dragoon Guards rode out to the area from Piershill barracks only to find everything quiet; but they remained nearby in Midcalder village three miles west of Balerno, until the threat of further violence had abated.

Such incidents were by no means unusual during the making of the Caley.

The Opening of the Edinburgh Branch

A partial opening of the Caledonian Railway took place on 10th September, 1847 when the section between Carlisle and Beattock came into use. Through services to and from Edinburgh were provided by the stage coaches of the Edinburgh-based firm John Croall and Company, who also provided a connecting service to and from Glasgow.

Fares on the 54 mile road journey between Edinburgh and Beattock were set by Croall at 14s. for outside passengers and 21s. for inside passengers. For the 39½ miles between Beattock and Carlisle the Caley charged 3s. 4d. third class, 5s. 6d. second class and 8s. 6d. first class.

The rest of the line opened on 15th February, 1848. The Board of Trade had certified the Edinburgh branch on 29th January, having failed it in December 1847 due to lack of adequate ballasting, fencing, gates at level crossings and drainage in cuttings.

The line opened that Tuesday without ceremony, though the previous day the Directors had travelled to Beattock over the railway and there toasted its future success during a private lunch.

The Scotsman approved this frugality on the part of the Board, comparing it with "the boldness of their expenditure for necessary and business purposes and the extraordinary courage and energy with which, in times when other directors faint and fail, they have pushed to completion an undertaking having more than a common share of difficulties, both natural and pecuniary."

The Scotsman went on to describe the new line. The three stations nearest to Edinburgh were "Slateford" (actually the Kingsknowe station of later years and still today), Currie, and Kirknewton – "which will supply the wants of the Balerno district to the south and the Mid-Calder district to the north."

Kirknewton station subsequently became known as "Midcalder and Kirknewton" and then simply "Midcalder", which it remained from the mid-19th century until several years ago when it was re-named Kirknewton! This station was the terminus for nearly all Balerno branch trains in the early years of the branch, after 1874.

"For this length," continued *The Scotsman*, "the line has been passing through a rich and cultivated country, and being on a higher level than either the Canal or the Edinburgh and Glasgow Railway, few of the beauties of the landscape are hid from the passenger."

The first trains to run close by Colinton, Juniper Green, Currie and Balerno were the six Anglo-Scottish trains (three each way) and four trains between Edinburgh and Glasgow (two each way) which ran daily in February 1848. Two cross-border trains ran to London and one to Carlisle only; while in the other direction two came from London and one from Liverpool. Services south of Carlisle were handled by other companies.

Most trains called at Currie and other intermediate stations. Between Currie and Lothian Road a third class single fare cost 5d., second class 10d. and first class 1s. From Slateford (Kingsknowe), fares were 3d., 6d. and 9d.

Through fares between Edinburgh and Glasgow were deliberately set at the rates charged by the Edinburgh and Glasgow Railway, but in competing against them the Caley were handicapped by the much greater length of their own line via Carstairs and the steep gradients which their trains had to overcome on the Edinburgh branch on either side of Cobbinshaw summit.

One train was known as a Parliamentary train because an 1844 Act required at least one service daily to provide third class travel to and from all stations on every line.

The first engines to run over the Edinburgh branch were those mainly built at the works of the Glasgow Paisley and Greenock Railway in Greenock. The Caley had taken over the Glasgow Paisley and Greenock company as well as several others in the Glasgow area. Greenock was to be the main Caledonian works until 1856, when St Rollox in Glasgow replaced it.

The Caley owned a total of 121 engines by 1850, either inherited from other companies or purpose-built. The most common design was the "single-driver"; this type of engine had a 2–2–2 wheel arrangement, with one very large driving wheel on either side. The design originated at the Crewe works of the Grand Junction Railway; Robert Sinclair, the Caley's first locomotive superintendent, copied it. "Single-drivers" were to serve the Caley well, and as late as 1875 four engines of that style were built.

On the Edinburgh line the first passenger trains consisted usually of four small carriages, just 18 ft long and 5ft 6in. high, each containing four compartments seating eight passengers and lit only by small door lights and quarter lights; three narrow slits above the doors provided ventilation. (These details were recalled by locomotive superintendent J.F. McIntosh in 1907.)

The railway was operated with primitive safety arrangements. There was no telegraph, and consequently no means for adjacent stations to communicate with each other. Train movements were organised on a rough-and-ready time-interval system, whereby a prescribed time had to elapse between the departures of successive trains in the same direction; for example, an express train could be followed five minutes later by a slower goods train, which would be unlikely to catch up with an express and run into it – but a goods train had to be allowed a start of 15 minutes over an express or ten minutes over a local passenger train. Many accidents inevitably occurred due to trains breaking down and being struck by following trains.

Passengers in the early days could travel in three different classes, and this remained so into the 1870s, when second class began to disappear. Unlike some companies who were reluctant to offer third class travel (other than the minimum required by law, namely one train a day on each line – hence the term a "Parliamentary" train), the Caley encouraged third class passengers from the beginning. They even argued with their English partners, the Lancaster and Carlisle company, on this point.

Life and Times

The Caley opened at a time of considerable social unrest and mass unemployment. On 7th April, 1848 the Board discussed an appeal from the Edinburgh Committee for the Relief of the Unemployed to take on as many men as they could. Fifty were given work near Slateford, making a junction for a Granton branch which the Caley still had hopes of constructing. The fifty men received wages of 1s. 3d. a day, or 7s. 6d. a week.

There were disturbances in Edinburgh in early 1848. In March a mob smashed windows and lamps and the military were called out to enforce order. In Glasgow the "bread riots" led to loss of life. Such was the climate of unrest that there were fears in some quarters of a popular uprising, not lessened by the news of revolutions that year in France, Italy and Austria. Indeed, 30,000 attended a mass meeting on the Meadows in April 1848 in support of chartism – popular suffrage.

The widespread unemployment had been caused in part by the consequences of the railway mania, which had bankrupted many businessmen. The spread of machinery in factories had also caused redundancies; while the influx of thousands of Irishmen and their families following the potato famine had swollen the competition for jobs and weakened the position of men and women still in work who might otherwise have protested about their harsh conditions.

The Irish were so numerous that of the 385 men constructing Threipmuir and Harlaw reservoirs above Balerno in the 1840s, 224 came from that country.

Lord Cockburn of Bonaly, referring in 1848 to the 10,000 weavers of Paisley who had been unemployed for a year, remarked: "Are not millions of starving people the necessary occasional sloughs of a very manufacturing nation?" In those days only the sick received assistance; the able-bodied poor had literally to starve if they could not find some way to get by.

To add to the troubles of the time Britain was swept by a cholera epidemic in 1848.

Early Setbacks

For the first two years after the railway opened, the headquarters of the Caley was in George Street, Edinburgh.

On the Edinburgh branch there were many early problems. On 2nd October, 1848 a report was submitted to the Board about "the lax discipline observed at the Edinburgh Station and the numerous complaints of want of civility and attention on the part of the officers of the said station."

As a result, the station manager Mr Mitchell was asked to resign, the alternative being dismissal.

The Edinburgh station was still only half-built when, at the beginning of January 1849, fire swept through the goods shed. By August the damage had still not been repaired and staff were granted two weeks' extra wages as a "gratuity" in recognition of their having "for the want of a shed suffered much exposure to the weather and been caused considerable additional labour."

As to the passenger terminus, in July 1849 concern was expressed that the ground floor had not been completed and that the part built was being damaged by exposure to wind and rain. It was consequently resolved "to put up so much of the arrival shed as there is iron work for on the ground."

There were problems too at intermediate stations. The poor state of Kingsknowe station was illustrated by a petition in February 1849 from "several gentlemen in the parish of Slateford urging the erection of a shed and platform" at the station. The Caley allocated £20.

The station clerk (that is, the station master) at Currie station was dismissed in May 1849 for his inefficiency and "irregularities" in his cash transactions.

At the end of 1849 the Caley found themselves in a state of financial chaos. A committee of enquiry consisting of non-executive shareholders was set up in September to examine the problems and reported in December.

The committee accused the Caley Board of wanton extravagance in buying up smaller railways and promising their shareholders guaranteed high dividends. It found that the Caley's accounts had been regularly mis-stated to disguise this state of affairs. Premium payments had been handed out to the contractors of the railway for an early completion of the line – which had not in fact been achieved! Train services had been inadequate from the outset; so short of engines had the Caley been that certain private traders who had been promised services to their works had been encouraged to buy their own engines and run them on the railway.

The committee even considered inviting one of the contractors, Thomas

Brassey, to take charge of the running of the whole network. It also noted that Edinburgh station still required work involving expenditure of £20,000.

The upshot was that a new Board was installed. Thereafter, slowly but surely, the Caley's finances were put on a healthier footing, so that with the exception of a period in the 1860s which led to stringent cost-cutting for some years and delayed the construction of the Balerno branch, the company continued to prosper.

On the recommendation of the Committee, the headquarters of the Caley was transferred in 1850 from Edinburgh to Glasgow. It was felt that, as the west of Scotland was the centre of activities, this was a proper choice.

It was not just within the Caley that the new railway caused teething troubles. Even on the roads there were problems. In October 1848 the turnpike trustees of Slateford district complained that horses using roads near where the railway passed were being frightened by the noise and smoke of engines.

The trustees wanted screens to be erected at such places to protect horses from the sight and sound of trains! The Board of Trade was called in, and an inspector visited the area. One problem spot was by the bridge carrying the railway over Slateford road; here he thought a screen would be "ineffectual to conceal the steam. The utmost that could be done would be to screen from view the working parts of the engine, which would appear to be of no avail."

The inspector felt screens might even be counter-productive. Horses might be more frightened if they could not see the cause of noise and steam than if they could. He concluded that it would be unnecessary to erect any screens since no accidents had yet occurred and horses were becoming more used to the railway – "and the remedy is even of a doubtful nature."

In these days humans as well as horses had to make adjustments to the new form of transport. One popular misconception concerned the potential dangers of travelling by train at considerable speed, the human body not being thought by some to be intended to move so fast.

Lord Cockburn was convinced rail travel could harm one. Of a journey to Dumfries in the autumn of 1850 he recalled;

> I was seized with what from its frequency seems to be an attack generated by railways, and reached Dumfries in great torture and great danger. I lay in the inn there (The King's Arms) twenty-three days before I could be brought back to Edinburgh, and never can forget the horrors, or the mercies, of the visitation.

His reason for interrupting a train journey from Edinburgh to Aberdeen at Dundee for two hours in 1852, was the memory of that experience — "Dumfries having taught me in September 1850 that too much railery is an unbecoming thing for an aged judge." When Lord Cockburn died at Bonaly in 1854, he had lived to be 74; a relatively old age despite his continuing "railery" from 1842 until that year!

An Accident at Slateford

The difficulties involved in getting things right first time when running a railway were illustrated by the following Caley minute of 30th September, 1852: "Currie. Reported its insufficiency and error of site. Ordered to take it down." It was re-erected in much the same location, off the present Currie-hill Station Road.

In January 1853 a new station was opened at Slateford to the east of the viaduct over the Water of Leith. It was named Slateford station, and the station already in existence three-quarters of a mile west, known hitherto as both King's Knowes and Slateford, now became uniformly King's Knowes.

The following June, as part of a company-wide station improvement scheme, the new Slateford station was allotted a "passenger shed" for £50, a goods shed for £400, a coal siding and "wharf" for £200 (a wharf being a platform) and a station master's house for £250. At the same time Currie station was allocated a station master's house for £300.

Meantime a serious accident occurred at the new Slateford station on 24th May, 1853. The 8 am passenger train from Carstairs to Edinburgh had arrived at the station as scheduled at 9.19 am, and half a dozen intending passengers had boarded, including several Colinton residents, when it was struck from behind by a mineral train consisting of 18 fully-laden wagons of coal.

Eleven passengers were injured, several of them seriously. Doctor Thomas Cunningham of Currie was summoned to their aid. The police also attended, and arrested the mineral train driver, Thomas Smith, who later stood trial at the High Court, as well as the driver and fireman of the passenger train.

Investigations revealed that the real cause of the accident was faulty Caledonian practice. It was a company rule that no mineral train should be allowed to leave any station within ten minutes of a stopping passenger train, and this rule had been broken at King's Knowes station on the morning of the crash when the station master authorised the mineral train driven by Thomas Smith to "proceed with caution" towards Slateford without stopping. But the station master was not held to blame; for it had emerged that he had no clock or watch with which to measure off the ten minute interval required between trains, and therefore had to guess it!

There were three signals in use on the Caley at this time. The displaying of a red disc (or red lamp at night) meant "Danger: stop", while a white disc or lamp meant that the line was clear. The caution signal, authorising a driver to proceed but with care, was given by a green disc or lamp; but at some stations there were no green discs available and it was usual for station masters to give a horizontal wave of the hand to indicate this signal. This was the case at Currie, King's Knowes and Slateford.

Driver Smith received this signal at Currie from station master John Bissell. Proceeding more slowly, as he stated in evidence later, he then took the train down the long gradient to Kingsknowe station. For brake power he had to rely on two brakesmen who were travelling on separate wagons; each had just a simple manual brake lever to operate.

The station master at Kingsknowe, James Campbell, had hoisted a danger signal after the passing of the passenger train minutes before. But now, hearing the whistle of the oncoming mineral train, he mistakenly estimated that ten minutes had intervened, and overruled his own danger signal by giving the "proceed with caution" sign with his hand.

The train ran on down the 1 in 100 gradient towards Slateford some eight minutes after the passenger train.

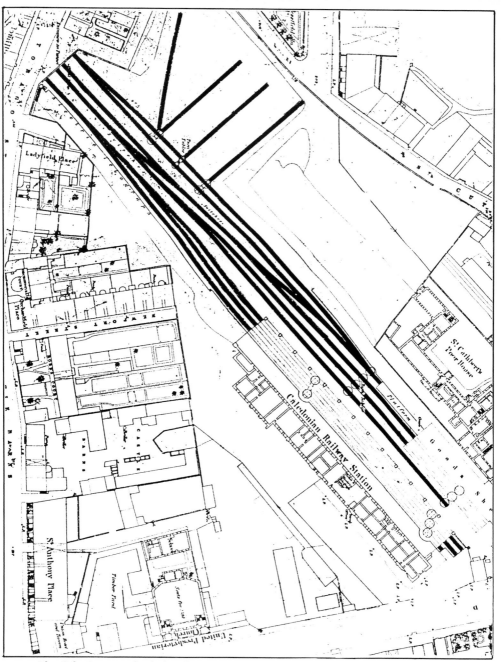

The Caley's original Edinburgh Station, opened in 1848 off Lothian Road. Note just one track serving the passenger shed; this divided into 3 tracks running through the shed and emerging on the other side. The adjacent Poor House was later knocked down to allow the opening of a new station (Princes Street) in 1870.

Reproduced from the 1852 Ordnance Survey map

The one and only employee at Slateford station was 15-year-old Robert Campbell, son of the Kingsknowe station master. Among his duties were selling tickets, attending to passengers' enquiries – and signalling. He had hoisted a danger signal immediately the passenger train arrived.

This signal was duly observed by the mineral train driver as he approached the viaduct but due to the momentum of the train down the gradient and the inadequacy of its brakes, he was unable to bring it to a halt before reaching the station. Meantime young Campbell had barely had time to warn the passenger train driver to move away before the crash occurred.

Of those injured, Edward Burton, an engraver from Colinton who had only just boarded the train, escaped through a window with a badly injured foot, which he returned home to treat with leeches.

Another passenger was Walter Marshall, a jeweller, who had boarded at Kingsknowe station. He was the tenant at the time of Hailes House. Two paper-millers from Colinton were also on board.

After spending two months in prison before coming to trial, the mineral train driver was eventually absolved.

It was almost certainly in consequence of the Slateford accident that on 19th July the Caley resolved to "get clocks put up at all stations and give time pieces to guards." Later, the introduction of the telegraph between stations would do away with the time-interval system altogether.

The Granton and Leith Branches

In September 1856 the Duke of Buccleuch came to the Caley with a proposal for a branch railway from the Caledonian main line at Slateford to Granton Harbour, which he owned and had built in the 1830s.

The Edinburgh, Leith and Granton Railway already served the port (it had in fact now been absorbed into the Edinburgh, Perth and Dundee Railway) but the Duke of Buccleuch wanted to secure quicker access to the west of Scotland than that roundabout line offered, incorporating as it did the Scotland Street tunnel. He invited the Caley to subscribe to his scheme and also to operate the line; the Caley agreed to work it, and subsequently also agreed to subscribe, putting up half the cost of £60,000. An Act was obtained for the branch the following year.

On 11th November, 1856 another accident occurred at Slateford, this time near the present station. Cattle from Gorgie farm strayed onto the line and derailed the engine and two carriages of the mail train from London. No-one was injured but 15 cows were killed and, as The Scotsman reported, "The locomotive and carriages are, of course, very much injured." For their alleged neglect the Caley dismissed the station master and porters at Slateford station. This evident harshness led local residents to submit a memorial praying for the men's re-instatement; but the Caley were adamant and the sackings stood.

Only slightly better treated was the Edinburgh station master of 1854 who was compulsorily transferred to the wilds of Beattock – hardly a promotion!

Great misfortune befell the contractor making the Granton branch in May 1860. Mr Morrison had begun work in 1858 but fallen well behind schedule when he approached the Caley in April 1860 for the loan of an old engine, the better to transport materials along the partially-built track. An engine was provided, in return for £30 to repair it. However on 29th May it was reported that sparks from the engine had set fire to cottages at Craigleith, halfway along the line, and caused damage put at over £450; Mr Morrison was later required to pay half of this bill!

The Granton branch was finally opened on 29th August, 1861. There were in fact two sub-branches, one running to the main western breakwater while the other served the older eastern pier. From this eastern section a connecting line was in due course built to the existing Granton railway – the line opened in the 1840s by the Edinburgh, Leith and Granton company (since re-named the Edinburgh and Northern and then absorbed into the Edinburgh, Perth and Dundee; in 1862 the North British company bought this concern in turn).

Though the Caley contemplated for a time operating a passenger service to and from Granton pier, the line in fact remained a preserve of goods traffic except for the period 1902–1942 when a private service of workmen's trains to and from Granton gas works operated.

In 1863 the Caley acquired full control of the Granton branch when they purchased the Duke of Buccleuch's half-share in it. Meanwhile another important branch, from the Granton line to Leith western docks (then the main docks) had been authorised in 1862, and this opened on 1st September, 1864. Only 2¾ miles in length, it cost the huge sum of £150,000 to make owing to the need to reclaim eleven acres of land from the sea at Leith. But the line was of vital importance to the Caley, who could at last share in the traffic at Edinburgh's main port.

The rival North British had been in Leith since 1862, after purchasing the Edinburgh, Perth and Dundee company; and in recent years the NB had indeed been a bugbear to the Caley, for they had foiled three separate merger proposals involving the Caley, the Edinburgh and Glasgow company and the Scottish Central Railway – the NB opposition being on the grounds that a monopoly would be created. It was therefore rather ironic that the NB themselves were allowed to merge with the Edinburgh and Glasgow Railway in 1865! Meantime the Caley set up mergers with the Scottish Central in 1864 (whose line ran between Stirling and Perth) and the Scottish and North-Eastern Railway in 1866 (whose line ran between Perth and Aberdeen) acquiring in the process an enlarged network stretching from Carlisle to Aberdeen.

A flurry of mergers such as these during the mid-1860s resulted in the existence of five powerful companies in Scotland who continued to dominate the scene until the 1920s. The Caley and North British were the biggest (and roughly equal in size) but the Glasgow and South Western, the Highland, and the Great North of Scotland Railways were considerable companies too.

Overall the railway system in Scotland had doubled in mileage in the decade up to 1864, from 1,000 to 2,000 miles. Many new lines had opened, among the major routes being the Highland Railway to Inverness and the Hawick–Carlisle railway, known as the Border Union. In the Edinburgh area the North British now had a system of lines to Granton, Leith, Musselburgh, Haddington, Hawick (with access to Carlisle) and Peebles, as well as the main railways to Berwick and Glasgow.

Among the many additional lines which were planned in a new railway mania that swept Britain between 1864 and 1866 was a branch up the valley of the Water of Leith from the Caley main line at Slateford to Balerno. But the seeds of the branch, thus sown, looked for a long time as if they had fallen on stony ground.

The Caley's advert in 'The Scotsman' of 12th October, 1870 inviting tenders for the construction of the Balerno branch.

Chapter Five
Planning the Balerno Branch

Slateford to Balerno. Submitted petition from proprietors of district, also plan by Messrs Bruce and Cunningham, A meeting asked. Meet Deputation at one o'clock on Tuesday next.

Thus on Friday 16th September, 1864 Archibald Gibson, the Secretary to the Caledonian Railway Company, made the first entry in the company minutes concerning the possible construction of a railway up the Water of Leith valley to Balerno.

In 1864 the valley was bustling with the activity of over twenty mills, including seven well-established paper mills. It was natural, in view of the resurgence of optimism eveywhere about the commercial benefits a railway could bring, that the thoughts of some local businessmen should turn to making a branch of their own. The district was already served by the Caledonian main line just a mile to the north but transporting goods over that distance to and from Slateford, Kingsknowe or Currie stations was a time-consuming and restrictive business; carts could only carry so much at a time and were slow.

Among the mill-masters and farmers who felt that nothing less than a purpose-built railway along the valley would suffice, Henry Bruce of Kinleith paper mill was well to the fore. He had taken over the mill in 1844 before the Caledonian main line was opened and had been able to see for himself how beneficial a railway could be, speeding up the transport of coal and raw materials to the mill and the dispatch of the finished product to his customers.

One advantage of a railway actually running through the river valley would be the potential ease of access. Many of the local mills were tucked away in hollows or on "haughs" (flats) by the waterside, and the lanes leading down to them were often steep and winding. The approach to Kinleith paper mill, for instance, was by Enterkins Yett, a long and steep road so-named because it was the main entrance or yett to the Woodhall estate across the river, formerly owned by the Cunninghams of Enterkin. Woodhall was in 1864 the home of Henry Bruce who rented it from Sir James Foulis.

There was support for the Balerno branch scheme from the landowners of the area whose estates were mainly farming land; the line promised better transportation of livestock and foodstuffs. It is conceivable also that the construction of the railway held out for some of them the promise of substantial compensation payments for land acquired.

The handling of passenger traffic on the proposed branch was not a major objective at this time. Nor was this unusual, for since the early 1850s goods traffic had in fact been the main source of revenue and profit on Britain's railways.

The impetus to make the line came from the paper-makers first and foremost, their mills being the largest. Apart from Henry Bruce there were David Chalmers of Kates mill (he had succeeded Cowan and Co.); Hogg and Co. of West mill in Colinton; Andrew Scott of Mossy mill, between Colinton and Juniper Green on the south bank of the river; Julius Beilby of Woodhall mill; Messrs Durham of Balerno mill; and Hill Craig and Co. of Balerno Bank mill.

They were joined by the owners of the nine grain mills, the five snuff mills and the flax mill above Balerno on the Bavelaw Burn,

The branch railway scheme had been well received; but now came the great practical problems of financing and then building the line. It was no secret that a host of promising-looking plans had failed before because of ignorance of the potential problems. Land could prove unexpectedly expensive to buy or difficult to excavate; the cost of materials and labour could also rise once construction was under way; even if a line was duly completed the traffic could fall well short of what was required. The consequences could be dire; many bankruptcies had resulted from the manias of the 1820s, the 1830s and especially the 1840s.

The promoters of the line decided for three reasons to approach the Board of the Caley. First, it was intended anyway to run the branch to the Caley main line at Slateford and this would have to be arranged. But the Caley were also to be invited to subscribe to the scheme – and to operate the line. The Duke of Buccleuch had made a similar approach in 1856 when proposing a branch to Granton. The idea was sound, for in this way engines and rolling stock could be hired rather than purchased; and while profits would be shared, so too would any losses.

So it was that on 16th September, 1864 the Caley Board found themselves studying the idea of a railway to Balerno. They then met a deputation of the promoters of the line – which took place, according to the minutes, on Friday 30th September – after which a civil engineer from the Edinburgh firm of B. & E. Blyth was sent to the district to examine routes and estimate the traffic potential.

On Thursday 6th October the Secretary informed the Board that a Balerno branch was expected to generate "£72,000 tons a year" – in other words goods traffic to that value. The Caley Chairman, Thomas Hill, also reported on the meeting with a deputation of the promoters.

The Board resolved to back the line to the extent of taking full responsibility for it themselves rather than merely contributing to it.

At the same time they approved plans for two other lines from Slateford. One was to link the Caley main line with the Edinburgh and Glasgow Railway; the other was a branch to Penicuik, due to run via Morningside and Liberton. As it turned out, neither was built.

The reasoning behind the Caley decision to take full control of the Balerno branch was spelled out later during proceedings held in Parliament to discuss the abandonment of the branch in 1869.

By that time the company had become caught up in a financial crisis and, seriously short of funds, were applying for authority to be relieved of the duty to make various railways of which the Balerno branch, to the great indignation of the local community, was one. The following exchange took place between George Cunningham, one of the two Engineers appointed by the Caley to plan the branch (George Bruce was the other and had carried out the original traffic survey), and a cross-examining counsel who was representing parties interested in saving the railway.

> Counsel: Originally the parties themselves proposed an independent line of railway, did they not?
>
> Cunningham: They did.
>
> Counsel: Was it not expressly at the instance of the Caledonian Company that they determined to forego their efforts to obtain this line, and handed it over to the Caledonian Company?
>
> Cunningham: That is so; they proposed that the Caledonian should be subscribers, but we find that it is a very great nuisance to have these small companies with local subscribers, and in the end we always have to buy them up. So in the end the Caledonian Company said, "We will promote a line ourselves."
>
> Counsel: But they were getting up a subscription, and were prepared to make an independent line themselves, when the Company interposed and undertook to make the line?
>
> Cunningham: That is so.

The Caley's approach, thus described by George Cunningham, was quite different from that of the North British and various other companies who tended to leave the hard work of planning and building branch lines to local promoters. They would then step in at a later date to buy up these lines, having for a time merely subscribed to and operated them. Thus the North British first leased and then purchased railways to Peebles, Dolphinton, Polton, Penicuik and Glencorse in the period between the 1850s and 1870s.

Once the Caley had given the go-ahead to the Balerno branch in October 1864 the two appointed Engineers, George Bruce and George Cunningham, set about planning it. Both were associates of B. & E. Blyth, a firm which had been set up in 1848 by Benjamin Hall Blyth, one of the first Scottish railway engineers. The firm's original premises at 135 George Street, Edinburgh are still in use today as the head office of Blyth and Blyth Partnerships – who still retain the original plans of the Balerno branch!

Bruce and Cunningham envisaged a double track railway terminating by Balerno bridge at the foot of Balerno village; no connecting line to the main railway further west was at this time contemplated. The branch was to cost about £80,000 though the overall cost was to be far higher thanks to heavy compensation payments. For, under an Act of 1845 protecting the rights of land-owners, wherever any part of a works was threatened by a railway the owner could if he so wished require the railway company to purchase the entire property. The Balerno branch was bound to interfere with a number of mills where there was little room for it to squeeze past them; and so the Caley, expecting large claims for damages, resolved to seek permission in their Bill for the line to raise £200,000.

Plans for the railway went on public inspection at the end of 1864. One mill-master, David Chalmers of Kates mill in Colinton Dell, complained that the mill would be ill-served by the branch, which was to run on the wrong side of the Water of Leith from his point of view.

Dissenting Voices

A more general protest against the Balerno branch was recorded in December 1864 at a meeting of the Heritors of Colinton Parish. The meeting was convened especially to discuss the railway.

The heritors were the local landowners who at that time had a collective responsibility for the upkeep of the church and its land, known as the glebe. A small section of this land was needed by the Caley where Colinton station was to be built. Among their other functions, heritors served on the parochial board which gave relief to the parish poor and until 1870 ran the schools.

Only three out of a total of twelve Colinton heritors were represented at the meeting, and two of these only in their absence. However, the two men thus represented by their agents happened to be the major landowners in the area. Sir James Liston Foulis owned the Woodhall estate though he no longer actually lived there; he was also officially the ninth Baronet of Colinton, despite the Foulis family's having sold the Colinton estate in 1800. Sir William Gibson-Carmichael owned the Hailes estate including Hailes Quarry, although he too was an absentee landlord. He was also the tenth Baronet of Skirling in Peebles-shire.

Andrew Grieve as owner of Hailes mill by Colinton church spoke for himself as well as for Sir James. The meeting was reported as follows:

> The clerk laid before the meeting Parliamentary Notice of the Balerno Branch of the Caledonian Railway, also a Form of Reply as to Assent, Dissent or Neutrality together with the plans of said branch railway. After due consideration of these, Mr Grieve for Sir James Liston Foulis, Bart of Woodhall and his Curators and himself stated the following reasons for dissenting from the proposed branch railway to Balerno.
>
> 1. Because the district is already served by the Caledonian Railway which runs parallel to and at a short distance from the proposed Branch with stations at Slateford, Kingsknowe and Currie.
>
> 2. This short branch would, it is believed, do greater injury to the amenity of residences and to the property of Heritors than other line [sic] of equal length; and without a much greater public necessity for it, compulsory powers should not be granted for its construction.
>
> 3. It has been said that it is the project of one or two papermakers on the Water of Leith engaged in the manufacture of cheap printing and other inferior paper out of Spanish grass or esparto, and other materials, the refuse from which is profuse and very offensive, and renders the bed of the stream for a great part of the year noxious and injurious to health, and when increased, as it would be by this Branch Railway together with the smoke and noise of Engines in the narrow valley, the residences of the Heritors on the water will become unhealthy. A clause in the Edinburgh Sewerage Act to compel these manufacturers to deodorise their refuse above Coltbridge was supposed to have been defeated by those who are now for their own purposes promoting this branch line; but it would be absolutely necessary to have such an enactment, and also to provide for consuming the smoke of the Engines if this line were allowed to be constructed.
>
> 4. In such a narrow district the introduction of a large number of Navvies might be productive of disorder and breaches of the Peace and of immorality in the villages to the great and lasting increase of the Parish burdens.
>
> For these and other reasons which could be named the Heritors of Colinton should give their dissent and opposition to the proposed Branch Railway. Mr Grieve accordingly moved that the Heritors' clerk be instructed to intimate to the Promoters of the Bill the Dissent of the Heritors therefrom. Which motion being seconded by Mr Dalziel was carried accordingly.

Evidently not every local landowner viewed the Balerno branch with favour! Equally clearly those heritors represented were not above taking advantage of their right to speak as guardians of the glebe by referring to their own personal interests and properties!

Their awareness of possible problems associated with navvies no doubt stemmed from the building of the Caley main line in the 1840s and was reinforced by regular reports in the press. Only three months earlier a riot had occurred among men making a branch to South Queensferry and the police had needed the help of the crew of a naval ship at anchor in the Forth to quell it!

The 1865 Act

The Bill for the Balerno branch was examined by a Parliamentary committee in late March 1865. Two other Bills dealt with at the same time related to proposed branches to Penicuik: one a Caley scheme, the other a North British scheme. All three planned lines were discussed in one package, as it were.

No opposition was presented to the Balerno branch, despite the Heritors' resolution of December 1864; so most of the argument centred on the Penicuik lines. But George Bruce gave brief details about the railway in passing. Both it and the Penicuik branch were to be double-tracked ("Nothing else would be suitable for that district") with a maximum gradient on either of 1 in 80. Both were to serve a large passenger traffic as well as heavy goods and mineral traffic.

The Balerno branch would incorporate sidings to "the various mills (grain and paper mills) upon the Waters of Leith."

When he was asked who had actually planned the railways, Bruce replied that he and Cunningham and others worked together. They had been consulted on "nine-tenths of all the contract works with regard to railways which have been going on in Scotland for the last four or five years."

After a vigorous and sometimes entertaining debate over the Penicuik lines, the Caley — who had been keen to gain a foothold in that district, with its rich mineral traffic — eventually lost out. One reason given by the North British in favour of their own line was the relative superiority of their Edinburgh station over the Caley's Lothian Road terminus. North Bridge station (later to be part of Waverley) handled 3,000,000 passengers a year, claimed the NB, while Lothian Road dealt with only 300,000.

The Caley retorted that Lothian Road was becoming increasingly central to Edinburgh as the city expanded westwards. They also deplored the longstanding refusal of the Edinburgh and Glasgow Railway Company to allow them to run their trains via the Haymarket Branch of 1853 to and from Waverley station.

The Balerno branch duly received the Royal Assent on 29th June, 1865. The railway was to terminate "near Balerno Bridge in the Parish of Currie by which the road from Currie by Newmills to Balerno is carried over the Water of Leith." It was required to open by 29th June, 1870, five years from the date of the Act. Should it not be ready then, a penalty of £50 for each day late would apply.

ANNO VICESIMO OCTAVO & VICESIMO NONO

VICTORIÆ REGINÆ.

✦✶

Cap. clxi.

An Act for enabling the *Caledonian* Railway Company to make a Branch Railway to *Balerno* in the County of *Edinburgh;* and for other Purposes.   [29th *June* 1865.]

WHEREAS by "The *Caledonian* Railway Act, 1845," the *Caledonian* Railway Company (in this Act called "the Company") were incorporated, and under the Powers of that Act the Company have formed (among other Works) a Main Line of Railway from the City of *Carlisle* to the City of *Edinburgh* : And whereas it would be attended with Advantage and Convenience to the Public if the Company were authorized to make and maintain a Branch Railway from their said Main Line near *Slateford* to *Balerno* in the County of *Edinburgh* : And whereas Plans and Sections showing the Lines and Levels of the said proposed Branch Railway, and the Lands which may be required to be taken for the Purposes thereof, with a Book of Reference to the said Plans, have been deposited for public Inspection in the Office at *Edinburgh* of the Principal Sheriff Clerk of the County of *Edinburgh* ; but the Objects aforesaid cannot be effected without the Authority of Parliament : May it therefore please Your Majesty that it may be

8 & 9 Vict. c. clxii.

[*Local.*]   25 *H*   enacted ;

Extracts from the 1865 Act authorising the Balerno branch. [*Further extract overleaf*].
Courtesy, Keeper of
the Records of Scotland
(BR/AP(S)/508)

15. The Branch Railway by this Act authorized to be constructed is,— *Description of Branch Railway.*

A Railway (to be called the "*Balerno* Branch") commencing by a Junction with the Main Line of the *Caledonian* Railway from *Carlisle* to *Edinburgh* near the Booking Office of the *Slateford* Station of that Railway, and terminating near *Balerno Bridge* in the Parish of *Currie* by which the Road leading from *Currie* by *Newmills* to *Balerno* is carried over the *Water of Leith*.

16. The Company shall, not less than Eight Weeks before they take in any Parish Houses amounting to Fifteen in Number or more occupied either wholly or partially by Persons belonging to the Labouring Classes as Tenants or Lodgers, make known their Intention to take the same by Placards, Handbills, or other general Notice placed in public View upon or within a reasonable Distance from such Houses; and the Company shall not take any such Houses until they have obtained the Certificate of a Justice that it has been proved to his Satisfaction that the Company have made known their Intention to take the same in manner herein-before required. *Lodging Houses not to be taken without Notice.*

A share capital of £150,000 was authorised, plus £50,000 in borrowings; a total of £200,000. (This 3:1 ratio of shares to borrowings was standard.)

One stipulation contained in the Act reads rather strangely today yet was another standard feature in those days. It was decreed that where fifteen or more parish houses "occupied either wholly or partially by persons belonging to the labouring classes as tenants or lodgers" were to be acquired, eight weeks notice must be given to the tenants. Presumably if no more than fourteen houses were to be taken the tenants had no rights to a warning!

The Balerno branch Act was just one of the many obtained by the Caley in 1864, 1865 and 1866. The most significant, perhaps, was for a line from west of Midcalder on the Edinburgh branch to the Glasgow branch near Cleland which was to give the Caley a new direct route between Edinburgh and Glasgow. An Act for a new Edinburgh station was also passed in 1866.

When the Caley and the Scottish Central agreed to merge on 6th October, 1864 (at the same meeting that approved the Balerno branch), to be followed by the union of the Caley with the Scottish and North Eastern in 1866, the significance was that the Caley now owned an almost uninterrupted line from Carlisle to Aberdeen. The exception was, curiously, a short stretch of North British track south of Larbert over which the Caley were allowed special running powers.

The Balerno branch, set against these great goings-on, was an insignificant undertaking – and this was about to cost its shareholders dear. The late 1860s saw the Caley becoming overstretched by so many liabilities, so that they were forced to default on some of them.

Just as in the 1840s, though to a lesser extent, a price was about to be paid for over-enthusiasm.

Delays – and Abandonment

No sooner had the Act authorising the Balerno branch been passed than the Caley began to show signs of dragging their heels over its construction.

Thoughts of a prompt start on the work were scotched when the Board deferred construction in September 1865 until the spring of 1866. This brought a complaint from Henry Bruce.

In December 1865 it was arranged that notices relative to the purchase of land for the branch be sent to local landowners. But they were not in fact sent; the order was cancelled in January.

However, on 13th February, 1866 a positive decision appeared to have been reached when the clerk to the General Committee of the Caley noted: "Balerno branch. Instructions asked as to whether the works of this branch are now to be proceeded with. Go on with the Balerno branch." But nothing happened other than that on one day the following July test bores were sunk along the line of the branch to determine the nature of the local soil and rock.

During the whole of 1866 and 1867 the only other steps taken with the Balerno branch in mind were the purchases of two properties. The acquisition of Hailes mill at Colinton in 1866 is rather puzzling, as the railway was to by-pass it through Colinton tunnel, and it was in fact later re-sold. The other purchase was of a cottage at Currie.

However, despite not going on with the construction of the branch the Caley did raise the £150,000 in share capital authorised by the Act. 1,500 shares of £100 value each were taken up in 1866 by the public, many by local people. It was to emerge later that the Caley duly spent this money but not on the Balerno branch!

The Caley were in fact facing a deepening financial crisis from 1865 onwards. A large number of expensive construction projects had been taken on and the company found that the funds required to carry them out were not available. Such as there were went increasingly only on major schemes such as the Cleland and Midcalder railway and the new Edinburgh station. The latter, even so, was successively scaled down in its proposed extent and grandeur in the late 1860s. The plan for a station hotel was dropped.

On 22nd October, 1867 the Caley Board met to consider the abandonment of various planned branches and other works in order to reduce their liabilities. A special committee of four company officers was appointed to study possibilities and decided to apply to Parliament for authority to abandon the Balerno branch, as well as other lines, "if arrangements can be made with millowners."

Subsequently an alternative plan was briefly considered whereby Parliament's permission would be sought for an extension in the time allowed to make the branch rather than abandoning it completely. However, no extension of time was applied for.

There was mounting disquiet among all Caley shareholders; their dividends had recently fallen very low. A committee of enquiry had once again been set up to examine the position, and its report was published on 4th January, 1868.

It recommended immediate savings be made through abandonments, and the installation of a new Board. It found that the old problem of unrealistically high guaranteed dividends which had plagued the company since the 1840s was at the root of the present crisis too. In the year 1865–66, out of a surplus of £713,179 (revenue of £1,397,560 less expenditure of £684,381) only £188,355 had been left after guaranteed dividends, debentures and debt payments had been made.

Among branches which the committee suggested be abandoned was a line to Corstorphine, which had been authorised shortly after the Balerno branch.

Powers to abandon the Balerno branch itself were initially to have been applied for in 1868. However, the Caley resolved instead to seek to raise new capital that year, and then apply for abandonments in 1869.

Not until 30th April, 1869 did Parliamentary proceedings get under way for the Balerno branch abandonment. But meantime there had been activity in other quarters among those who were not prepared to lose the railway without a fight. As can be imagined the original subscribers to the branch were not happy with the performance of the Caley so far; the company had accepted their subscriptions but had been conspicuous only by their absence for four years.

Henry Bruce for one was not prepared to let the Caley away with reneging on their promise; on 13th April, 1869 the Board had discussed a letter from him, and noted: "If the line can be made for £50,000 or £60,000 at the outside it may not be unadvisable to make it."

When the case came to Parliament later that month, the millowners and local landowners retained a counsel to oppose the abandonment and speak on their behalf.

But the first to address the hearing was the counsel for the Caley. After attempting to justify the spending of the share capital raised for the branch he did admit: "We have spent this money, and perhaps wrongly spent this money."

But he insisted that the Caley had not raised money from the branch under false pretences. He was echoed in this by George Cunningham, the next to appear. He was by now a partner in the re-styled Blyth and Cunningham, following the death of the firms's founder Benjamin Hall Blyth in 1866. He stressed that only the Caley's "pecuniary difficulties" had prevented the line being built, despite the inherent problems its construction involved, what with very steep banks and rocks abounding.

Of the original plan for a double track branch he commented that it had perhaps been laid out more expensively than necessary.

The counsel for the protesting mill-owners then cross-examined Cunningham. Was it not true that several mills had been enlarged in the last year or two in expectation of the Caley building the railway? Cunningham agreed. And had not several mill-owners recently offered to forgo their right to demand the fullest compensation (under an 1845 Act) whenever the railway was to encroach on part of their property – so that the Caley would not be put to as great expense as originally intended? Cunningham agreed. Suddenly there was a hint of an agreed compromise in the air. Clearly the two sides had consulted in advance. The question of the Caley building a single track branch was next raised, and Cunningham agreed the suggestion had been made and was feasible.

"Have you any doubt," asked the counsel for the mill-masters, "that to any company who made that line for £60,000 that would be very remunerative?"

"I have no doubt that there would be a very great traffic upon it. I believe that the Directors would not have abandoned the line if they had not been very hard up."

The next witness to appear for the Caley was Christopher Johnstone, who had been the general manager at the time the branch was originally planned. Under cross-examination he was questioned in detail about the vital importance of the railway to the local mills. The general manager agreed that there were many of these and several had been enlarged with the coming of the railway in mind, and that they gave very valuable trade to the railway.

Following his insistent questioning of Mr Johnstone on 5th May, 1869, the counsel representing the opponents of the abandonment returned to the hearing the next day to conduct the opposition case.

On behalf of 56 "owners, occupiers, and lessees, and mill-owners, and traders, and farmers upon the Balerno branch" he argued that the Caley had badly let down those who had originally proposed the branch. The large share capital raised for the branch had been "misapplied and misappropriated to other purposes, and not one particle of the line has been made, though some little progress was made in the purchase of property."

The Caley should not be permitted to abandon their 1865 undertaking without at the same time being required to make fresh plans for the branch. The question of a single track line had been raised and the Caley had agreed that it could be built for £60,000 and thereafter run at a profit. As a further incentive counsel's clients, the local property-owners, had generously offered to waive their rights to the fullest possible compensation where the railway affected their land.

In conclusion the counsel suggested that the Caley could consider themselves lucky not to be asked to construct the double track railway originally proposed, on the strength of which the share capital had been raised.

Before the counsel, Mr Johnson, could call any witnesses (one was to have been Henry Bruce of Kinleith paper mill) the Caley intervened to state that they accepted the opposition case in full. It was then decided that proceedings should be adjourned to allow consultations between the two sides to take place.

On 7th May, 1869 it was announced that the abandonment Bill would be passed, but only as a formality, to cancel the provisions of the 1865 Act and wipe the slate clean, as it were. The Bill would contain clauses requiring a new Act to be obtained for a single track Balerno branch.

The abandonment Act was officially passed on 26th July, 1869. Under it the Caley were to return to Parliament for authority to make a line "terminating to the westward of Newmills farmsteading in the parish of Currie" and "proceeding in or nearly in the course and direction" of the 1865 line.

The Caley were to complete the branch within two and a half years of obtaining a new Act; which, as it turned out, was passed on 20th June, 1870.

The sum of £60,000 was to be deposited in a bank within a year of the abandonment Act and only to be used on the Balerno branch. In effect the Act treated the Caley rather like an errant schoolboy who had been trusted with the shopping-money but returned home empty-handed; there was no question of the same degree of trust being given now!

Indeed a more sober spirit now infused general railway company thinking after the wild excesses of the mid-1860s. The North British, like the Caley, had recently had their wings clipped after revelations of corrupt practice. Dividends had been paid out of capital to disguise how bad things were. A new Board had been brought in.

Fresh Plans – and further Protests

Until 1869 the Balerno branch was envisaged as a railway running west from Slateford and terminating at Balerno.

But on 12th October, 1869 approval was given to the idea of a connecting line, linking Balerno with the Caley main line at Ravelrig further west. This would enable traffic, especially goods traffic, to run directly between stations on the branch and the central belt or the west of Scotland.

The effect of adding this new section of line to the plans was to turn the Balerno branch into a loop line. "Railway no. 2", as the new section was described, was to leave the existing proposed branch a quarter of a mile east of the planned Balerno terminus (the short ¼ mile length of track thus detached later became the spur to Balerno goods station, with the passenger station being erected at the top of the new section) and run down to the Caley main line at Ravelrig at a steady gradient of 1 in 70 for a length of 1¼ miles.

When the complete revised plans were put on public inspection at the end of 1869 they included few changes from the 1865 plans. But one amendment caused some heated debate. This was a heightening of the railway by means of a large embankment, which was to carry it at a gradient of 1 in 50 between Currie church and the river and enable it to cross the road approaching Currie brig from the south, rather than go under it on the level as formerly planned.

The amendment had been made to save money, since under the old plan it was to have been necessary not only to raise the approach road but to build an entirely new bridge over the Water of Leith. Savings of £2,000 were involved.

But the thought of a large railway embankment so close to the church aroused the ire of some locals including Sir William Gibson-Craig, second Baronet of Riccarton and a venerable public figure. He protested first to the Caley and then in a letter to *The Scotsman* newspaper published on 12th February, 1870, and at the same time – rather late in the day – poured scorn on the whole branch.

Although Sir William was not involved in selling his own personal land for the Balerno branch, he was one of the Currie parish heritors from whom the Caley needed to buy the land on which to build the controversial embankment. And like his father with whom the Caley had had problems in

1845 he was a man to heed, for at the age of 72 he was a former Lord of the Treasury and present Lord Clerk Register in Scotland.

In his letter to *The Scotsman* Sir William noted angrily of the embankment:

> It will be only thirty or forty yards from the manse and church, and close to the school and schoolmaster's house, blocking up all these buildings most injuriously, and making both the accesses to them and to the southern part of the parish almost unsafe. I need not say that a railway and station within a few yards of a parish school is most objectionable and even dangerous.

(The school was at that time the building to the immediate north of the church; the railway station would be separated from it by a road – Kirkgate – and several cottages.)

Sir William condemned the Balerno branch in its entirety for three reasons. Firstly the four communities which it was to serve were "all small and poor villages". Secondly many of the local mills would not be able to benefit from the railway by reason of being on the opposite side of the river from it – and anyway Kinleith paper mill was the only one of any importance.

Thirdly the district was already adequately served by the main Caledonian railway. Sir William likened the relative positions of the branch and the main line to the figure of a strongbow, the branch being the string and the main line the bow; he commented that "no part of the bow is above a mile from the string, and the greater part of it is not half that distance." Sir William concluded with a warning:

> Too many of the great railways have been deeply and irretrievably injured by unremunerating branches, and I do not believe one has ever been proposed which was less required or which would be more certainly unproductive.

The Caley reacted to the publication of Sir William's letter by sending George Cunningham to Currie to meet him and several other residents who had voiced concerns similar to those of Sir William at the Caley's half-yearly meeting a few days before.

Cunningham attempted to mollify them. But he evidently failed, for the following August, after the final Balerno branch Act had been passed in June, it was Henry Bruce's turn to launch an angry outburst.

In a letter to the Caley Chairman he echoed all Sir William's misgivings. He threatened that if the branch were built as planned the Caley would have to "pay sweetly" in compensation. He himself, despite being a shareholder, would offer evidence against the company in any arbitration cases.

Of the controversial embankment at Currie he wrote:

> Had I known that such a change on the levels was to be made, I never would have consented to the Abandonment Bill. The line now proposed will ruin the church, manse and schoolhouse, and the accesses to the new Currie Station will be worse than anything I know of existing in the Kingdom.

From the Caley point of view, though the new Act had been safely obtained and Bruce's criticisms could not alter that, it was clearly desirable that an important present and future customer should not be at odds with them.

They turned again to George Cunningham, more or less quoting him in their reply to Bruce. Cunningham suggested that the original scheme for a line on the level and a new bridge over the river, with high access roads, could be revived provided the local road trustees and the heritors joined in:

All the parties are interested in having the road and bridge improved, and I have no doubt would at once consent to the alteration of the levels, though I have little hope that any of them will put their hands in their pockets.

He stressed that the embankment, though adding fifteen feet to the height of the railway, would still carry it well below the level of the manse garden wall and so would not be as intrusive as feared. He also condemned Henry Bruce for his attitude – for had he not been one of the advocates of a cheap, single track line in 1869, yet here he was demanding expensive alterations?

Cunningham replied to another criticism made by Bruce to the effect that too many mills would be by-passed by the railway (just as Sir William Gibson-Craig had asserted) by remarking that only one mill-owner had complained; this was David Chalmers of Kates mill who had also protested about the 1865 plan!

On 20th June, 1870, following the briefest of proceedings in Parliament in early May, the second Balerno branch Bill was given the Royal Assent. It was a reflection of how much more economically the railway had been engineered that gradients of 1 in 50 were authorised in the Act, compared with a

---

4. Subject to the provisions of this Act the Company may make, in the lines and according to the levels shown on the deposited plans and sections, the Railways and other works hereinafter described, and all proper stations, approaches, works, and conveniences connected therewith

15 respectively; and may enter upon, take, and use such of the lands delineated on the said plans, and described in the deposited Books of Reference, as may be required for that purpose. The Railways and other works hereinbefore referred to and authorised by this Act are:—

  (1.) A Branch Railway (in this Act called the "Balerno Branch")
20   five miles and one hundred and twenty-seven yards or there-
    abouts in length, commencing by a junction with the main
    line of the Caledonian Railway leading from Carlisle to
    Edinburgh, near the south-western end of the viaduct by
    which that line is carried over the Water of Leith, near the
25   village of Slateford, and terminating near the bridge over
    that river called Balerno Bridge:

  (2.) A connecting Branch Railway (in this Act called the "Balerno
    Connecting Branch") one mile two furlongs and sixty-six
    yards or thereabouts in length, commencing by a junction
30   with the said Balerno Branch, about six chains westward
    from Newmills Corn-mill, and terminating by a junction with
    the said main line of the Caledonian Railway, about seven-
    and-a-half chains eastward from the $93\frac{1}{2}$ mile post from
    Carlisle on that line:

(Power to make and maintain certain Railways and other works and to acquire certain lands.)

Extract from the 1870 Act re-authorising the Balerno branch. The spur from Balerno to Ravelrig is now also authorised (para.(2)).

Courtesy, Keeper of the Records of Scotland (BR/AP(S)/57)

maximum of 1 in 80 under the 1865 Act. Curves of seven-chains radius were also permitted.

The Act provided that a financial penalty should be imposed on the Caley if the railway did not open on time – that is, by 20th December, 1872 – with each day's delay to cost them £50 for a limited period (in fact until five per cent of the total cost of the works had been set aside). This penalty, however, need not be paid if the delay was due to circumstances outwith the Caley's control, though lack of funds would not be considered an excuse!

In the event the Balerno branch opened twenty months behind time on 1st August, 1874. But there is no record of any penalty being paid and since the contractor later reported that the contract was "with difficulty got through" due to an unexpected rise in cost of materials, it may be that this was reckoned to be a circumstance outwith the Caley's control.

The contract for the Balerno branch was advertised in *The Scotsman* and other newspapers on 12th October, 1870. Interested parties were asked to attend at Slateford station at 10.30 am on 27th October, where they would be met by an engineer and shown along the course of the branch.

On 22nd November, 1870 the offer of Charles Brand and Son to build the line at a price of £42,134 13s. 6d. was accepted. The firm were then employed in Ayrshire constructing a branch for the Glasgow and South-Western Railway Company.

The New Edinburgh Station

A new passenger terminus was opened by the Caley on 2nd May, 1870, a little to the north of the existing Lothian Road station. The latter was converted for goods-only use.

Known as Princes Street station, the new building was a simple wooden shed 150 yds long, into which ran three tracks of rail. Trains arrived by the most westerly track and departed by the track nearest Lothian Road, with the centre track reserved for spare carriages. There were just two platforms, which extended for 100 yds clear of the station shed to the south.

It was ironic that the station should be a humble wooden structure. When first planned in September 1864 at the height of the boom in ambitious railway schemes, it was intended that the new station would be an elegant stone structure complete with a hotel – and that it would answer the critics. For as *The Scotsman* had reported on 17th September, 1864, "the present station is confessedly inconvenient, ugly, and confined, and much complained of by passengers."

In fact plans for the station had been shelved for most of 1865 while the Caley discussed with their Edinburgh rivals, the Edinburgh and Glasgow Railway and the North British Railway (who merged that year), the possibility of a general central station. This plan, however, fell through.

The Act for a new station was obtained in 1866. One major functional purpose it was to serve was to accommodate the anticipated increase in traffic between Edinburgh and Glasgow when the Cleland and Midcalder railway opened. This had been authorised in 1865 and opened in 1869.

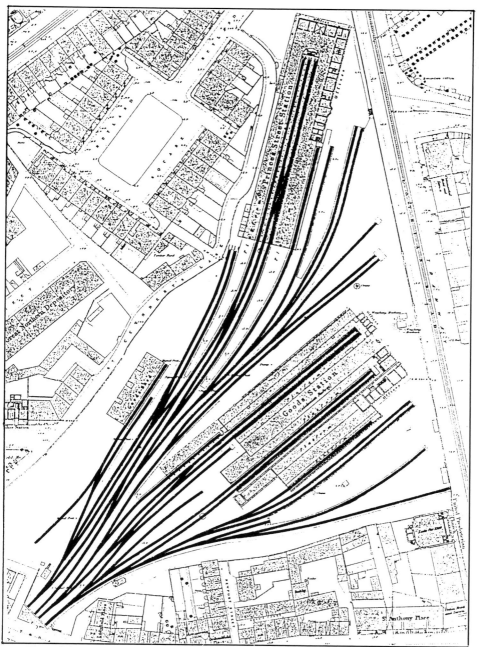

Plan of the Caley's second Edinburgh passenger station, opened in May 1870. (*Plan dated 1877*.) The new terminus was little more than a wooden shed. Trains arrived by the track nearest Rutland Square and departed from that nearest Lothian Road, the centre track being for spare carriages. (Note diamond crossing between the latter two.)

But as the financial crisis of the late 1860s developed, the Caley had to cut costs and the Edinburgh station became a casualty. The plan for a stone building was dropped; the station hotel was scrapped.

To make room for the station, a large number of buildings were demolished. The poor house, next to the 1848 station, was knocked down and an alternative site found at Craiglockhart (the new building opened in 1867 and accommodated over 600 people). Beyond the poor house was the Scottish Naval and Military Academy which had trained generations of officers for service in the East India Company and in government. The attached Riding Academy was also knocked down.

Also demolished were St George's Free Church, erected only in 1845; Brae House (an old mansion); and a number of houses in Rutland Street, at the north-eastern end. St Cuthbert's Lane, which ran from Torphichen Street to Lothian Road, emerging between the church and the academy, was diverted to end at Rutland Street. Lothian Road itself was raised considerably so that it was level with the station instead of dipping to a hollow opposite Castle Terrace as formerly.

When the Cleland and Midcalder railway opened for passenger traffic on 9th July, 1869 the need for the new Edinburgh station became pressing. There were now 16 trains running each way between Edinburgh and Glasgow daily and only one track was available at Edinburgh for passenger trains, whether arriving or departing. The other line was goods-only.

In making the new station the Caley took the chance to reduce the problem of access by quadrupling the railway lines from as far west as Dalry Junction, where a new signal box with 42 levers "understood to be the largest in Scotland" (*Scotsman*) was opened. Between the signal box and the stations a new mineral depot was provided at Morrison Street.

Princes Street station was set quite far back from Princes Street, in fact. A large triangular space whose sides were the station façade, Lothian Road and Rutland Street was left for horse-carriages to draw up in. (The later station, opened in 1894, came much closer to Princes Street.)

The station opened on 2nd May, 1870 with quite a lot of work still in hand. Subsequently extra sidings were laid between it and the goods station, where new facilities including a costly grain store were provided.

In the twenty or so years between its opening in 1870 and its demise in the early 1890s the second Edinburgh station provoked numerous complaints, just as the first had, for its general shabbiness. Indeed when Sir William Gibson-Craig wrote to *The Scotsman* to criticise the Balerno branch in February 1870 he suggested that the money for the branch "would better be spent on a substantial Edinburgh station instead of the wooden shed which is now erecting." Sir William made this comment in his draft letter, which is still preserved among family papers – but he tactfully removed it from the final copy!

Chapter Six

Construction Of The Balerno Branch

By the beginning of 1871 the Caley had officially spent £7289 on the Balerno branch despite the fact that work had not yet begun on making it. These costs were mainly Parliamentary and planning costs and also included the purchase of two properties.

Construction of the branch began in April. Meantime the contractors Charles Brand and Son applied to the Caley for permission to have their men conveyed to and from the district daily by train as the navvies were mainly lodging in Edinburgh. The Caley agreed and granted special weekly fares.

Some men, however, lodged locally. The contractor's agent, who was the man in charge at the site, William Duncan, boarded in Juniper Green. He had been employed by Brand since working on the Sutherland Railway in the mid-1860s, along with his brother. Many of the men, like these two, were from the north of Scotland. Though no record survives to indicate the total number of navvies working on the line, it can be guessed from figures for other similar lines that about 200 men were involved, working on different sections simultaneously.

Charles Brand himself was a man of over 70 who had embarked on a long career building railways in the 1840s after starting out as a mason in the town of Montrose in the 1820s. Until 1867 his firm, in which his elder son James was a partner, had worked only in the north of Scotland. James Brand was later to describe how and why the firm first ventured into the south in memoirs written for his children in 1901:

> In the autumn of 1867 we tendered for the Ayrshire lines, two contracts, one which extended from the Muirkirk branch of the Glasgow and South Western Railway above the Lugar Iron Works through Cumnock, passing down to join another branch six miles from Ayr. I was very unwilling to take this work, as there was still the Caithness line to make in the north, as well as the Dingwall and Skye, and I could have had at least amongst them £200,000.
>
> But your grandfather was eager to get work in the south and thought that if I did not go then, as I was approaching forty, I might never go into a wider field. It was a mistake and he was sorry, as the work was heavy and we were not trained to estimate in that country, and we lost all the money we had made.
>
> However, I did not lose heart, and I took a little contract from the Caledonian called the Balerno branch, which, as prices rose in the line of trade in 1870, was with difficulty got through, and at a loss.

The Balerno branch involved 28 bridges large and small, the long tunnel at Colinton, and many cuttings and embankments. As the Water of Leith kept the line company for much of the way, a number of retaining walls had to be built along the riverside notably at Juniper Green and Newmills. At Newmills the river even had to be diverted slightly to allow room for the railway.

In order to safeguard the operation of various water mills where the railway was to run close by, the Engineers specified in the contract:

> No interference to be caused to flow of water in any lade, byewash or other stream so as to cause interference to the working of any mill unless with consent of owners: contractors to be answerable for any damages.

In fact Woodhall paper mill was put out of action for a fortnight in May 1872

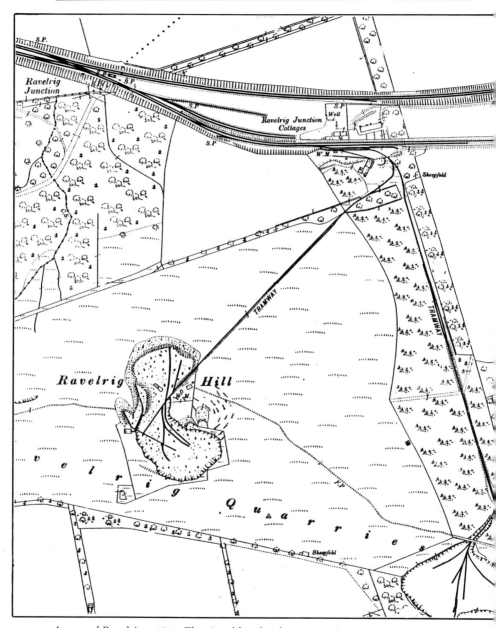

A map of Ravelrig c.1914. The signal box has been recently re-erected between main and branch lines, from its previous position to the north of the main line (*opened September 1912*). Ravelrig Platform was just to the west of the junction (off the map). By this time only two quarries are served by tramways, the westernmost having ceased working.   *Reproduced from the 1914 25" Ordnance Survey Map*

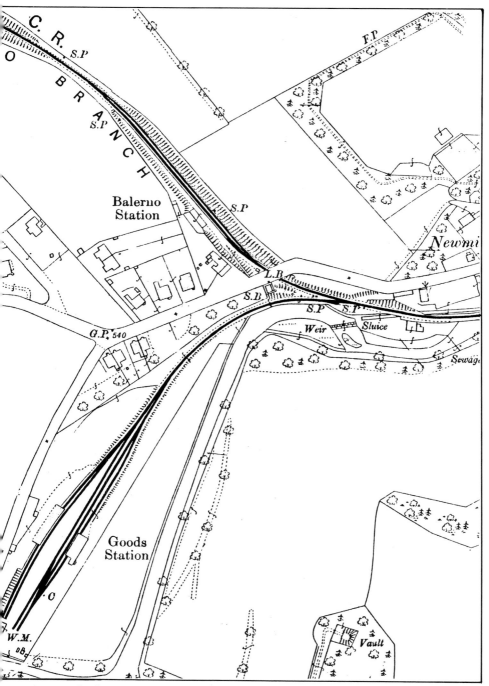

The map of Balerno Station.   *Reproduced from the 1914, 25" Ordnance Survey Map*

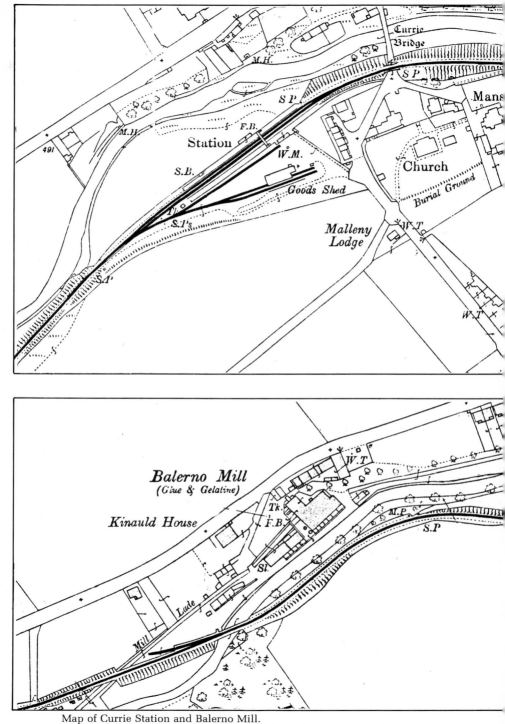

Map of Currie Station and Balerno Mill.
Reproduced from the 1914, 25″ Ordnance Survey Map

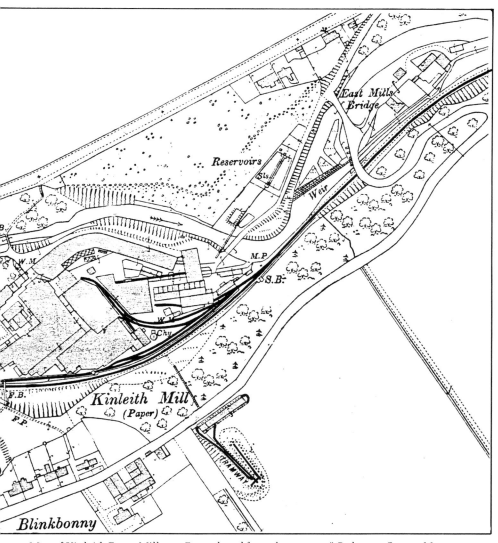

Map of Kinleith Paper Mill.   *Reproduced from the 1914, 25" Ordnance Survey Map*

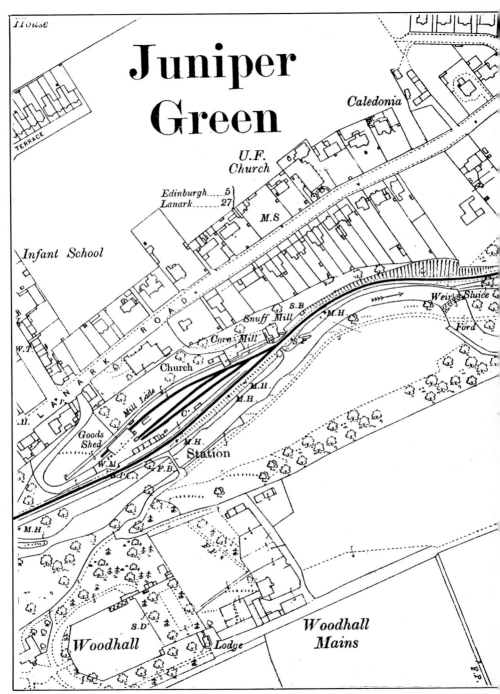

Map of Juniper Green Station.

Reproduced from the 1914, 25" Ordnance Survey Map

The Balerno branch showing the entry to the sidings at Kinleith mill, with the Water of Leith on the right. Photographed on the 8th November, 1952. *D.L.G .Hunter*

A CR wagon at Kinleith mill c.1914, with esparto grass being unloaded.
Courtesy, Edinburgh City Libraries

The electric shunter at Kinleith mill, seen here in 1953. This was bought by Henry
Bruce & Sons in 1902 and was still in use in 1965.   *W.S. Sellar*

First of the two special trains on 19th April, 1965, crossing the Water of Leith,
between Juniper Green and Currie, west-bound.   *David S.G. Stirling*

A view looking east at East Mills Snuff mill (closed 1920), between Juniper Green and Currie. The railway here crosses the Water of Leith. *Courtesy Mrs J. Tweedie*

East Mills Snuff mill was situated between the river and the railway on the south bank. The wall of the railway branch is visible. Just out of the range of this photograph, is the bridge taking the line over to the north bank and on towards Juniper Green station. The mill is now demolished, having closed in 1920.

Royal Commission on Ancient Monuments, Scotland

Newmills meal mill was by the goods junction at Balerno. It was open until 1920. Earlier, the Caley acquired it in 1872, when purchasing land for the branch (which ran directly behind it).   *Royal Commission on Ancient Monuments, Scotland*

Juniper Green showing the disused signal box (this closed in 1889 at the time of the line's conversion to tablet operation). Watts snuff mill can also be seen, which closed in 1940. This view looks east.   *Courtesy Mrs J. Tweedie*

Woodhall paper mill immediately west of Juniper Green. Dating back to the 18th century, it was expanded considerably in the mid-20th century. It was closed in 1984 and is now demolished.

Courtesy Royal Commission on Ancient Monuments, Scotland

A good view in 1934 of Juniper Green station, looking east and showing well the acute curve of the platform.   *L.G.R.P., courtesy David and Charles*

JUNIPER GREEN STATION & ST MARGARETS PARISH CHURCH

Two views of attractive Juniper Green station in Caley days. The footbridge in the foreground was over the Water of Leith. *Top: Lens of Sutton bottom: Royal Commission on Ancient Monuments, Scotland*

THE STATION.

A view of Juniper Green station (looking east) appearing rather forlorn in its last days as a goods station on 19th January, 1952. The wagons in the goods yard behind the old station building can just be seen. The level crossing in the foreground was used by traffic to and from Woodhall paper mill.   *D.L.G. Hunter*

Juniper Green looking west, 1961. The large shed visible was a dispatch shed belonging to Woodhall paper mill, situated further west. This shed was erected on the site of Juniper Green station, which had closed as a goods station in 1958.

David S.G. Stirling

In the middle of winter, January 1954, a freight train (with 0−6−0T No. 47163)
approaching Juniper Green from Colinton. *W.S. Sellar*

Near Juniper Green (passing Inglis mill) is seen the last special on the branch in April
1965. Note the interesting wooden footbridge. *W.S. Sellar*

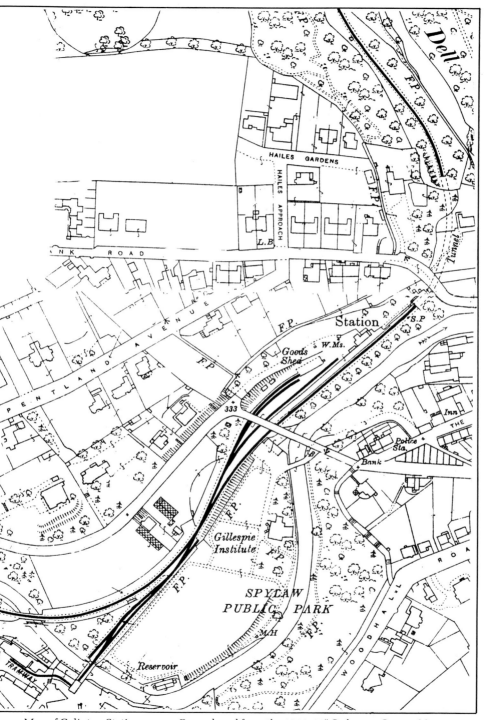

Map of Colinton Station.   *Reproduced from the 1914, 25" Ordnance Survey Map*

Map of Hailes Platform.   *Reproduced from the 1914, 25" Ordnance Survey Map*

Station Master George Melrose of Currie Station, in the handsome uniform of the Caledonian Railway. Note the flower in his button-hole! (*see* Chapter Ten)
        Courtesy Mrs J. Tweedie

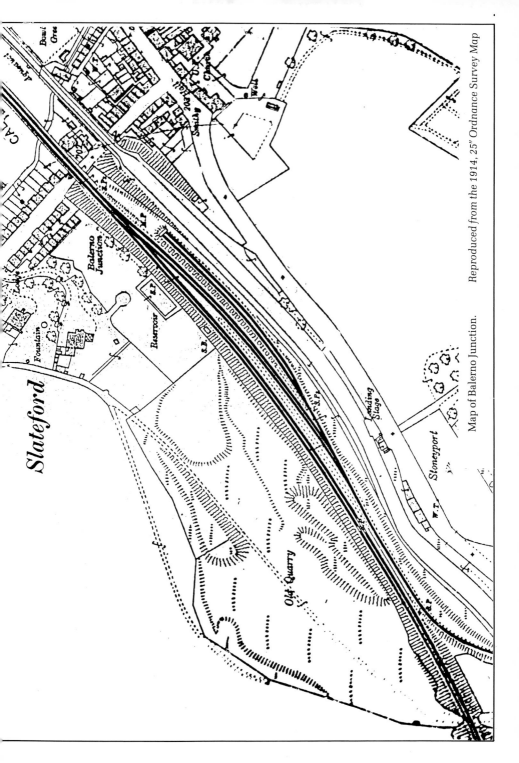

Map of Balerno Junction.

Reproduced from the 1914, 25" Ordnance Survey Map

when the mill-lade was blocked up. The Caley paid the mill-master damages of over £50 which was no doubt then deducted from Brand's payments.

The many bridges involved in the building of the Balerno branch included four over the Water of Leith, the most substantial of these being at East Mills between Currie and Juniper Green; the estimate of its cost was over £1100. But perhaps the most elegant bridge was that at Upper Spylaw between Juniper Green and Colinton, which was built on the skew unlike most of the others.

Six of the bridges crossed over or under local roads, including two over and under the Lanark Road at each end of the branch. Most of the others were small affairs built across streams, farm tracks and mill-lades.

A fifth bridge over the Water of Leith was never built; it was to have carried an access road directly from Colinton village over to the station. In 1872 the Caley cancelled the plan to make it, in favour of subscribing to a new bridge proposed by the local road trust which was duly erected further west and stands to this day.

Brand and Son let the ironwork required for several bridges as a sub-contract. It was taken by a young Glasgow engineer William Arrol, who had only recently set up in business on his own, and had capital funds of £250. He subsequently moved on to be the main contractor on the Forth Bridge, on the opening of which he was knighted in 1890. His Dalmarnock ironworks, erected in 1872 and subsequently enlarged, was the largest structural steel-works in Britain.

The masonry of the bridges on the Balerno branch was built by Brand and Son who obtained stone from several quarries which they opened in the district.

Cuttings and embankments were linked together under the specifications for the branch for the reason that material excavated in making cuttings was then used to build the embankments.

The heaviest section of cuttings was on the line west of Balerno, where they continued for half a mile before giving way to a long embankment. At either end of Colinton tunnel cuttings to a depth of 40 ft were required.

Dynamite was used to blast both rock cuttings and the 150 yds-long Colinton tunnel. It was then a recent innovation, powder having formerly been used. In order to insert a charge, teams of three men drilled holes in the rock-face, one alternately holding a "jumper" or drill while the other two hammered it.

In the specifications for the contract the Engineers insisted: "In rock cutting the Contractors shall take all necessary precautions to avoid injury to life or property by blasting or otherwise."

Embankments were built by a traditional method known as "tipping" whereby wagons of earth or rock were run at speed along temporary rails to the head of the embankment before being tripped by a piece of timber laid across the line, causing the contents to be up-ended over the edge. The traction was provided by horses which were expertly unhitched from the wagons at the last possible moment.

The Balerno branch was built entirely by manual labour. Though mech-anical diggers known as "steam navvies" were beginning to come into use at the time, James Brand later recalled that the firm used one for the first time in 1876 at Strathaven Junction.

The contract for the Balerno branch was meticulous in its detail. Brand and Son were obliged to supply thirty gradient boards and twenty-two mile posts (including half-mile and quarter-mile posts). "These mile posts shall be of the best memel timber, well-cleaned, shall receive three coats of white lead and oils and shall be lettered and numbered as the engineer may direct."

Even footpaths, of which 1,300 yds were to be made, were to conform to strict specifications, being "three feet wide and covered to a depth of four inches with engine ashes, the price to include all cutting and banking not exceeding two feet in depth"!

The main costs of making the branch were estimated as follows:

Table of Costs (Estimates)

Bridges:	£8126	17s.	10d.
Embankments/Cuttings:	£7722	3s.	4d.
Permanent Way:	£5407	3s.	9d.
Stations/Junctions:	£5142	16s.	6d.
Retaining Walls:	£4338	15s.	0d.
Culverts and Ends:	£3514	7s.	0d.
Drains and Fencing:	£2709	11s.	8d.
Colinton Tunnel:	£2400		
Road Alterations:	£1100	4s.	0d.
Other Items:	£906		
Total:	£41,367	19s.	1d.

(The difference between this total and the overall contract price of £42,134 13s. 6d. was accounted for by another undertaking – the replacement of Ravelrig level crossing on the main line by a bridge – which was separate from the branch.)

The "other items" comprised ditches, footpaths, level crossings and so on.

The fairly large sum allocated to road alterations arose from the need to raise and lower road levels wherever the railway ran over or under roads. At Newmills the line of the Lanark Road was to be diverted north to allow sufficient room by the riverside for Balerno signal box and the junction of the branch proper with the spur to the goods yard.

As to stations, these were to be laid out at the following cost:

Colinton station:	£447	17s.	0d.
Juniper Green station:	£486	16s.	0d.
Currie station:	£946	7s.	0d.
Newmills station:	£83	3s.	0d. (includes goods junction)
Balerno station:	£612	13s.	0d. (i.e. the goods station)

Currie station alone was to have two tracks, allowing trains to cross. Timbers were to be laid between the rails to enable passengers to cross from one platform to the other; there was to be no footbridge. One was eventually erected at the station in 1884, ten years after the opening of the branch.

Land Acquisitions

Under the 1870 Act the Caley were granted powers of compulsory purchase over the land required to make the Balerno branch, these powers remaining in force until 1872. But many of the 44 agreements were only eventually reached through the process of arbitration, and more than a third were concluded after the railway opened in 1874.

The Fleming brothers of Upper Spylaw snuff mill received an award of £60 for their "loss of amenity" as late as 1882.

The final list ot settlements ranged from £4000 to £1! This sum was given to William Hill as compensation for "a bit of garden ground" which he occupied (but did not own) at Millbank near Boag's mill.

James Gowans, the tenant of Redhall quarry in the same area, was paid £1450 for the loss of rock which he was unable to excavate as a result of the Balerno branch running too near; the line had to be protected. (James Gowans opened a new quarry to the north of the Caley main line nearby in 1873 with which he had similar problems in later years.)

The several arbitrators involved in land deals could make a tidy income out of these cases. One such was George Glendinning, the factor to the Earl of Morton's Hatton estate, who was called on in half a dozen awards. To George Stirling, the tenant of Newmills farm, he allocated £10 as a result of "damage to oats when surveying" and £6 because this surveying work had caused the "loss of two days of four horses and two days of ten people at harvest." Stirling eventually received £276.

The tenant of nearby Pilmuir farm, George Davidson, received sums for the "loss of unexhausted manure" (£39 2s. 0d.) and "a heap of broken stones" (£8) as part of his settlement of £600. But the major items in these settlements and others were payments for "severance" and "detour" – the loss of the land itself and the nuisance of having fields broken up into small parts.

In purchasing Newmills mill at Balerno in 1872 the Caley also acquired the ancient "multures, sequels and pertinents" of the mill, the formal right to deduct payments in grain or cash from customers at the mill! (Newmills mill had in fact only recently burnt down; it was subsequently re-erected.)

The Caley had eventually to pay out over £27,000 for land for the Balerno branch. Eight major landowners received over £1000. The biggest payment was £4000 to Sir James Liston Foulis of Woodhall, while £2973 was paid to Major Francis Scott of Malleny, £2600 to Sir William Gibson-Carmichael of Hailes, £2434 to the Earl of Morton for land along the Ravelrig section, £2188 to the governors of James Gillespie's school for land near Spylaw, £2272 to Henry Bruce of Kinleith, £1173 to John Inglis of Redhall and £1005 to Dr John Stuart of Newmills.

Colinton Bridge

Shortly after the construction of the Balerno branch was begun the Caley appointed a police constable to the line, as required by law. He remained on hand for three years from July 1871 until August 1874 when the branch opened, supervising the behaviour of the men. Caley capital accounts show that he was paid a wage of £1 per week while quarterly payments of "boot money" and "uniform money" were also made.

The other regular wage-earner apart from the contractor was the Inspector of Works. His job was to monitor the quality of the work being done. His opposite number in the contractor's staff was the head ganger whose interest, it has been said, was to see that the work was economically done while the inspector had to see that it was not *too* economically done!

Each "side" also had engineers on hand. For the Caley James H. Cunningham was the Resident Engineer; he was an assistant with Blyth and Cunningham. Brand and Son also had a Chief Engineer. Both men made detailed reports on the work as it progressed, measuring excavated material for payment, their notes being compared and eventually matched.

Building a railway also involved numbers of men in secondary capacities. There were the quarriers who produced the stone for use in masonry; carters taking stone and other materials to wherever they were needed; a smith to sharpen tools at the specially erected smithy; stores staff; and so on.

On 7th February, 1872, with the Balerno branch well under way after ten months, a decision taken by the local road trust meant a last-minute change in the plans of the Caley for an access bridge to Colinton station.

The trustees resolved on that date to erect a new bridge over the Water of Leith west of Colinton village, with special access roads; this would allow the old brig with its awkward aproaches to be by-passed. The Caley were amenable, as the village station could be easily reached from the north end of the bridge. They agreed to contribute £1500 to its cost.

The road trustees involved were those of the Calder, Slateford and Corstorphine Trust; they now persuaded the Lasswade and Wrights Houses trustees, who administered the existing road through Colinton, to contribute £600.

Charles Brand and Son, being already on hand, applied for and won the contract to build the new bridge at a price of £2414, the access road to cost a further £1200. The bridge was completed in 1873. Railway tracks were then laid under the three most northerly of its eight arches, one being the branch proper, the others being sidings running from west of the bridge into Colinton station.

Special Engines

So steep were the gradients on the Balerno branch, and so sharp the curves, that the Caley decided to commission special engines to be built to operate on it.

On 6th May, 1872 the permanent way and traffic committee instructed the locomotive superintendent, Benjamin Conner, to take tenders for two bogie engines for the branch.

The advantage of a bogie engine was in the manoeuvrability it offered; but at the time this was a most unusual departure for the Caley and it illustrates the very particular conditions pertaining on the branch.

On 3rd July the stores committee secretary minuted:

Bogie engines for the Balerno branch. Submitted tenders. Accept the tender of Neilson and Co. for two engines at £2400 each, to be delivered in April 1873.

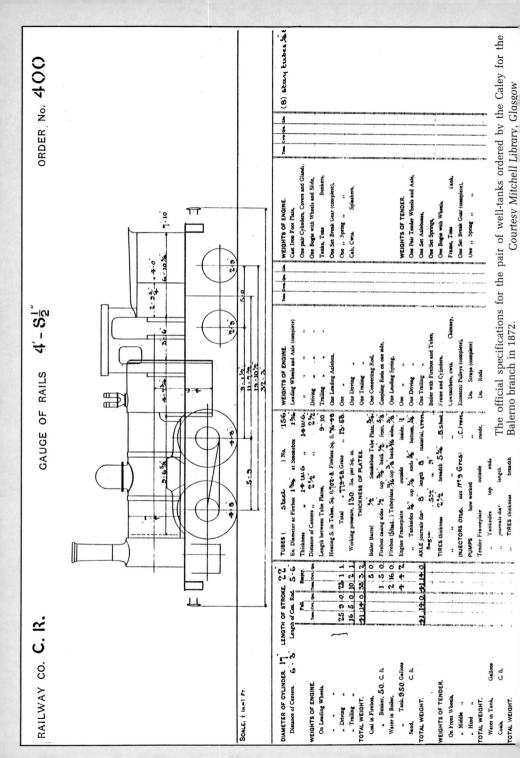

The official specifications for the pair of well-tanks ordered by the Caley for the Balerno branch in 1872.

Courtesy Mitchell Library, Glasgow

The engines were delivered and evidently proved satisfactory, for two more were ordered that year and built in 1874.

At this time the Caley were ordering most of their new locomotives from external works rather than building them at St Rollox. Most were supplied by the two main Glasgow builders, Neilson and Co. at the Hyde Park Works in Springburn or Dübs and Co. at the Glasgow Locomotive Works in Polmadie.

The four engines (no more were built) were additionally unusual for the Caley in that they were the first passenger tank engines to be built since 1851; they had outside cylinders as was usual then; but the water tank's position directly above the bogie was another distinctive feature.

Each engine was just 33 ft 1¾ in. long from buffer to buffer. With their short wheelbase and 0−4−4 design they were designed to be compact enough to handle the twisting Balerno line but also responsive enough to be able to get away quickly from the intermediate stations.

Very minor alterations were made on the second pair of engines, the wheelbase being extended and the sanding arrangements adjusted.

The main specifications of the engines were as follows:

Cylinders:	17 in. x 22 in. (Later re-bored to 18 in. x 22 in. in 1882.)
Driving wheels:	4 ft 8½ in. dia.
Bogie wheels:	2 ft 8 in. dia.
Well tank capacity:	950 gallons
Coal capacity:	30 cwt.
Boiler barrel:	10 ft 0½ in.
Tubes:	1¾ in.
Heating surface − tubes:	702.8 sq.ft
− firebox:	76.48 sq.ft
Grate area:	13.58 sq.ft
Working pressure:	120 lb.
Weight − full:	42 tons, 3 cwt, 2 qrs.
− empty:	33 tons, 11 cwt, 3 qrs.
Length over buffers:	33 ft 1¾ in.

The engines were originally delivered to the Caley bearing the numbers 488, 489, 490 and 491, though these were later changed to 167, 168, 169 and 170, in 1881. The first pair, built in 1873, were initially sent to work around Perth and Stirling respectively; but when the Balerno branch opened in August 1874 they and the later pair (completed that year) were based in Edinburgh.

The Balerno branch timetable being such that, at least in the early years, just one engine could handle most of the services on a shuttle basis, there was obviously not enough work on the branch for all four engines. Generally engine No. 491 was assigned to the Balerno branch to be supplemented when required by another of the class, the remainder being found other duties. Engines Nos. 489 and 490 in fact appeared regularly on the Leith branch, while No. 488 was most often employed on shunting work.

The Completion of the Branch

Work on the Balerno branch had fallen well behind schedule by the

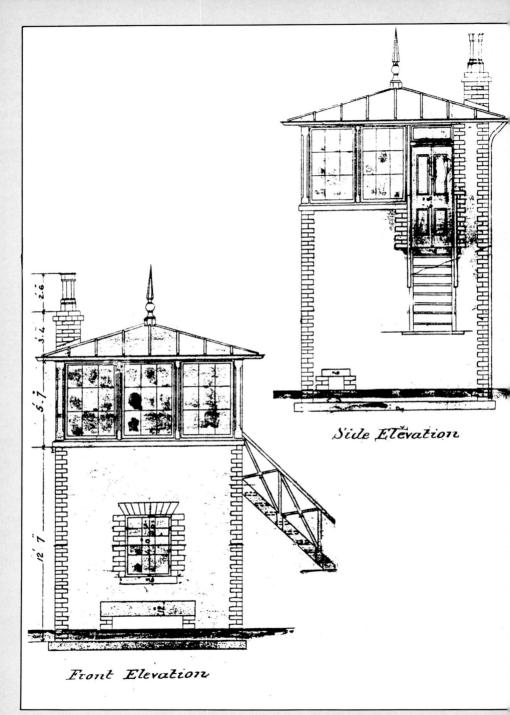

Side Elevation

Front Elevation

Drawings of the signal box at Balerno Goods Junction (dated 1874).
Courtesy Blyth and Blyth

autumn of 1872, a time when according to the original timescale the line should have been about to open. Nonetheless in October 1872 the Caley asked the Board of Trade for permission to begin using the two main line junctions, with a view no doubt to transporting stores and materials as far along the line as it was made.

An inspecting officer, Colonel Hutchinson, approved this, subject to several provisos. Foreseeing a danger of vehicles running back from the branch to the main line at Balerno Junction (the junction near Slateford), he asked that a temporary safety point be interlocked with the signals there. At Ravelrig Junction he requested a locking bar be attached to the facing points for safety and noted that "other points and signals connected with the branch and worked from the pointsman's cabin are not completed, but will be presented for inspection when the branch is ready for opening."

The Balerno branch had been due, under the 1870 Act, to open not later than 20th December, 1872. The deadline however passed with the railway a very long way from completion. On 10th December, 1872 the Caley's finance committee discussed a complaint from Henry Bruce about the delay and advanced him £1,000 towards the settlement of his land compensation claim.

Not until 1873 did work begin on the various buildings along the line. Three Edinburgh contractors undertook respectively the stations (including the two goods sheds at Currie and Balerno); the station masters' cottages at Colinton and Balerno (while those at Juniper Green and Currie were bought as existing properties); and the signal boxes at the four branch stations and at the main line junctions.

Charles Brand and Son's contract for the stations had included the laying-out of platforms but not the actual offices and sheds.

A former engineer once highlighted the gulf in scale between the navvies' task of creating the railway itself and the erection of these later offices and signal boxes:

> These were the responsibility of a building contractor, who brought from the city a race of workmen — joiners and plumbers, slaters and painters — who wore overalls and worked neatly, and whose ways and outlook had as much in common with those of the men on public works as the sardine industry has with whaling.
>
> Duncan Kennedy: *Birth and Death of a Highland Railway.*

The first buildings to be erected were the main line junction signal boxes at Balerno Junction and Ravelrig Junction, which were installed in February 1873.

On 25th February, 1873 the Caley made a slight amendment to their plans for the branch when they authorised double track junctions to be made with the main line. This entailed two tracks being laid for several hundred yards from either end of the line before merging. The Board of Trade were consulted; the inspector asked for several safety features including the interlocking of the proposed points on the branch near Ravelrig Junction with signals on the main line.

This interlocking of signals with points was an innovation being widely introduced. Its purpose was to prevent accidents which might otherwise

Any reply to this communication should be
addressed to—
THE ASSISTANT SECRETARY,
RAILWAY DEPARTMENT,
BOARD OF TRADE,
LONDON, S.W.,

The following letter and number should be
quoted in the reply, and the letter marked plainly
on the outside of the envelope.

R 6715

BOARD OF TRADE,

(RAILWAY DEPARTMENT,)

Draft

LONDON, S.W., *18 October* 1872.

SIR,

I am directed by the Board of Trade to acknowledge the receipt of your letter of the *18th Instant*, giving notice that it is intended to open for public traffic *the Balerno & Ravelrig Junctions* and requesting that an early inspection may be made.

In reply I am to inform you that the Board of Trade have appointed *Colonel Hutchinson RE* to make the inspection as soon as he conveniently can.

I am to add that the usual month's notice of the Company's intention to open the work for public traffic is dispensed with in this case upon condition that should the *Junctions* in question be brought into use before such inspection has taken place, any requirements which the Inspecting Officer may make shall be complied with, and that the Inspecting Officer shall be at liberty to make a re-inspection of the work at any subsequent time.

I am,

SIR,

Your most obedient Servant,

W R Malcolm

The Secretary of the

Caledonian

Railway Company.

A reproduction of the Board of Trade's reply to the Caley's request for authorisation to begin using the junctions of the Balerno branch with the main line.
Courtesy Public Record Office, MT6/111/6; & British Rail.

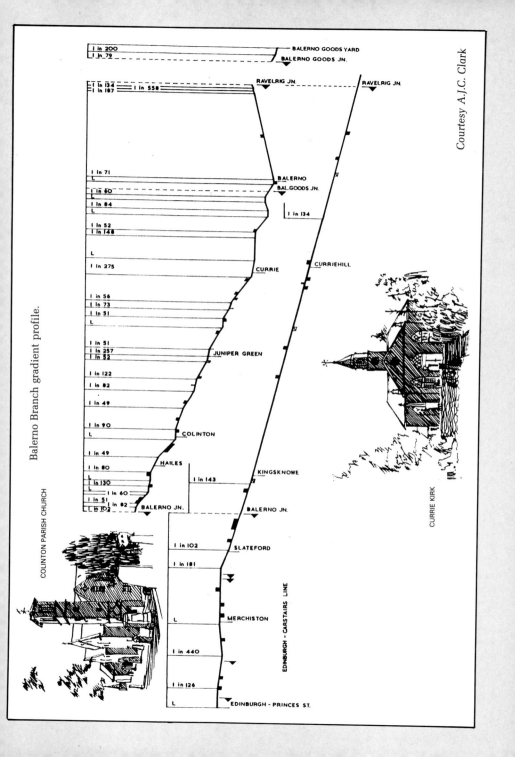

Balerno Branch gradient profile.

Courtesy A.J.C. Clark

occur through human error as a result of a signal being set one way without the points being correspondingly adjusted, or vice versa. Locking bars were provided to hold the points in position as trains passed over.

In April 1874, with the opening of the Balerno branch at last in sight, the Caley authorised the construction of new sidings at Midcalder station 2½ miles west of the branch on the main line – for it was intended that most of the branch trains would terminate there. The new siding accommodation would be needed for branch trains to wait between trips, and for shunting.

On 13th June the Caley's Secretary, Archibald Gibson, informed the Board of Trade in London (as required by law) that it was the intention of the company "to open for the public conveyance of passengers their Balerno Branch Railway in one month from this date".

On 1st July he wrote again, as required, to advise the Board that the line would be "sufficiently completed for the safe conveyance of passengers" as from 4th July, and to invite an inspection of it in the ten days thereafter. Next day, the Board of Trade appointed Colonel Rich to carry this out.

Rich inspected the branch some time in the middle of July and submitted his report on 23rd July. He summarised the lay out of the railway, commenting with approval on the construction of bridges and the tunnel, noting that the sharpest curves on the lines – those of seven chains' radius – were protected with guard rails, and that the rails used were of the double headed type. 1000 tons of these had been supplied by the Caley to Charles Brand and Co. in 1873, at a cost (to the Caley) of £13,500.

Rich also remarked, on the subject of curves: "There are some private road crossings on the railway that should be carefully looked after as they are very dangerous through the sharp curves on the line obstructing the view."

He reserved his main comments for signalling arrangements, ordering a number of alterations at the three junctions – Balerno Junction, Ravelrig Junction and Balerno Goods Junction, where a locking bar was called for. But he did not insist that the opening of the railway be delayed for these alterations, and noted that the Engineers had agreed to make the most important changes at once.

Rich's final sentence, though, caused a flurry of exhanges between the Board of Trade and the Caley in the next few days. He authorised the line subject to "a satisfactory undertaking as to the proposed mode of working" – a reference to the Caley's plan to work the branch by a system of telegraph messages passed between signalmen over three sections or "blocks" of railway, and known as the Absolute Block Telegraph System. This procedure is described in the next chapter; it was designed to ensure that two trains never entered the same section of line and inevitably collided on the single track. Rich suggested the system be re-inforced in one of two ways: either by the Caley agreeing to a procedure known as "train staff" working, which involved train drivers having to carry a unique section staff on each trip (and since there was only one staff, this meant that no other train could be inadvertently allowed on a section), or by the insertion of a new clause in the agreed method of working. This clause was to the effect that "only one engine in steam or two coupled together" could enter any section at any time. In fact, this did not involve any change in proposed working, but merely spelt it out in greater detail.

The Caley understandably chose the latter option, for it obliged them only to revise the wording of their initial undertaking – and they were by this time in a hurry to get the branch open at last. Having been told by letter on 29th July, 1874 that the Board of Trade would need the mode of working to be duly altered, the Caley confirmed in a telegram the next day that the "one engine in steam" provision would be agreed:

> Undertaking as to working Balerno Branch on the absolute block telegraph system and that only one engine in steam or two coupled together shall be on the line between certain points at the same time will be sent you by tonight's post. We propose to open the line for passenger traffic on first August.

The next day, 31st July, the Board of Trade wired the Caley to accept their new undertaking. The way was cleared for the railway to open.

On the line itself, all was virtually ready. Though one or two works were not quite finished, such as the two goods sheds, at Currie and Balerno, many of the minor details had been seen to. On 31st July, 30s. was paid for station name-boards!

Staff had been appointed. The station master at Currie station was to be John Tonnar, who had until then been station master at the village's main-line station (now re-named Curriehill). Another man moving only a short distance was Charles Campbell, who was to be Balerno's first station master; he was currently station master at Slateford.

A young man who was later to become something of an institution in Colinton was appointed there; John Kerr was still there 44 years later.

With opening imminent, there was interest in the future and potential of the Balerno branch. On 8th July, 1874 *The Scotsman* had sounded favourable: "Along the whole course the line passes through pleasing river scenery, and at several points there is excellent feuing ground, to which the opening up of railway communication will no doubt give additional value."

The Final Cost

The cost of the Balerno branch was not fully paid until several years after the line opened. For one thing the contractors Charles Brand and Son remained on hand for a year to maintain the railway and the Caley, according to standard practice, withheld ten per cent of their contract fee until that period was up.

Final payments of compensation to landowners and tenants were settled as late as 1879, many cases going to arbitration. Sir James Foulis accepted the sum of £4000 for his land on the Woodhall estate in 1878 and the North British Railway the sum of £244 for their land at the Union Canal in 1879.

Eventually the cost of making the Balerno branch emerged as a little over £134,000. The following table breaks this down into construction, land, legal and preliminary costs:

Preliminary costs (1865–70):	£7263 2s. 11d. (Parliamentary; planning)
Construction costs (1871–75):	£95,609 13s. 10d.
Land/compensation costs:	£26,824 13s. 11d.
Legal/interest charges, etc:	£5720 2s. 4½d.
Less: sale of land:	(£1343 17s. 9d.)
Total cost:	£134,073 15s. 3½d.

The figure deducted for sale of land refers to Hailes mill at Colinton which the Caley sold in 1876, its original purchase being one of the costs incurred between 1865 and 1870. The total for 1865–70 includes the cost of Parliamentary proceedings in 1865, which covered the Penicuik Bill, but excludes the cost of proceedings for the Abandonment Bill in 1869 and the 1870 Bill. The inclusion of the Penicuik costs probably roughly balances out the exclusion of the latter.

The actual construction of the Balerno branch accounted for 75 per cent of total costs, whilst land and compensation costs represented 20 per cent. This was a typical result.

The cost per mile of the branch was fairly typical also at £22,000. As to the scale of the undertaking it may be of interest to compare the cost of two other major works in the Edinburgh area in the 1870s; Fettes College was opened in 1870 at a cost of £150,000 while St Mary's Episcopal Cathedral near Haymarket was completed in 1879 for £110,000.

The following table breaks down the construction costs incurred in making the branch. It shows that Charles Brand and Son received over £57,000 for work done, considerably more than the original contract price. (The figure excludes what the firm received for building Colinton road bridge, which was paid out by the local turnpike trustees and included a £1500 contribution from the Caley.)

Final Table of Construction Costs

Contractors:	£57,391 11s. 11d.
Stores/materials:	£22,660 16s. 6d. (rails etc)
Signalling:	£3763 16s. 3d.
Stations:	£2814 8s. 1d.
Station houses:	£2355 17s. 7d. (at Colinton and Balerno)
*Engineers:	£2325
Signal boxes:	£883 2s. 4d.
Branch telegraph:	£569 13s. 5d.
Inspector of works:	£541 15s. 9d. (salary 1871–75)
Switches/crossings:	£461 9s. 0d.
Station cranes:	£200
Police constable:	£193 16s. 3d. (wages 1871–74)

Other payments included the £1500 towards Colinton road bridge, £154 15s. 6d. for alterations to the private railway serving Ravelrig quarry, and £45 15s. 0d. for digging a well at Balerno station in 1875!

---

* Blyth and Cunningham, the Engineers, had previously received £3401 5s. 5d. in the period 1865–70 for drawing up plans, some of which pertained to the Penicuik line however.

Chapter Seven
Early Days

On Saturday 1st August, 1874 the Balerno branch railway opened to all traffic. Almost ten years had passed since the Caley had first discussed the application from the local millowners and landowners for help with their plans for a line.

The opening of the branch was not attended with any ceremony. After such a long delay in its construction the Caley were no doubt simply relieved to see it at last earning revenue – and glad not to have to answer any more of Henry Bruce's and others' complaints.

A one line entry in the minutes of the Caley's traffic committee noted merely: "Balerno Branch. Reported opening for passenger traffic on 1st inst."

The first passenger trains to run over the branch were the 7.50 am from West Calder to Edinburgh and the 8 am from Edinburgh to Midcalder, which crossed at Currie station – the only passing-place on the line – at 8.25 am.

However, the first operational train of all was the goods service of that Saturday. This was perhaps appropriate, for the branch had after all been conceived to provide for the interests of the various mills in the district. No timetable in fact survives to record the goods service of 1874; but it was invariably the case throughout the years the Balerno line was open that the daily goods train was the first on to the branch in the morning. And of course in the 1870s and until quite recently, Saturday was merely another working day, so all the local mills were open as normal.

Sometimes goods sevices were allowed to begin operating on new railways weeks or months ahead of the first passenger services, because less rigorous safety standards were demanded for goods working. But on the Balerno branch goods and passenger services began on 1st August – as confirmed in a circular sent by general goods manager James Thompson (later Sir James and Chairman of the Caley).

There was one aspect to the opening of the railway which perhaps led to its being greeted a little less excitedly than was usual on such occasions. This was, in fact, not the first time the local community had received a new line – indeed Currie already had its own station – and therefore, while the opening of the branch was a major event, there was not the usual degree of novelty about it – for one thing, the trains on both main and branch lines were turned out in the same Caledonian Railway livery, already very familiar. And then, one of the branch trains was actually an existing main-line service between Glasgow and Edinburgh, diverted on to the branch between Ravelrig and Slateford (and on Saturdays it continued to run via the main line rather than the branch).

However, there must have been considerable excitement at the new railway not just among the commercial interests for whom it was of great potential but for the local populace, to whom the sight of those colourful little trains with their brand-new tank engines weaving along by the riverbank must have been a real fascination.

It has never been questioned that Caley livery was among the most colourful and attractive of any company. At that time passenger engines were turned out in dark blue (later, at the turn of the century, a sky-blue shade was also used), lined with a black band edged in white, while the footplate facing, steps and tender underframes were painted an attractive crimson-lake (also edged in white and black); the chimney, smoke-box and engine underframes were black. Goods engines were a dark olive-green with black lining. (In the 1880s this was replaced by black with red lining.) Carriages were an all-over crimson-lake; until 1873 they had carried a cream band along their upper panels, but this was then painted over – it was later resumed on main-line stock in the 1890s.

The Caley's imposing crest, based on the arms of Scotland, was always proudly displayed between the initials "C" and "R" on the tender or the tank sides of passenger engines.

The First Timetables

The first trains to flash blue and crimson through the leafy glades lining the Water of Leith ran in the early morning of Saturday 1st August, 1874 as part of a service of six trains in the up direction (from Edinburgh to Midcalder) and seven trains in the down direction. The service operated daily except on Sunday – and indeed it was to be 1913 before any Sunday trains ran on the branch.

Of the seven down trains, two came from beyond Midcalder: the first of the morning left from West Calder (six miles west of Midcalder on the line via Shotts to Glasgow, opened in 1869), while in the afternoon a train originating in Glasgow, as mentioned above, travelled the branch on its way to Edinburgh. Its route was not via the Shotts line but via Carstairs and the long way round.

On Saturday only, an extra branch train ran from Princes Street to Currie and back – the first of many excursion trains to operate on the line, and the first of a number over the years which terminated at Currie.

All other up trains terminated at Midcalder at this time. Why the Caley thus ran Balerno branch trains to and from Midcalder station leaves room for speculation; it seems unlikely there can have been much local traffic between there and stations on the new branch, for the respective industries of the two districts drew their workforces from the local population. Midcalder station itself served only the small villages of Kirknewton and Midcalder. Yet the Caley evidently had their reasons, for Balerno branch trains continued to run to and from Midcalder for several more years, though decreasingly so.

Most likely the explanation is that the Caley were seeking to cater to through traffic between the west of Scotland and the Balerno branch, and using Midcalder station as a staging-post.

But there was also one practical advantage in running branch trains to and from Midcalder station – for they could at least turn there! Until 1899 there was no turning facility at Balerno; and even when trains did begin terminating there increasingly in the 1880s they had still to descend all the way to Ravelrig Junction so that engines could get round their carriages!

In fact the Caley did consider installing a turntable at Balerno in early 1874 – presumably at the goods station – in the belief that the Board of Trade would insist on one. Evidently the Board did not: for it was never put in. The timetable during that first month of opening was as follows:

August 1874

						SO		
Princes Street 8.00	10.05	2.30	4.10	6.45	8.15	8.30
Slateford 8.06	10.11	2.36	4.16	6.51	8.21	8.36
Colinton 8.13	10.19	2.43	4.23	6.58	8.28	8.43
Juniper Green 8.18	10.25	2.48	4.28	7.03	8.33	8.48
Currie 8.25	10.33	2.55	4.35	7.10	8.40	8.55
Balerno 8.31	10.40	3.01	4.41	7.16	–	9.01
Midcalder 8.45	10.55	3.15	4.55	7.30	–	9.15

				SX					SO
Midcalder 8.05	8.50	11.35	3.05	3.25	5.45	7.35	
Balerno 8.17	9.02	11.47	3.17	3.37	5.57	7.47	–
Currie 8.25	9.09	11.54	3.24	3.45	6.04	7.54	9.00
Juniper Green 8.31	9.15	12.00	3.30	3.51	6.10	8.00	9.06
Colinton 8.36	9.20	12.05	3.35	3.56	6.15	8.05	9.11
Slateford 8.45	9.29	12.14	3.44	4.05	6.24	8.14	9.20
Princes Street 8.50	9.35	12.20	3.50	4.10	6.30	8.20	9.25

SO: Saturdays only; SX: Saturdays excepted.

The 8.05 am train from Midcalder to Edinburgh in fact left from West Calder at 7.50, calling at Newpark station at 7.56. This service was hauled by an engine which ran out specially from Edinburgh via the main line to take charge of it; and this procedure whereby empty trains beginning or ending their duties at Balerno or stations further west ran out or returned via the main line continued to apply thereafter.

Most of the other branch services were hauled by the regular Balerno branch engine – No. 491 – which shuttled to and fro during most of the day. This engine had the branch to itself except in the morning when the 7.50 from West Calder crossed it at Currie, and on Saturday evenings when a second train ran out to Currie and back, being passed there at 8.55 pm by the regular train on its last trip of the day to Midcalder.

The 3.05 pm train from Midcalder to Edinburgh also crossed the normal branch train, but on the main line west of Ravelrig Junction. This was the service which ran all the way from Glasgow. It comprised two distinct sections: one which left South Side station at 12.35 pm, the other Buchanan Street station at 12.45 pm, the two trains being joined at Motherwell. All told, the journey time of this roundabout service from Glasgow via Carstairs and the Balerno branch to Edinburgh was over three hours. This compared unfavourably with the fastest Caley train between the two cities, which took one hour and forty minutes but ran via the shorter Cleland and Midcalder line and then the main line east of Ravelrig Junction.

Surprisingly, the Caley only operated seven trains over that shorter route of 46¼ miles, while six ran via Carstairs, covering the 56¼ miles on that route in between 2½ hours and 3¼ hours. Before the Balerno branch opened, the 3.05 pm from Midcalder was one of these and ran via Curriehill. It continued to do so on Saturdays after the branch opened.

Why the Caley should have re-routed this service along the new branch in August 1874 without providing a similar service in the opposite direction is a mystery.

Then, in November 1874, they did so – but at the same time they cut the overall number of services on the Balerno branch to just four each way with an additional service on Saturday. Two of these (in each direction) now ran between Edinburgh and Glasgow, being formerly main-line services; and this meant that only two Balerno branch trains in each direction were being operated as part of a specific "branch-only" service.

More changes were to follow in December, when the branch's link with Glasgow ended. The two inter-city services both ways were axed from the branch, and re-routed back to the main line. This ended the "Glasgow connection" for good on the Balerno branch, after just four months. The Caley compensated by laying on additional services to Midcalder and back – but overall the number of passenger trains working the branch was still just four each way.

This represented a poor service which, it must be assumed, stemmed from poor demand among the local population. Yet if the Caley were disappointed at the level of response, they would also accept that they had simply been too optimistic early on, and that the true level of demand had now been found. Things were likely to improve as the mere presence of the railway stimulated commercial and perhaps residential traffic in days to come. Indeed, the December 1874 service, which continued throughout 1875, gave the lowest-ever frequency of trains; from 1876 on, new services would be added regularly.

Trial and error were inevitable aspects of starting up a railway. That also seems to apply to the Caley's short-lived approach of diverting previous main-line trains to run over the Balerno branch between August and November 1874; the Balerno branch was not really a suitable alternative to the main line, as shown by the fact that diverted trains took 20 minutes longer to cover a mere extra mile of distance over the route!

Operating Restrictions

The key to the safe and efficient operation of the Balerno branch was the practice known as "absolute block telegraph" working, whereby the line was divided up into three blocks or sections and the arrival and departure of trains on each section was controlled by signalmen at either end, who exchanged telegraph messages with their opposite numbers. The whole aim was to prevent the possibility of two trains ever colliding on the single track line; rigid observance of block working would ensure that only one train was ever on a given section at any time.

The three sections into which the Balerno branch was divided were between Balerno Junction and Currie (a distance of 3½ miles), between Currie and Balerno (1¼ miles), and between Balerno and Ravelrig Junction (also 1¼ miles). There were thus four signal boxes involved in the exchanging of telegraph signals: these being Currie and Balerno, where two-way communication was required, and at the junctions with the main line – Balerno Junction signal box was in touch with Currie, Ravelrig Junction signal box with Balerno.

Coded telegraph signals were exchanged by the sounding of a bell or gong incorporated into a "block instrument" at each end of a section (linked by wire to the other instrument). The bell sounded at the "up" end of a section, the gong at the "down" end; these are traditional railway terms, indicating "towards London" and "away from London" – so "up" on the Balerno branch was to the west, "down" towards Edinburgh.

The number of times a bell or gong sounded indicated to the signalman at one end of a section what was happening at the other end. In practice, each exchange began with a single ring – a call for attention, acknowledged in kind – before the type of train awaiting clearance to enter the section was indicated. The most common codes were three, four, five or six rings: indicating a passenger train, goods train, mineral train or empty train respectively. The signalman receiving the message then accepted or refused the train with his own signal; obviously if he knew another train was still to clear the section (perhaps having failed to appear after a breakdown) he would refuse it.

If accepted, the train would be signalled to enter the section by the dispatching signalman, who then informed his colleague that it was on its way, by giving two rings. The signalman in advance would then alter an indicator fixed in the block instrument to remind him that the section was occupied; only when the train had cleared it would he turn the indicator back to "off".

The Balerno branch was worked in this way until 1889 when a more sophisticated system based on drivers carrying special section "tablets" which had first to be released from electrically-interlocked block instruments, was introduced.

Of course, not only passenger trains but the branch goods trains were subject to block working rules. The goods train made two round trips over the railway daily; it was able to by-pass passenger trains at Balerno or Currie sidings (or at Currie passing loop) without infringing regulations, but could not do so at Colinton or Juniper Green sidings, otherwise there would be two trains in the long section between Balerno Junction and Currie – which was forbidden.

One restriction in the operation of the Balerno branch referred to coaches, which were required to be four-wheeled due to the sharp curves in the line; six-wheeled carriages were banned. This restriction lasted until 1929! As late as 1920 a new stock of carriages was ordered for the Balerno branch which, despite their modern fittings and electric lighting, were still four-wheelers.

The carriages of the 1870s, however, were far from luxurious. In these days seats were still hard-backed in third class vehicles, being little more than benches (first class seating was padded). Lighting was provided by oil lamps which were inserted in holes in the roof; at dusk each day they were taken out to trains and put in place by a railwayman or lad who first had to clamber up on the roof of each coach. (By day the lamps were stored away and the sockets in carriage-roofs were blocked up by a kind of plug.)

In the 1880s lighting of carriages by gas was widely introduced by the Caley, with old coaches being re-equipped and new ones being fitted with gas; but oil-lit carriages lingered well into the 20th century.

On Balerno branch trains first class and third class accommodation was always carried. Second class accommodation, which was phased out on Britain's railways between the 1870s and 1880s, never was, though it was available on the Caley main-line service to and from Edinburgh at the time the branch opened.

Other restrictions on the Balerno branch from its opening concerned speed and the maximum length of trains (with a view to safe braking). A limit of 15 mph was imposed − even in the 1960s this had risen only to 20 mph − and trains were restricted to 18 vehicles, including brake vehicles. All brakes at this period were worked manually by guards or special brakesmen riding in brake-vans; automatic air or vacuum brakes were increasingly fitted by the Caley from 1882 onward (mainly air brakes) after successful trials in the 1870s.

Fares on the Balerno branch trains were initially set at these rates:

	3rd single	1st single	3rd return	1st return
Colinton−Edinburgh	3½d.	8d.	6d.	1s. 2d.
Juniper Green−Edinburgh	4½d.	10d.	8d.	1s. 5d.
Currie−Edinburgh	6d.	1s.	10d.	1s. 8d.
Balerno−Edinburgh	7d.	1s. 4d.	1s.	2s. 3d.

Passengers who travelled from Currie to Edinburgh actually got a better deal if they caught a main-line train from Curriehill station where the fares were 5d. or 9d. or 1s. (single) and 9d. or 1s. or 1s. 6d. (return). It was not many months before the Caley made the fares at both stations the same and also permitted passengers to depart from one and return to the other if they wished.

Between Midcalder station and Princes Street fares were the same whether passengers travelled in branch line or main line trains.

The Railway and the Community

For a new railway to become fully integrated into the life of the community which it served could take months if not years. Old habits died hard; and though some residents between Colinton and Balerno had grown used to rail travel thanks to the Caley main line the great majority had not − for several reasons.

Since most local people worked locally at the mills, on the farms or in service, there was in fact little need for them to travel − by whatever means. Moreover a ten hour working day six days a week left them little time to do so. The only free day was Sunday, when there were no trains!

Wages of £1 a week and often a lot less (some workers at Kinleith paper mill received 4s. a week in 1875 for a 60 hour week) also meant that train journeys were out of the question; a return trip to Edinburgh from Currie cost 10d., representing over a fifth of a wage of 4s.

According to the 1871 census there were 3,426 people living in the district bordering the new railway from Stoneyport in the east to the farms round Balerno. Of the 1,452 of these listed as employed, nearly all worked locally. The main categories were: 484 mill workers and labourers, 196 domestic servants, 172 agricultural labourers, 66 retailers, 46 joiners, masons or slaters, 44 carters, 44 gardeners (i.e. in service), 39 yarn bleachers or flax dressers (at Malleny Mills flax mill), 39 tailors or shoemakers, 35 quarriers and 30 millers.

There were also 25 farmers, 18 blacksmiths, 14 mill-wrights and 13 teachers, while among a handful of "professionals" were five ministers and just two doctors. "Officials" comprised two police constables, at Colinton and Currie, four village postmasters or postmistresses, two of whom doubled as shoemaker and grocer respectively, and two post-runners.

There were relatively few people in the district from whom the Caley could reasonably expect regular custom for the passenger trains on the Balerno branch. They were the people who had a reason to travel, as well as the time and the money to do so: the paper-millers, the grain-millers, the farmers, the retailers, all of whom might have need to do business with their suppliers and customers in town or further afield.

There were evidently enough of these (plus the few gentry, professionals and other persons of means) to support the service of four trains each way which was running at the start of 1875 and for most of that year and which thereafter began to expand slowly. The expansion would continue, with some hiccups, for sixty years until twenty trains were running each way in the 1930s.

The Balerno branch itself played a key role in attracting passengers. It gave easy access to an attractive country district and encouraged city-dwellers to come and live locally and commute to work.

Colinton and Juniper Green expanded very rapidly in the late 19th century, undoubtedly due in large part to the railway. But this trend had in fact started even before the branch opened. Currie and Balerno, on the other hand, showed little growth during this time. Being further away from Edinburgh this was understandable.

But these two villages, particularly Balerno, were also relatively poorer than Colinton and Juniper Green. In the early 1870s Currie and Balerno formally declared themselves a "special water district" and a "special drainage district" respectively in order to be assisted in upgrading basic facilities. Until 1872 Currie villagers got all their water from St Mungo's well by the church: that year water was piped to the main street for the first time. Not until 1875 was it first supplied to any private dwellings.

In 1872 Currie also experienced a smallpox outbreak. But Balerno had even more problems: the local medical officer remarked during a typhoid outbreak in 1877 that the village was in fact seldom free of the disease due to the prevailing unsanitary conditions. The village had no drainage at all until 1873.

The problems of Balerno were exacerbated by some of the villagers' attachment to the domestic pig! In 1879 and 1880 the medical officer decreed that the numerous pigstyes (and several cow-byres) within the village should be removed as being a health hazard.

Though such statements are hard to associate with Balerno today, they illustrate that the village which gave the new railway of 1874 its name had perhaps the least traffic potential in the early years.

Another problem in the area was pollution from the mills, particularly Kinleith where Henry Bruce was in constant "hot water" with the parochial board. He was eventually prevailed on to build a 280 ft high chimney in 1878 to carry away fumes, but complaints still persisted.

Colinton was by no means free of this nuisance. The minister complained frequently in the early 1870s about the smoke and smell emanating from the pasteboard mill erected by George Smith next to the manse in 1870 and also about the dust from Hailes mill on the other side of the manse! It was even agreed at one time that a new manse should be found or built in a more healthy location; but fortunately Stevenson's erstwhile holiday home has survived.

Village Populations 1871—1901

	1871	1881	1891	1901
Colinton	c.200	224	476	782
Juniper Green	716	1018	1321	1607
Currie	249	255	313	338
Balerno	490	474	619	695

This expansion may have benefited the Balerno branch, but it caused resentment in some. George Reith wrote in *The Breezy Pentlands* in 1910 that Juniper Green "is being rapidly annexed, and its rustic characteristics destroyed, by Edinburgh villadom" while Colinton too was "suffering from the invasion of villadom, which, in some repects, is worse than a German one."

The Transport Scene

The opening of the Balerno branch inevitably took traffic from the local roads. On 6th October, 1874 the clerk to the local Turnpike Trust noted:

> The opening of the new line of railway from Slateford to Balerno and Currie having caused considerable alteration in regard to the traffic in that district, it was stated that it might probably be requisite to make some alteration in the check toll bars. There were produced two letters from parties interested in the district, offering to pay the sum of £40 per annum in order to avoid the erection of a check bar at Balerno station, and it was stated that there was a probability of further payments being offered for a like purpose.

As £40 was a very large sum, the parties who stood to gain from such a deal would have to be very regular users of the station — no doubt the goods station — such as Hill Craig and Co. of Balerno Bank paper mill, or the roperie company at Malleny Mills, or perhaps the local coal merchants and carriers, Henderson, George and Craik.

But the days of the tolls and toll bars were now numbered: they were abolished in 1882. In the first half of 1874 the three bars on the Lanark Road had drawn average weekly takings of £8 (Slateford), £13 (Currie) and between nothing and 6d. (Little Vantage): the once busy Lang Whang was now clearly virtually deserted.

In the early 1870s there was an important development in road transport in Edinburgh when the Edinburgh Street Tramways Company was set up in 1871 to operate horse-drawn tram routes in the city. Ten lines were laid by James Gowans, who was not only the lessee of Redhall quarry and various other quarries but a former railway engineer: he had designed the North Berwick and Bathgate railways among others. (He was also a renowned architect, and created a number of interesting houses using intricate stone patterns: the cottages he built for his Redhall quarriers can still be seen in Redhall Bank Road.)

The tramways flourished and expanded. On the day the Balerno railway opened, The Scotsman reported that receipts on the trams during the last half-year – mainly in 2d. fares – had been almost £23,000, up by £5,000.

But the trams posed no threat to railway services extending outside Edinburgh, such as the Balerno line. On the railways themselves, various openings and alterations took place in the first half of the 1870s. On the Caley a new station had been built at Slateford in 1871, on the site of the present station, and the former station converted to goods-only use: it stood at the east end of Slateford viaduct (no trace of it remains today). New signalling and telegraph arrangements were made for Slateford, Kingsknowe and Curriehill stations between 1874 and 1875 under a company-wide improvement scheme.

Elsewhere around Edinburgh, new branches to Penicuik and Roslin (later extended to Glencorse) were opened by the North British in 1872 and 1874. Early in 1872 the North British had almost merged with the Caley before at the last minute rejecting the move.

Kinleith Paper Mill Siding

Official Caley statistics in early 1875 showed the company maintained 746 miles of line, up by 6 from the last half-year (the six miles of the Balerno branch); and owned 622 engines, 1513 carriages and 32,239 wagons. The Caley were declared to be in sound financial health.

A ticket platform was opened west of Princes Street station at this time, where passengers on incoming trains had their tickets checked. It was situated between Morrison Street and Grove Street.

In March 1875 the Caley made plans to open the first mill siding from the Balerno branch. It was to serve Kinleith paper mill and would give Henry Bruce, at last, the direct access to the railway which he had so long and impatiently sought. Meantime he employed a "station man", David Wilson, (whether at Currie or Curriehill is not known), to deal with the various shipments of goods and materials, all of which had to be carted to and from the mill.

Colonel Hutchinson of the Board of Trade examined the plan for the new siding. He reported with some concern:

> This siding junction is situated on a gradient of 1 in 50 and in the event of any vehicle breaking away it would run down to the junction with the main line at

Slateford, a distance of about three miles. Being a single line it is inexpedient to introduce any catch siding, but there is one already existing in connection with the junction with the main line.

I would therefore suggest that the Company be informed that this siding junction can only be approved of, on condition that when shunting is going on at it, no train shall be allowed to leave the junction with the main line at Slateford for the Currie Station.

In fact this provision was already guaranteed by the working of the block telegraph system.

As it turned out, a catch siding was installed at the paper mill siding. It served to divert any wagons which broke away, before they reached the branch.

When Colonel Yolland inspected the completed siding in June he stipulated that "the catch siding should be lengthened and provided with a mound of earth at the end, or have buffer stops of some kind to prevent an engine or other vehicle, moving in the siding and over-running the points, from falling into the stream below."

This requirement, however, prompted an objection from Blyth and Cunningham, who had designed the siding. There being so little room for the catch siding, a mound of earth at its end would foul the actual branch.

Yolland replied that it would suffice for the rails at the end of the siding to be turned up, stressing that his only concern was for the welfare of the train crew should any engine fall into the Water of Leith and also for the expense the Caley would be put to in recovering it!

A signal box was erected beside the branch at Kinleith. It was manned only when a train called at the mill.

In July 1875 the former station man became known as a "sidingsman", and another was also taken on.

A station man also featured among the fifty employees at Balerno mill. William and James Durham, who ran the mill at Kinauld, had actually asked the Caley for a works siding in 1874 shortly before the branch opened; their request had been initially turned down, then granted; but in fact the siding had not been built.

The mill's station man was based at Curriehill station on the main line until 1879. On 3rd May that year the new owners of the mill informed their suppliers: "In future please forward all goods to Currie Station." A special siding had been provided there. However, just three years later Balerno mill closed down. It remained disused and latterly ruinous until being re-opened as a glue works early this century with, in due course, its own siding at Kinauld.

Charles Brand and Son, the contractors, finally left the Balerno branch in the autumn of 1875. But the firm were already busily engaged in projects elsewhere. They had undertaken several new tramways around Glasgow in the early 1870s, simultaneously with the Balerno branch, and also carried out four railway contracts in the west of Scotland in the mid-1870s. Between 1877 and 1880 they built new docks at Grangemouth.

Thereafter the firm continued to construct railways, docks and harbours, eventually setting up in London in 1920 and becoming involved in building part of the Underground network. Charles Brand and Son are still operating today as part of the French Kier Group: direct descendants of the young Montrose mason who decided to venture into railway-building in the 1840s.

A Chapter Of Accidents

A number of accidents and incidents that occurred on the Balerno branch between 1875 and 1880 were virtually the only blemishes in an otherwise excellent safety record.

On 26th November, 1875 an engine working at Balerno goods yard was very slightly damaged, in what can have been no more than a bump. However, the driver was reported and his case came before the traffic committee, whose clerk minuted:

> Engine 393 damaged to the extent of 12s. at Balerno on 26th November. The driver, John Millar, had only four days to run in order to complete his premium period. Millar bears a good character and this is said to be his first offence. Instructions asked as to marking his card whereby he would forfeit £5. Millar to pay 12s. and *not* mark card.

The scheme of premium payments had been devised in 1873 to encourage the avoidance of accidents, then very frequent. Drivers, firemen, goods guards, station masters and yardsmen received £5 if, during a period of a year, they had not "caused, contributed to, or by any neglect failed to prevent" an accident. Passenger guards and pointsmen received £3.

The above minute illustrates two sides of Caley management. Though the final decision was taken out of humanity, nevertheless the committee did consider withholding the large sum of £5, about five weeks' wages, from a driver guilty of causing damage estimated at a mere 12s!

On 29th June, 1876 another incident occurred near Colinton. The only casualties were two sheep, but the Board of Trade regarded the occurrence seriously enough to report on it:

> When a passenger train was approaching Colinton tunnel the driver observed a number of sheep on the line. He endeavoured to frighten them to the side, but they ran into the tunnel, where they were overtaken by the engine. Six of the sheep were run over, two of which were killed. The fence was in good order, and it cannot be ascertained how the animals got on to the line.

These were times when fatalities on the railway were treated almost as routine. At the Caley's weekly Board meeting, six or seven were regularly listed, these being usually individuals such as yardsmen who had been trapped between wagons or passengers killed crossing a line at any of the many stations where there was no footbridge. A woman was thus killed at Kingsknowe in August 1876; just weeks before, a surfaceman was killed at Ravelrig Junction.

On 4th April, 1877 the 6.20 am Balerno branch train from Princes Street to Midcalder was derailed between Currie and Balerno, while rounding a right hand bend on the approach to the bridge over the river.

No one was injured and no damage was done but the Board of Trade reported:

It appears that as the passenger train was running round a sharp curve of 6¼ chains radius on an ascending gradient of 1 in 50, at a speed stated not to have exceeded 12 miles an hour, and with the steam shut off, the rails spread under the wheels of the engine, and first its right wheels and then almost all the remaining right wheels of the train dropped inside the right or low rail, the left wheels remaining for the most part on the left or high rail, the engine having run altogether a distance of about 80 yds after first leaving the rails.

The investigator concluded that the accident had been caused by the loosening of the spikes in the chairs (the chairs were metal attachments fitted to the sleepers, on which the rails lay) as the engine passed over. As a result, the track spread under its wheels and these dropped inside the right-hand rail. The inspector added that the fitting of a check rail round the inside of the curve would probably have prevented the incident.

The other notable feature of the Balerno branch apart from the sharpness of its curves was its steep gradients. It was these that contributed to the most serious accident to occur on the line. Coincidentally, a 6.20 am up train running from Princes Street to Midcalder was once again involved.

Just before 7 am on Saturday 24th April, 1880 this train, which consisted of a tank-engine and eight carriages (the first being a brake carriage) plus a brake van, collided with a goods train at Ravelrig Junction. The goods train was the 3 am from Paisley to Leith and had arrived at the junction as usual to drop off several wagons at the junction sidings, which could only be reached by trains coming partly onto the rails of the Balerno line.

At 6.54 am the goods engine had stopped on the junction facing points (set for the branch) while the three wagons next to the tender were uncoupled, ready to be dropped. In setting the points, the interlocking compelled the junction signalman to set the points further up the Balerno branch, where the single line forked so as to allow a double junction with the main line. In other words, the points had been set as though the goods train was about to run up the hill to Balerno.

The signalman at the same time moved the two nearest signals on the Balerno branch to danger. This was to warn the driver of the 6.20 am branch train, which was expected shortly, that the line was not clear. The branch train should then come to a halt at the second signal, the junction home signal.

The Ravelrig signalman later reported that it was quite common for the 6.20 am Balerno branch train to be thus held up by the shunting goods train.

Meanwhile, the branch train had arrived on time at Balerno station at 6.49 am. It was due to depart again at 6.52 am, but at 6.50, to the surprise of the driver, the guard gave the starting-signal. The driver, who had set his watch by the clock at Currie station, now wrongly assumed that the Currie clock was slow and that the guard had the right time: in fact the guard's watch was two minutes fast.

Leaving Balerno ahead of time, the driver now set the train down the 1 in 70 slope towards Ravelrig Junction. He and the guard later gave conflicting evidence as to the speed of the train at this time, though it emerged that it was too great. The driver claimed: "I kept on my steam till just before catching sight of the Ravelrig distant signal, the usual practice, and my speed was no higher than usual when I shut steam off."

But the guard contradicted this. "I first thought the speed too high when I saw the home signal at danger, but the speed from the top of the hill was greater all the way along than usual."

According to the driver, Alexander Stavert, when he rounded the curve beyond Balerno he found the distant signal at danger and accordingly told the fireman to apply the brake, ready to stop at the home signal.

> My speed would not have exceeded 15 or 16 miles an hour when I shut off steam; the application of the break did not check the speed in the least; and when nearing the distant signal, and observing that it was rather increasing, I looked over the side, and seeing the wheels skidding, I reversed the engine and ordered the fireman to slack off his break, and at the same time applied steam the reverse way."

This only briefly checked the speed of the train before the wheels began skidding again. The driver then applied sand to the rails in front of his wheels but without any effect, before whistling three times for the guard to apply his brake: in fact the guard was already doing so.

There were just two hand brakes available on the train: one on the engine, the other in the guard's van. The situation was made worse by the van's brakes being defective. Later the Board of Trade investigator recommended the fitting of an efficient continuous brake on all Balerno branch trains.

When the train, now out of control, arrived at the fork in the branch it was diverted onto the same track as the goods train because of the interlocking described above. A few moments later the two trains collided.

Seeing the oncoming passenger train, the goods driver had just had time to try to set his engine back before it arrived, but had not succeeded. He and his fireman jumped off the train before the collision.

Two passengers and the branch train guard were injured in the collision which damaged both engines, two carriages and two wagons. A signal post was also knocked down. On Monday *The Scotsman* reported that Stavert had been arrested. (He was not tried; but it can be assumed he was dismissed.)

Stavert, it emerged, had been working on the Balerno branch for four months along with his fireman, while the guard had been on the branch for four years. The latter further incriminated Stavert when he reported that after the crash "The driver said he had a good mind to run away. He said he had come rather smart from Balerno, the rails being greasy. I had never seen any difficulty before in stopping." (The greasiness was due to a shower.)

In concluding, the investigator Major-General Hutchinson largely blamed the driver's excessive speed for causing the accident but also cited three other factors: the inadequacy of the branch train's brakes, the interlocking of two sets of points (which he deemed unnecessary) and the negligence of both the guard and the driver as well as the Balerno station porter in permitting the train to run ahead of time.

When Dugald Drummond took over as the locomotive superintendent of the Caley two years later, he instituted a major programme for fitting trains with automatic continuous brakes. By 1884 strict rules applied to Balerno branch trains as to the number of brake vans and brakesmen to be carried, whereby in fact an extra brake van and brakesman would have been carried in the centre of the train concerned in the 1880 accident.

A Day on the Balerno Branch

One summer's day in 1876 a group of friends enjoyed an excursion to the Pentland foothills above Balerno, travelling there and back via the Balerno branch. Afterwards one of them wrote an account of the day, which was published in the *North British Advertiser* on 21st September.

The writer, A.C.R., was enthusiastic about the railway:

> Although the Balerno branch of the Caledonian Railway has been open for fully two years, we still meet many of the good folks of Edinburgh who seem scarcely aware of its existence – who, at any rate, have no practical acquaintance with the beautiful district through which it passes.

Promising that the scenery along the branch "will not fail to gratify all lovers of the picturesque who feel inclined to go and see it," the writer went on to tell of his own day.

Catching the 10 am train at Princes Street Station, he travelled as far as Colinton station before getting out to enjoy a stroll to Bonaly, then return to the line at Juniper Green station to catch the early afternoon train to Balerno, where the remainder of the day was spent.

The 10 am train stopped briefly at Slateford station, then set off again across the viaduct over the Water of Leith, where the neighbouring aqueduct was admired.

> The railroad here is considerably below the level of the canal, but in a minute or two the train takes a sharp turn to the left, and we find ourselves crossing the latter – a proof of the steepness of the gradient we have ascended.
>
> We have now reached the branch line. Following pretty closely the windings of the Water of Leith, we proceed at a moderate pace up the valley, and, as the engine puffs along on its circuitous track, beautiful little glimpses of the scenery open up at every curve.
>
> Passing the extensive paper works of Messrs Chalmers at Kate's Mill, the line takes exactly the form of a semi-circle, and then we enter Colinton Dell, decidedly the most picturesque "bit" on the railway. Indeed, with the single exception of Roslin, there is not a more romantic glen in the neighbourhood of Edinburgh.

Admiring the view over to the wooded grounds of Colinton House and down to the river winding below, the writer commented that the only eyesore was the excessively dirty colour of the water.

The train then whistled before entering Colinton tunnel and drawing up at the station. The little party got out for their walk to Bonaly, and meantime sent on a hamper in the train to Balerno, to be picked up later.

> As we go from the station we observe a beautiful road leading westward in the direction of Juniper Green. Diverging from the Lanark Road near Curriemuir End, this road was opened about three years since as a new access to Colinton, which it approaches by a handsome stone bridge of eight arches. Commanding an uninterrupted view of the valley and the hills, and admirably adapted for feuing, it is surprising there are as yet no signs of building. We can hardly conceive a more charming situation for country villas.

It was not many years before houses had in fact sprung up all around here. After admiring Bonaly and climbing up onto Torphin hill to enjoy the extensive views over Edinburgh and the Forth, the writer and his party then strolled down towards Juniper Green station, along a footpath taking them past Woodhall Mains farm.

We arrive at the station just a few minutes before the two o'clock train for Balerno makes its appearance, not having time of course to take a stroll through the village.

Juniper Green, however, is well worth a visit. Its situation being elevated as well as beautiful, it has no lack of good fresh air, and is now becoming (thanks chiefly to this railway) a very favourite summer resort.

The writer briefly referred to the section of the branch line he had not travelled over, between Colinton and Juniper Green. Woodhall grain mill, a little below Juniper Green station, was well known for its product "Hunter's East Country Oat Meal". (John Hunter had been the mill-master here for nearly 50 years; he was also the farmer at Woodhall Mains.)

The two o'clock train duly arrived at Juniper Green and the party got in.

Starting punctually at the advertised hour, we pass, on the left, between Juniper Green and Currie, the opening of a beautiful little wooded glen appropriately named the "Poet's Glen". On the opposite side are the paper mills of Woodhall and Kinleith, the latter being very extensive and one of the most complete in the country.

At Currie, which may be considered the principal station, there is a double line of rails to permit trains to pass. Moving onward, we notice another paper mill, Messrs Durham's, and to the south is the picturesque ruin of Lennox Tower, an occasional residence of the unfortunate Queen Mary, and a favourite hunting-place of her son James VI.

The line, keeping for the most part close to the river, still passes through very pretty scenery till we reach Balerno, highly pleased with our railway journey. Here we get our little hamper of pic-nic necessaries we had asked the guard to convey hither from Colinton station. Having secured two native youngsters to carry it, and feeling refreshed by our rest, we march merrily en route for the Harelaw reservoir.

Passing through Balerno about ten minutes after leaving the station at Newmills, the writer felt that the village was "not particularly attractive in itself, but in the vicinity there are many delightful walks, and when better known it will no doubt become a popular resort."

For the remainder of their day the little party picnicked above Balerno, near Harlaw reservoir, before reluctantly deciding to head for home by the last train, the 8.51 pm from Balerno. The journey home was in the gloaming, Princes Street being reached shortly after sunset.

In reflecting on the excursion, A.C.R. summed up the feeling of the group:

After today's delightful experience, and knowing we have not nearly exhausted the beauties of the Balerno Railway, we determine at no distant date to pay it another visit.

So far, without much fatigue, we have feasted our eyes on some lovely land-scapes, and inhaled a stock of oxygen worth a score of M.D. prescriptions.

The enthusiasm of these early passengers on the Balerno branch was later to be echoed in thousands more who, during the 69 years that the line remained open, took the opportunity to enjoy the attractive scenery along its route.

However, A.C.R.'s observation that Currie station was the principal station on the branch was mistaken; for though it alone had two platforms it was always the quietest station where passenger traffic was concerned. Traffic returns, available from 1883 to 1922 when the Caley last operated, show that between 10 and 15 per cent of all passengers bought their tickets at Currie – which was, after all, the smallest village.

Yet Currie station produced more revenue than any of the other stations. This was, however, due to its being credited with the traffic to and from Kinleith paper mill siding, which was in fact separate.

The branch train timetable in 1876 showed that services had now been restored to their original levels. Six trains ran daily in each direction, of which all but one served Midcalder. The exception was the last train of the day, which ran to Balerno and back. There was also an additional train to Currie and back on Saturday evenings only.

The Goods Service

On 3rd July, 1876 an important new section of railway was opened by the Caley. Known as the Wester Dalry Branch, it linked the main line at Dalry west of Princes Street station with the North British line west of Haymarket. It meant that all Caley services to and from Edinburgh could now use Princes Street station; previously those to and from Stirling and further north had had to use Waverley.

The 1877 Caley service timetable (which, unlike the public timetable, listed goods trains and operational practices) is the oldest available record of the Balerno branch goods service. It shows that a morning and afternoon goods service was provided for customers on the branch.

Departing at 7.03 am from Lothian Road, the train called at all stations and Kinleith siding before arriving at Ravelrig Junction at 8.30 am, where it remained until 9.15, no doubt to leave goods for collection at the junction sidings and also to uplift wagons for delivery to points along the branch.

The train then returned to Kinleith paper mill, calling en route at Balerno and Currie, remaining at the mill from 9.45 to 10.00 am. It then returned to Ravelrig Junction, again calling at Currie and Balerno. Currie and Balerno were the centres of goods traffic.

After shunting at the junction from 11.10 to 11.30 am, the train set off back to Edinburgh, calling at all stations but not Kinleith this time, arriving back at 1.40 pm.

The afternoon service left at 2.10 pm and reached Ravelrig Junction at 3.50, omitting Kinleith siding; the final journey back began at 4.10 and included a third visit to Kinleith siding, the train arriving at Lothian Road at 6.10 pm.

As to the engines which took charge of the branch goods trains in the early years, the reference in November 1875 to engine 393 being damaged at

A view from Colinton station, looking west on the 25th April, 1953. Note the siding in the background serving Scott's porridge oats mill. Trains ran right through the company's buildings and then crossed the river beyond to reach the main mill. Also note the station sidings in the foreground, diverging from the branch proper at the same junction as the oat mill siding. *D.L.G. Hunter*

Sidings points west of Colinton station in 1961. The ground frame is visible to the left, with the catch siding to the right. The bridge was built at the same time as the railway. *D.S.G. Stirling*

Colinton station in 1934 with several passengers awaiting the arrival of the branch train. Note the selection of wagons in the goods yard and the coal wagon belonging to the local coal merchant, Hastie (wagon No. 10).   *Mowat Collection*

Colinton station in 1912 showing the tall, disused signal box in the distance. This view shows plenty of activity and a well used service.   *Courtesy Mrs J. Tweedie*

The Colinton Tramway. From 1926 trams ran to the terminus at the top of Bridge Street, Colinton. In this scene the competition to the railway is illustrated not only by two trams but also the van and lorry. *N.B. Traction Group Collection*

The last excursion to the branch is seen with No. 78046 standing at Colinton station on the 19th April, 1965. *W.A.C. Smith*

BR Standard class 2, 2−6−0 No. 78046 hauls the last passenger train to visit the Balerno branch on 19th April, 1965. This was the second visit by the excursion that day − another group of enthusiasts had travelled the line several hours earlier. This scene is in Colinton dell. *David S.G. Stirling*

Winter is well established as the branch train approaches Hailes platform from Colinton. *E.B. Wilson*

LMS No. 11273 pulling goods train from the Balerno branch at Balerno Junction on 24th June, 1933. Note the small platform where the signalman and driver exchange the branch section tablet. This 0−6−0T engine was still working the branch in the 1960s as BR No. 47163. *W.E. Boyd, Scottish Record Office*

The 'Balerno Pug', CR No. 169 seen here at Slateford station (east-bound) on the 24th April, 1925 (although in LMS days, the locomotive is still in CR livery). This engine was withdrawn in December 1934. *W.E. Boyd, Scottish Record Office*

A view of Merchiston station in 1934. *Mowat Collection*

An unusual view in 1934 of the LMS (ex Caley) station and yard serving Granton Gas works. The regular Granton branch is to the right. This branch opened in 1861 and carried only goods traffic apart from the private service for gas works employees, which ran from 1902 to 1942. Note the small signal box at the end of the wall and very acute curves into the gas works. *L.G.R.P., courtesy David and Charles*

Barnton station photographed in 1934. The Barnton branch was opened in 1894 and closed to passengers in 1951.   *L.G.R.P., courtesy David and Charles*

The station approach to Barnton station seen here in 1950, just a year before the branch closed to passengers (only 10*d* first class and 6½*d* third class to Edinburgh). The Balerno branch had closed to passengers in 1943 and the Leith branch in 1962. This station was originally called Cramond Brig from 1894 to 1903.

L.G.R.P., courtesy David and Charles

The LMS (ex Caley) station at Leith. The Leith branch opened to goods traffic in 1864 and to passengers in 1879 – five years after the Balerno branch opened.

L.G.R.P., courtesy David and Charles

The extensive goods yards at South Leith on the 22nd June, 1934.   *Mowat Collection*

Balerno would suggest that a class of 0–4–2 goods tender engines was involved.

No. 393 was one of 64 engines in this class built between 1861 and 1866. They were hardy creatures, many lasting well into this century; the last was withdrawn in 1916 after 50 years of running. The engines had outside cylinders. They were also originally fitted only with weatherboards for the protection of the driver and fireman, though cabs were later added.

All the engines were built outside the Caley, 34 of them by Neilson and Co. and 30 by Dübs and Co. No. 393 was a Dübs engine of 1866 (the first ten of the Dübs engines were the first order ever completed by that famous firm).

The original class numbers were 216–227 (Neilson & Co., 1861), 243–254 (Neilson & Co., 1864), 272–281 (Dübs & Co., 1865), and 387–416 (Dübs & Co., 387–406; Neilson & Co., 407–416; 1866).

The engines were remarkably small for the heavy duties they handled; the 1866 Dübs engines had a wheelbase of just 13 ft 10 in. and weighed 27 tons 15½ cwt. Their usefulness in working a tight, twisting line like the Balerno branch was enhanced by their small tenders, which were four-wheeled. This also applied to a later (final) class of Caledonian 0–4–2 engines, of 1878/1881, (30 in all, Nos. 670–679 and 700–719), which carried on working the Balerno branch goods service into the 1930s. All were built by Dübs and Co.

Many of the 1860s class were re-built at one time or another; No. 393 in 1873 and again in 1886 when Drummond turned it into a saddle tank.

The 1877 timetable listed working arrangements on the Balerno branch. Three of the branch signalmen worked twelve-hour shifts (from 7 am to 7 pm), the exception being at Balerno signal box (7 am to 6 pm).

It was the branch passenger trains that handled the delivery and collection of mail and parcels. Three up trains carried mail to Colinton and a fourth to Currie in the afternoon; while one down train collected mail at both Currie and Colinton and another at Colinton only.

Kates Mill Siding

On 9th August, 1878 the Caley sought the approval of the Board of Trade for a siding in Colinton Dell to serve Kates paper mill on the other side of the river. Most likely the impetus for the plan had come from David Chalmers, the owner of the mill, who had taken an interest in the railway both in 1865 and in 1870, and had complained each time that Kates mill would be ill-served by it.

The fault lay not with the Caley so much as with Nature, for the mill was simply in an awkward location, difficult to reach by road as well as rail. In the event a bridge over the river and a track up to the siding had to be built.

There was little space to make the siding, with the steeply sloping ground to either side of the railway. Major-General Hutchinson reported:

> This is an awkward junction in the midst of steep gradients on a single line. I have seen the Engineer of the Caledonian Railway with reference to it and it appears that there is a sufficient amount of level space for a goods train to stand on while working at the proposed siding and that in the event of a breakaway there are

runaway points at the junction with the main line. Under the circumstances the proposed arrangements need not be objected to.

The completed siding was approved on 31st March, 1879. Trains were to call only when required – no times were set. A signal box was erected below the siding on the north side of the branch, and a telegraph installed. Like the cabin at Kinleith paper mill it was to be manned only at such times as a train was visiting the siding.

Kates mill siding was in use for just eleven years before, in 1890, fire destroyed the mill. It was never re-built and so the siding fell into disuse.

Further west on the Balerno branch a water tank was erected at Currie station in 1879. Standing at the west end of the platform, it enabled engines stopping there to have their tanks replenished. Water tanks were installed shortly afterwards at Curriehill station and Slateford, where water was piped at considerable expense (over £800) from the Union Canal.

On 1st August, 1879 the Leith branch opened to passenger traffic, having been in use since its opening in 1864 as a goods-only line. Its passenger services were to outnumber those of the Balerno branch from the outset, so popular did it prove.

Stations were erected at Murrayfield, Craigleith, Granton Road, Newhaven and Leith, where the station became known as Leith North to distinguish it from the North British station, North Leith!

On the same day as the Leith branch opened to passengers the Caley's great new terminus in Glasgow also opened. Glasgow Central became the terminus for the Caley's Edinburgh–Glasgow trains a month later. The opening of this long-awaited station in the Caley's heartland – for they were always a west of Scotland force in the same way that the North British were firmly rooted in Edinburgh – must have boosted morale in the company. The Caley indeed ended the decade of the 1870s in a healthy and flourishing state, a far cry from ten years earlier.

Contrastingly, their Edinburgh rivals, the North British, were left to ponder the impact of the collapse of the Tay Bridge on 28th December, 1879.

Chapter Eight

The 1880s

The Railway Workers

On 27th April, 1880, three days after the accident at Ravelrig Junction involving a Balerno branch train, the minutes of the Caley's traffic committee recorded a "Memorial for improved passenger train service on the Balerno branch. Manager to report." The request, one assumes, was not for fewer train crashes to occur but for more services to be provided.

By 1881 there were in fact seven up trains and eight down trains running over the branch every day. Two trains now ran only as far as Balerno and back, a third ran only to Currie and back, while the rest still served Midcalder. But a trend was growing; and within several more years nearly all services would begin and end at Balerno.

On Saturdays only, one of the up trains which normally terminated at Balerno ran on to Midcalder and returned thence. There was also a late Saturday train to Balerno which returned empty via the main line.

The census of 1881, which was the first since the Balerno branch opened, showed that 47 men in the villages and hamlets of the district owed their living to the railway.

One or two of them worked on the main line but most on the branch. Hardly any of them were native to the area, which was not at all unusual as men had to take work wherever they could find it.

Seven men came from Ireland including two brothers by name McWeenie, surfacemen living in Colinton. The elder brother had emigrated in the early 1870s; a son had been born in Ireland in 1872, his other children in Balerno, Juniper Green and Slateford from 1874 onward.

Other men came from all over Scotland. John Gordon, a signalman at Currie, was from Conon Bridge in Ross and Cromarty and was lodging in Rosebank cottages with a signalman from Dumfriesshire and a porter from Lanarkshire. The three station masters listed came from Leadburn, Ayrshire and Perthshire (respectively John Kerr at Colinton, John Tonnar at Currie and Charles Campbell at Balerno).

Forty of the men were incomers; just seven were native to the district. Since many of the new arrivals had brought families with them, the increase in the local population arising from the opening of the Balerno branch was of the order of 150 – a sizeable figure, given that the overall total was under 4000. It can be seen how important a railway was to the community over and above the services it provided.

The largest three groups of workers listed were the porters (ten), platelayers (nine) and surfacemen (eight). All ages from 18 to 81 were represented, with the Curriehill level crossing keeper (on the main line) the oldest, but only by four years from a platelayer living in Currie. The latter, David Bishop, aged 77, was a local man; his grandson, also called David Bishop, was a foreman platelayer on the railway – and in later years became the manager at Balerno goods station. The youngest employee listed as working on the railway was the son of a paper mill worker, John Johnston aged 18, who was a clerk at Juniper Green station.

Dugald Drummond; New Engines

On 1st July, 1882 a new station appeared in Balerno branch timetables. Merchiston station was actually on the main line, roughly mid-way between Princes Street and Slateford stations, and had been built to cater for residents recently settled in new housing nearby. (During that year, the city boundary was extended to take in the district and station.)

Merchiston station had been proposed in 1879, but delayed until suitable access roads had been made. These included Harrison Road and Harrison Gardens (then Bonaly Road) to east and south. The station, which was quite modern for the time in being supplied with gas as well as water, cost over £2000 to build.

The Caley's service timetable for July 1882 noted:

> Balerno branch: All trains, Up and Down, will call at Merchiston, and the intermediate times of several of them will be slightly altered. The Down trains will discontinue calling at Edinburgh Ticket Platform.

The latter provision resulted from the transfer of ticket-inspecting from the special platform opened just seven years earlier to the immediate west of Princes Street station (between Grove Street and Morrison Street) to Merchiston. At this time Princes Street was an open station – though in time ticket-checking was transferred there. Passengers on the Leith branch meantime had their tickets inspected at Murrayfield station, as Merchiston was not on that route.

1882 was an important year in the history of the Caley in that a new locomotive superintendent, Dugald Drummond, arrived from the North British, where he had already proved a great success since 1875. Drummond made his mark with new classes of engine, including 4–4–0s (two types), 0–4–4 tanks and the remarkable 0–6–0 goods tender engines known as "Jumbos", of which 244 were to be built between 1882 and 1897 (81 of them by Drummond's successor McIntosh) and no fewer than 238 would survive into British Railways days in 1948!

Drummond's engines were a radical departure from those of his predecessors Sinclair, Conner and George Brittain (1876–82) in having inside rather than outside cylinders, plus other innovations such as Ramsbottom safety valves on the dome, closed splashers, improved cabs, etc. Even after he left the Caley in 1890 his basic ideas were carried on with modifications by succeeding superintendents.

He was responsible also for major programmes to equip engines with the Westinghouse air-brake and to provide gas-lighting in rolling stock; many new carriages were built, including a large class of four-wheeled coaches 28 ft 6 in. long which were to become the main stock on the Balerno branch in later years and up to the 1920s; and he pioneered the heating of carriages with exhaust steam piped under seating. He also altered goods livery to black lined with red.

The 0–4–4 tank-engines designed by Drummond for passenger duty were known as the '171' class and were in time to become familiar on the Balerno branch service. Built in four separate batches of six (with the first ordered in 1883 and delivered in 1884, and successive orders completed in 1886, 1889

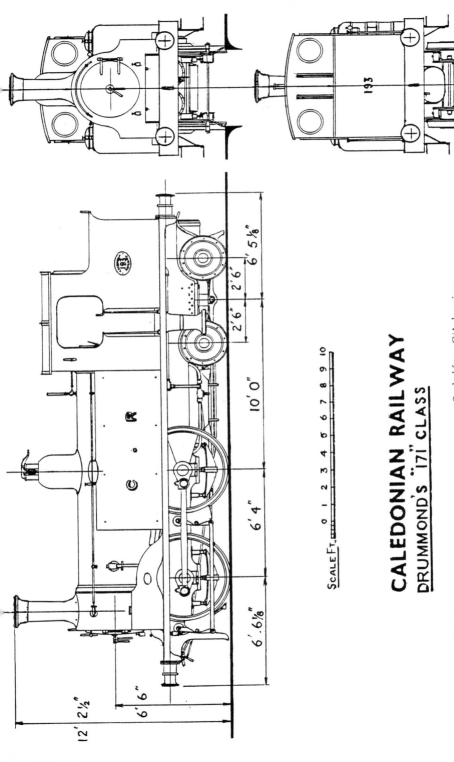

CALEDONIAN RAILWAY
DRUMMOND'S "171" CLASS

SCALE Ft. 0 1 2 3 4 5 6 7 8 9 10

Scaled from G/A drawing.

Courtesy W.D. Stewart
and Caledonian Railway Association

and 1891), the class was derived from a design of 4−4−0 tank-engines which Drummond had built on the North British − the '72' class. The dimensions of their cylinders (16 in. x 22 in.), driving wheels (5 ft diameter) and boiler-barrel were identical.

The 24 engines were all built at St Rollox. Slightly larger capacities were allowed on the second twelve, which could hold 855 gallons of water (up from 830) and 1¾ tons of coal (up from 1¼ tons). Overall length was just 29 ft 3¼ in. The '171' class engines were to become familiar on rural branch services throughout the Caley network; they were on the Balerno branch in the 1890s and perhaps before although it is uncertain when they first appeared on the line.

The class, which was turned out in passenger blue livery and Westinghouse-braked, was numbered as follows: 1884 batch: Nos. 171−176; 1886 batch: Nos. 177, 178, 228−231; 1889 batch: Nos. 222−227; 1891 batch: Nos. 189−194.

The 1882 extension of Edinburgh's boundary mentioned above was followed by new tram-lines extending along Polwarth Terrace to Colinton Road and to Dalry. That year, road tolls were abolished and the toll-houses at Slateford (which had been shifted west in 1876, to near Robertson Avenue), Currie and Little Vantage closed.

Traffic Figures

The earliest traffic returns relating to the Balerno branch still surviving are those for 1883.

They show that Colinton and Juniper Green stations handled three-quarters of the passenger traffic on the line but that Currie and Balerno stations nominally contributed the lion's share of receipts thanks to the goods traffic to and from the local mills and quarries.

1883 traffic returns	Colinton	Juniper Green	Currie	Balerno	Total
Passengers booked	38,464	38,280	17,154	23,235	117,133
Passenger receipts	£747	£872	£579	£753	£2951
Goods receipts	£1310	£1285	£4113	£3171	£9879
Total receipts	£2057	£2157	£4692	£3924	£12830

There is no mistaking the relative importance of the daily goods service on the Balerno branch.

Most of the goods traffic in fact involved goods and minerals received, rather than dispatched, despite the substantial shipments of paper from the mills, particularly Kinleith. For one thing the mills themselves took delivery of large quantities of raw materials − esparto and lime mainly − and for another the whole community required coal.

As to the passsenger service it can be roughly calculated that with eight down trains running each day, on average each train picked up nine passengers at Balerno station, seven at Currie and fifteen each at Juniper Green and Colinton. This however is only an approximation since some passengers will have booked to travel in the up direction and of course not all trains were equally busy.

However this pattern was consistently maintained over later years. Colinton and Juniper Green, the main centres of population, regularly provided about 37 per cent of passengers each, Currie ten per cent and Balerno about fifteen per cent.

Figures were quoted in returns for passengers arriving as well as departing from branch stations. This figure until about 1912 was always a slightly bigger total, except at Juniper Green: there the figures were equal. The explanation may be that the other three villages were noted as accesses to the hills and visitors came out by train to Colinton, Currie and Balerno and then returned homewards by other means.

Ravelrig Platform

As the need arose, the Caley would make various additions and improvements to their facilities at stations and elsewhere on the Balerno branch. In 1878, for example, an additional waiting room was provided at Currie station, and in 1880 a water supply at Colinton station. The platform at Juniper Green was extended in 1884, and in the same year a footbridge was erected at Currie for the first time, enabling passengers to cross the line in safety. A weighbridge was also installed; and at Balerno goods yard the loading bank was lengthened.

The same year, 1884, a completely new platform was opened at Ravelrig Junction, a short way west of the actual junction. The platform (actually there were two, one to each side of the main line) was the idea of an officer in the Volunteers, the equivalent of today's Territorial Army, whose men regularly came to exercise near Ravelrig; Captain Belfrage initially approached the Caley in July 1883 with his suggestion, and was told the platform could be provided if he would contribute towards the cost. Belfrage agreed, and donated £70 out of the eventual total cost of £169.

Ravelrig Platform opened on 4th April, 1884. For a short time it was visited by quite a large number of trains, as the Caley evidently wished to find out if there was sufficient local demand to justify a regular service over and above the occasional traffic provided by Volunteers. Thus, between Monday and Thursday four trains altogether called (two up, two down) of which three were Balerno branch trains; on Fridays four up and three down trains, seven in all, called, one of these being a Balerno branch service; and on Saturdays, no fewer than twelve trains were scheduled to stop at the platform (six each way), with one of them a branch train.

However, demand was obviously low, for within weeks most services had ceased calling. Indeed, few people lived nearby; apart from the railwaymen in the junction cottages there were just a handful of farm-dwellers, none of whom would be likely to wish to travel often. Thereafter it became the established pattern over many years that one train in each direction called at the platform daily; a morning down train, collecting passengers for Edinburgh – and an evening up train, dropping them off again. Both ran to and from town via the main line, and so Ravelrig Platform ceased to feature in Balerno branch services.

But branch trains resumed calling at the platform much later when, for a time in the 1920s and 1930s, the Caley's successors, the LMS, laid on a curious occasional service of trains which ran to Balerno via the branch before returning to Princes Street via Ravelrig Junction and the main line. In the 1920s one of these services ran daily, as well as another on Saturday afternoons; the latter lasted into the 1930s. And in the same era, the opening of Dalmahoy Golf Club in 1927 a little to the north of Ravelrig Junction gave the old platform a new use; in time the platform surfaces were upgraded and a sign erected announcing "Ravelrig Platform for Dalmahoy G.C.".

Rules and Regulations

The Caley regularly issued instructions relating to the operation of various lines and sections in their system. These were published either in footnotes to the service timetables or in an occasional appendix of rules.

In 1884 a variety of restrictions and regulations were given for the Balerno branch. The most complex concerned brakes. By now the branch was worked by a mixture of trains, some with automatic brakes, some with manual brakes. In the former case it was noted:

> Trains not exceeding ten vehicles to have brake vehicle in front, and one on rear, and one guard in rear brake. Trains consisting of more than ten vehicles, and not exceeding fifteen, to have one brake vehicle in front and one on the rear, and a guard in each.

For trains without continuous automatic brake even more stringent rules applied, viz:

> Trains consisting of not more than seven vehicles to have a brake vehicle in front and one on the rear, and one guard to work the rear brake. Trains consisting of more than seven vehicles, and not exceeding fifteen, to have one brake vehicle in front and one on the rear, also a brake vehicle in the centre; to be worked by two guards, one in the rear brake, and the other in the centre brake.

If this last restriction had applied in 1880, the branch train involved in the accident at Ravelrig Junction would have been better braked and the crash perhaps avoided.

The Caley stressed that no train on the Balerno branch must carry more than fifteen vehicles. The speed limit of fifteen miles per hour still applied.

With the branch becoming busier the signal boxes along the way were open longer during the day in 1884. Balerno signal box was manned from 6.20 am to 9.30 pm – more than fifteen hours – and Currie signal box almost as long, from 7.20 am to 9.50 pm. The signal boxes at Colinton and Juniper Green on the other hand were only in use for the movement of the branch goods train in and out of the station sidings. In their many free hours, the signalmen at these places would have helped out around their respective stations, issuing tickets and so on. The signal boxes at the main line junctions were manned 24 hours a day.

All drivers on the Balerno branch were required to observe a code of warning whistles to be sounded as they approached stations or junctions. These indicated their intentions to the signalman and station staff.

Thus one whistle (in fact the Caley "whistle" was a distinctive deep toot from the days of ·Drummond on!) indicated that a train was proceeding normally along the branch while two whistles meant it was bound for sidings. There were further options at the main line junctions; at Ravelrig Junction one whistle indicated a main line train passing through, two whistles a Balerno branch train (in whichever direction), while three or four whistles indicated respectively a train visiting the west or east sidings (the east sidings were reached from the Balerno line). To complicate matters two "cock crows" meant a train was bound for the stone sidings of Ravelrig Quarry!

Among general rules and regulations in 1884 signalmen on various lines were instructed to listen out at one o'clock each day for a time signal based on the firing of the one o'clock gun at Edinburgh castle! They were then to "regulate their clocks accordingly." This applied to Balerno branch men.

A number of stations were designated "footwarmer stations"; here staff were to keep supplies of footwarmers ready to issue to passengers in winter. Princes Street and Midcalder stations were the nearest footwarmer stations to the Balerno branch. Whether they were issued to passengers on branch trains is unclear but they may well have been. Since 1872 third class as well as first class travellers had been entitled to them.

At this time Dugald Drummond had recently begun using a new means of providing heat to carriages whereby hot exhaust steam was piped through them. Carriages were converted at a cost of £12 each but not on the Balerno branch where steam heating was introduced only in the early 1920s.

Caley staff were ordered to check their footwarmers regularly as they were prone to rust at the water-level! In October 1878 1300 footwarmers had been replaced as they were worn out; it was noted that this was half the total.

The Quarry Railways

A new branch line opened in south-west Edinburgh in December 1884. The Edinburgh South Side and Suburban Junction Railway formed a semi-circle leaving the North British line west of Haymarket to run under the Caley Granton branch and main line in quick succession, before continuing via Morningside and Newington and re-joining the North British at Portobello.

The railway was operated independently until the North British acquired it in 1885. But when it was first proposed in 1880 the Caley had applied for a junction with it at Slateford and a fifty per cent stake in it, without success.

Between 1883 and 1888 the Balerno branch railway was re-laid with steel rails, which had been superseding iron rails everywhere since the 1870s.

Colinton and Juniper Green stations were provided with goods sheds for the first time in 1886 and 1885 respectively. At the time goods traffic was still mainly handled at the other two stations though in later years Colinton's share would be boosted by the arrival of A.&R. Scott Ltd, a large oat-milling firm, at West Mills in 1900.

Maps of the late 19th century show a whole network of private railways on the hillside above the Balerno branch between Balerno and Ravelrig Junction. There were three separate quarries here, all connected by rail to two loading banks adjacent to a long siding which ran parallel to the branch line. It diverged from the branch close to Ravelrig Junction.

The first quarry railway dated from 1869 (before then a siding had been provided to the main line nearby, in 1865). Since 1869 additions had been made; and in 1886 the lessees of Ravelrig Quarry applied to the Caley for a loan of old materials in order to extend their sidings still further.

Perhaps the most spectacular private railway was that serving the eastern quarry at Hannahfield. It ran in a straight line, at a very steep gradient, rising more than 300 ft in under half a mile to a height of over 800 ft and entering the quarry in an unusual way: for, the Balerno branch being on the north side and the quarry being excavated from the south, a cutting had to be blasted through the rock-face so as to allow the tramway and its wagons access to the workings.

The quarry railways were worked by means of horses pulling wagons up and gravity letting them run down again to the loading bank by the Balerno branch. Obviously several brake wagons would have to be attached on the downward journey to prevent a wagon-train going out of control. Small locomotives may also have been used on occasion; and several men were listed in censuses of the 19th century as "engine driver at quarry" – though most likely this referred to the stationary engines which were employed to pump water out of quarry workings.

Around the turn of the century, an alteration was made in the layout of the Balerno branch below the quarry lines so as to reduce the length of the double track section of the branch and turn the spare set of rails into a new stone siding of considerable length.

Quarrying was by then confined to the two easternmost quarries – the other, known as Shade's Quarry, having been closed. Meantime, however, another quarry further west, on Kaimes Hill, was thriving and had been connected to the Caley main line by its own siding in 1895; its output was invoiced at Balerno station. In 1910 stone traffic thus attributed to Balerno reached a peak of 60,000 tons.

The abandonment of quarrying on Ravelrig Hill in the 1930s allowed Nature to turn the old network of tramways into attractive, grassy paths, kept in neat order by grazing sheep. However, after a gap of fifty years stone is once again being quarried and soon those relics of a bygone age will be obliterated, except for the faded track leading up to Hannahfield, which is not to re-open.

The Railway Races to Edinburgh, 1888

The celebrated races between London and Edinburgh which took place during July and August 1888 arose from the fierce competitiveness of the two sets of railway companies which operated their respective routes. The Caley were the Scottish link in the West Coast route, the North British in the East Coast route.

The racing was called off eventually by an agreed truce, after the West Coast companies had reduced their through-time from 10 hours to 7¾ hours, and the East Coast allies from 9 hours to the same 7¾ hours. Thereafter new journey times of 8½ hours and 8¼ hours respectively were put into effect. The whole episode was started by the West Coast companies' concern over the East Coast route attracting traffic thanks to the recent opening of the Tay Bridge and the imminent opening of the Forth Bridge.

While it lasted, spectators had the opportunity of seeing engine No. 123 careering past Ravelrig, Curriehill or Kingsknowe at breakneck speed en route from Carlisle to the capital setting undreamt-of records on several occasions.

CR No. 123 was an engine unique on the Caley in her 4−2−2 wheel arrangement; she had been built two years earlier for showing at the 1886 Edinburgh International Exhibition, held on the Meadows, by Neilson and Co., after which the Caley had bought her to use in normal service. Thanks to the performances recorded by her during the races, she became the pride of the line afterwards!

No. 123 achieved her most famous run on 9th August, 1888 when the 100.6 miles between Carlisle and Edinburgh were covered in 1 hour, 42 minutes and 33 seconds, at an average speed of nearly 60 miles per hour. This was despite the obstacles in the way − namely Beattock summit as well as Cobbinshaw summit on the Edinburgh branch. Between Midcalder Junction and Curriehill station the train, which included four coaches, ran at 70 mph.

CR No. 123 is preserved today at the Museum of Transport in Glasgow. One of her last outings was from Glasgow to Edinburgh and back on 19th April, 1965, via the Caley line through Curriehill, when she conveyed enthusiasts to the Balerno branch and other parts − though No. 123 herself did not visit the branch.

Another outbreak of racing occurred in 1895, but on that occasion the target for the rival alliances of companies was Aberdeen, not Edinburgh. The Caley worked their trains via Stirling and Perth, of course.

But in the summer of 1888 not all trains in the vicinity of Edinburgh travelled so fast. In their own way, those that conveyed parties of deprived children from the slums of Edinburgh along the Balerno branch to Harmony House in Balerno for a fortnight's holiday were equally worthy. As The Scotsman reported in August that year, twenty children at a time were taken in, with ten coming and going each Saturday; they were ferried between Balerno station and Harmony House in a donkey cart. The Scotsman praised the work of the home, where

> ... dwining children from the closes and back streets of Edinburgh can feel heaven's light and heaven's love nourish their poor little bodies and souls.
> There is a strong element of hope in every effort made to save such little ones, and already the blessings diffused among them through Holiday House are bearing fruit. The children carry back to their city life new feelings, higher aims, better thoughts. They have felt God's sunshine and handled His flowers without reproof, and seen His everlasting hills, and known the happiness of real child life − so different from the life they lead at home.

Did the Balerno branch ever give more pleasure to passengers than it did to those youngsters of a century ago, eager in their anticipation of a holiday as the train rattled along beside the picturesque river? And did it ever carry more sorrowful travellers than the same children returning home a fortnight later?

In 1888 the first of several petitions from residents of Balerno was submitted to the Caley, asking for the goods station there to be converted to handle passenger services too; the residents felt that, with most branch trains by now terminating at Balerno rather than running through to Midcalder, there was no longer any justification for the passenger station remaining on its existing awkward site at Newmills, at the top of the Balerno−Ravelrig section.

The Caley, however, saw things differently, agreeing only to make minor improvements to the present passenger station. Further requests from the inhabitants in 1891 and 1895 were also rejected; in 1891 the cost of shifting passenger facilities to the goods station was put as £2735. The Caley most likely felt that goods traffic was too profitable to be hampered by having passenger traffic crowding into the same location, with the additional need to provide a means of turning engines.

Train Tablet Working

The safe operation of the Balerno branch from its opening in 1874 until 1889 was achieved under the absolute block telegraph procedure described earlier, whereby train movements were controlled and monitored by messages passed between block instruments located at Balerno Junction, Currie, Balerno and Ravelrig Junction.

Block working on its own was a very unusual practice on single lines within the Caledonian network. Much more common was the procedure known as "train staff and tickets" working; this also involved the use of blocks or sections of line, but with an extra factor, whereby trains working any section had to carry a special staff (a rod-shaped object) unique to that section – and only when the staff became available could another train enter the section from the other end. "Staff and ticket" working was employed when two trains were to run consecutively over a section in the same direction; then, the first driver was given a ticket after being first shown the section staff (to confirm it was at the right end) while the second driver accepted the actual staff.

The defect of the system was in the event of late running of trains, when it might be desirable to alter schedules – and the staff would be at the "wrong" end of a section. It then had to be physically retrieved, on horse or on foot, to allow working to proceed!

It seems likely that the Caley had feared this problem in 1874 when opting not to use staff and tickets on the Balerno branch, because with so many of the trains running to and from Midcalder (and some at first to and from Glasgow) late running might indeed have caused frequent hold-ups.

In 1878 a new method for working single line railways was patented by Edward Tyer and adopted for the first time by the Caley two years later. The electric tablet system proved so successful that its use thereafter became widespread, and it was eventually installed on the Balerno branch in 1888−89.

The system involved special instruments at each end of a section being electrically inter-connected and containing a stock of section tablets, which were to have the same role as section staffs. The interlocking of the instruments meant that, when a tablet was withdrawn and given to a driver, the circuit between them was locked so that no other tablet could be got out until the first was replaced. The act of replacing the tablet allowed both instruments to be unlocked again.

The system therefore guaranteed that only one train could gain access to any section at a given time; and its advantage over the absolute block telegraph procedure was that it was proof against human error.

For each section of line several tablets were made, which enabled two or more trains to travel in the same direction consecutively.

On the Balerno branch, tablet working was proposed by the Caley in July 1888 at the same time as a new siding to the West paper mill at Colinton was authorised. The Caley expected that the Board of Trade would press for the siding to be worked by tablet and that consequently the whole branch would have to be converted to the new system.

By January 1889 work on the conversion was complete, and the Caley issued instructions to the signalmen at Balerno Junction, Currie, Balerno and Ravelrig Junction (for the previous sections still applied). The new list of telegraph signals included the following principal codes:

Preparatory signals:	3 bells: passenger train offered.
	4 bells: goods train offered.
	3 bells (2, pause, 1): light engine offered.
	4 bells (2, pause, 2): engine and brake offered.
Train tablet signal:	5 bells.
Departure signal:	2 bells (Train entering section).
Arrival signal:	6 bells (Train leaving section).

As before, signals for up and down trains were distinguished by bells and gongs, bells sounding at the up end of sections and gongs at the down end.

The sending of the train tablet signal of five bells or gongs required the signalman at the other end of a section either to accept the train by responding with one bell or gong or to refuse it with five bells or gongs. If accepting, he had to wait while his colleague began the operating procedure whereby the circuit between the two block instruments was unlocked – but this had to be achieved by joint actions.

Naturally, at the two intermediate signal boxes on the Balerno branch – Currie and Balerno – two tablet instruments were installed, giving contact with colleagues on either side. For the Currie signalman, in particular, powers of mental concentration would be required at those times when two passenger trains were crossing at the station, for he then had four tasks to carry out quickly: the arrival of each train had to be reported in turn, to the signalmen at Balerno Junction and at Balerno, whereupon the two section tablets involved would be replaced in their respective instruments; and then the departure of each train had to be authorised, with the same tablets being re-issued, only this time to different drivers.

The four signal boxes on the Balerno branch not involved in tablet working – namely those at Colinton, Juniper Green, Kates mill and Kinleith mill – were all made redundant by the new system. Ground frames were installed at these locations, to be locked and unlocked by the appropriate section tablet, and containing levers which opened and closed the various siding points (*see below*).

Tablet working continued thereafter on the Balerno branch until the line closed. In 1901 the number of sections was increased to four when Juniper Green station was made a tablet station. With the closure of the branch to passenger traffic in 1943, the system became virtually redundant because there was no longer any prospect of more than one train (the goods train) working the line at any time; but even so, the branch continued to operate as a single block, and the signalmen at Balerno Junction and Ravelrig Junction still exchanged tablets with drivers on the goods train.

The original cost of the 1888–89 conversion work was £333. Curiously, when the Board of Trade authorised tablet working on the branch at that time they stipulated that, should it prove an unsatisfactory method for any reason, the Caley must "revert" to staff and tickets working – which had never in fact been used! However, this was only a standard expression: it dated back to the days when tablet working was still experimental and staff and tickets were viewed by the Board of Trade as the logical alternative or fall-back.

Colinton Paper Mill Siding

The new siding to West paper mill near Colinton opened in March 1889. Its construction, at the request of the mill's owners, Messrs McLeod and Birrell of Colinton Paper Company, involved a new railway bridge being built over the Water of Leith to give entry for wagons into the mill – which, like Kates mill, was located on the "wrong" side of the river in relation to the branch. However, wagons alone – not engines – were permitted to use the bridge.

West Mills had once been a complex of three distinct mills, making paper, grain and flax. The flax mill had by 1889 long since gone; but Messrs King still ran their grain mill to the west side of the paper mill; the two were so close that in days of water-power both had relied on the same mill-lade for a supply.

The proposed new siding was given initial approval by the Board of Trade in September 1888. But, as at Kinleith and Kates mills, Major-General Hutchinson had reservations about the site; he was concerned by the steep gradient in the Balerno branch near the planned works. He insisted from the outset that whenever a shunting operation was to involve a train not being completely off the actual branch because of its length, then the engine must be at the lower end (the eastern end) as a guarantee against wagons being able to break away down the incline towards Slateford.

Approving the completed siding on 8th February, 1889, Hutchinson re-iterated this point by limiting trains to 20 wagons so that they might be completely off the actual branch and within range of a catch siding, unless the train was proceeding towards Edinburgh – that is, with the engine at the lower end.

CALEDONIAN RAILWAY.

CODE OF SIGNALLING

FOR

SINGLE LINES

WORKED BY

TRAIN TABLET.

1. The Bell applies to Up Trains, the Gong to Down Trains.
2. The Outdoor fixed Signals must always be kept at "Danger", except when it is necessary to lower or turn them off for a Train or Light Engine to pass, and before any Signal is lowered or turned off care must be taken to ascertain that the Line on which the Train or Light Engine has to run is clear.
3. No Signal is to be considered complete until the proper acknowledgment of it has been received. Should the Signalman in the Box to which the Signal has been sent not reply, the Signal is to be repeated at short intervals until the acknowledgment is obtained.
4. No Signal is to be cancelled until after it has been acknowledged.
5. All Signals are to be given slowly and distinctly, the Plunger being pressed well home. Should an indistinct Signal be received, the "Repeat" Signal is to be given, when the Sending Signalman will repeat the last Signal given by him.
6. No Train or Light Engine must be considered out of Block or clear of a Section until it has passed forward in steam into the onward Section, or has been shunted clear off the Main Line.
7. When the Train or Engine last signalled, carrying the last Vehicle Indicator, has arrived at the Box, the Arrival Signal must be at once sent to the Box from whence the Train or Engine departed, and the Train Tablet Instrument must be put into its normal condition, in accordance with the Code of Working.
8. The Train Tablet, immediately on being received, must be placed in the slide, lettered side downwards, and passed into the Instrument.
9. When the Section is clear, the normal position of the Train Tablet Instrument shews the word "In" on white ground of both discs.
10. The Tablets are raised and lowered in the Cylinder by means of a screw connected with the large circular knob, and the gauge over the Cylinder indicates when a Tablet is in position to be drawn out.
11. The time of all Trains or Empty Engines must be immediately entered in the Train Signal Book within the proper columns, and any irregularity in the working and the cause of any detention to Trains or Engines must be noted at the time in that Book, and at once reported to the Inspector of the District. The number of each Tablet used must also be entered in the Train Book.
12. No private Signals are to be given between Signalmen.

CODE OF WORKING THE TRAIN TABLET INSTRUMENTS.

👉 TRAINS DEPARTING.

PREPARATORY SIGNAL—

Passenger Train,	**3** Beats on Bell or Gong.
Goods or Mineral Train,	**4** do. do.
Engine and Brake,	**4** do. do. thus—2 pause 2.
Light Engine,	**3** Beats on Bell or Gong, thus—2 pause 1.

TRAIN TABLET SIGNAL—

5 Beats on Bell or Gong.

When acknowledgment of 1 Beat is received, push the Bell Plunger and keep it home till Indicating Needle falls to Zero. Release the Plunger, wait till Upper Disc moves from "in" to "out," then draw out Slide, and give Tablet to Engine Driver.

DEPARTURE SIGNAL—

2 Beats on Bell or Gong.

ACKNOWLEDGMENT—

8 Beats on Bell or Gong.

Then push Bell Plunger, and keep it home till Indicating Needle falls back momentarily to Zero. Release the Plunger, and when Upper Disc moves from "out" to "in," push empty Slide back into the Instrument.

TABLET SLIDE IN SIGNAL—

1 Beat on Bell or Gong.

👉 TRAINS APPROACHING.

ACKNOWLEDGMENT—

3 Beats on Bell or Gong.	
4 do. do.	
4 do. do. thus—2 pause 2.	
3 do. do. thus—2 pause 1.	

ACKNOWLEDGMENT—

1 Beat on Bell or Gong. When Indicating Needle is deflected draw out the Slide—it comes empty—as far as possible. This unlocks Lower Disc, and causes Indicating Needle to fall back to Zero. Turn Lower Disc from "in" to "out", push the Bell Plunger, and keep it home till Indicating Needle falls back momentarily to Zero.

5 Beats on Bell or Gong if not prepared to take on the Train.

ACKNOWLEDGMENT—

2 Beats on Bell or Gong.

ARRIVAL SIGNAL—

8 Beats on Bell or Gong. When Acknowledgment is received, and Indicating Needle shews a constant current on, push Slide, with Tablet received, back into the Instrument. Turn Lower Disc from "out" to "in," and push the Bell Plunger, and keep it home till Indicating Needle falls back momentarily to Zero.

ACKNOWLEDGMENT—

1 Beat on Bell or Gong.

BELL AND GONG SIGNALLING.

			ACKNOWLEDGMENT.	
CANCELLING SIGNAL.—To be sent when it becomes necessary, from any cause, to cancel the Signal previously given.	**7** Beats on Bell or Gong.			**7** Beats on Bell or Gong.
REPEAT SIGNAL.—To be sent when an indistinct Signal has been received.	**8** Beats on Bell or Gong.			Repeat the last Signal sent.
STOP TRAIN AND EXAMINE.—To be sent to the Station in advance when anything is observed wrong with a passing Train. Should a Train become divided in running, and pass a Box in two portions, the Signalman must repeat the 9 Beats when the second portion passes him, and in this case the Signalman in advance must act as he may consider best in the circumstances.	**9** Beats on Bell or Gong.			**9** Beats on Bell or Gong.
RUNAWAY VEHICLES.—To be sent to the Signal Box in the rear, or advance, as soon as the breakaway is observed.	**10** Beats on Bell or Gong.			**10** Beats on Bell or Gong.
INSPECTOR'S SIGNAL.—To be sent by the Inspector when Testing the Instruments. This Signal must only be given when the Section is clear.	**12** Beats on Bell or Gong.			**12** Beats on Bell or Gong.

GENERAL MANAGER'S OFFICE,
GLASGOW, January, 1889.

JAMES THOMPSON, *General Manager.*

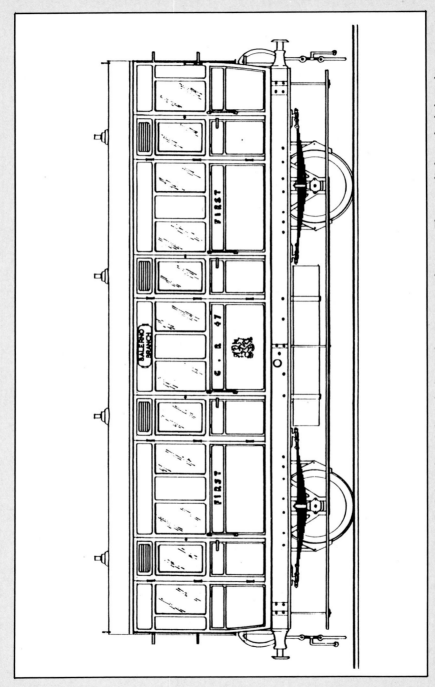

A first-class carriage as used on the Balerno branch from the late 19th century into the 1920s. These gas-lit four-wheeled coaches were a Drummond design of the 1880s, 28 ft 6 in. long.

Courtesy A.J.C. Clark

The Caley duly instructed that no train of more than 20 wagons should use the siding. In any event the weakness of their own new bridge meant that it was desirable to have the engine at the lower end as it was prohibited from going on the bridge.

Drivers were instructed that three whistles must be sounded to indicate use of the paper mill siding, while two whistles were required for the ordinary station sidings at Colinton. (The new siding junction and the existing one were in fact very close together, so it was of help to the Colinton staff to hear the distinguishing whistles and know exactly where a train was bound.)

Both junctions were worked by a new tablet frame installed close by, to be operated by a "porter-pointsman", one of Colinton station's staff. The frame contained four levers; two to open and close the points for the paper mill siding and two to do the same for the station siding points. It could only be used after first being unlocked with the branch tablet for the section between Balerno Junction and Currie. The Caley directed:

> When using the sidings, the porter-pointsman must get the train tablet from the driver, and deposit it in the tablet frame, with the notch to the back and the lettering to the top, after which the points can be unlocked by turning the handle to "Points Unlocked", as directed in the frame. When work has been completed, and the points properly set for the main line the handle must again be turned to "Points Locked", as directed on the frame. This will free the tablet and allow it to be withdrawn; and it must be handed back to the driver before starting.

Major Plans for Edinburgh

There was an unusual happening in January 1889 in the vicinity of the Balerno branch when an earthquake of minor proportions caused some strange effects.

The clock at Currie, reported *The Scotsman*, stopped between 6.50 am and 6.55 am; the signalman at Ravelrig Junction felt the signal box shake; a number of people complained of feeling unwell; while "A railway porter at Curriehill who has felt earthquakes abroad says he was at once aware of what had occurred by the trembling of his house and an accompanying sudden noise of low sound."

But the biggest reverberations that year in the Caley, at least around Edinburgh, were caused by the unveiling of three major new projects.

In October the company gave the go-ahead for a new Edinburgh station to be built on the site of the existing one. It was not before time; after more than forty years of operating trains in and out of the city the Caley had still succeeded only in erecting two "temporary" wooden stations.

George Cunningham, by this time the Caley's Consulting Engineer, was asked to design the new terminus, his fee to be three per cent of the eventual cost.

In November plans for an extensive network of lines running to the eastern docks at Leith were approved. The Caley's existing branch to Leith, which dated from 1864, was handy for the older western docks but was linked to the Albert Dock and Edinburgh Dock further east (opened in 1869 and 1881 respectively) only by a single tramway owned by the North British. So a new branch was to be constructed from the established line.

More strikingly, though, the Caley also planned to get to the docks by an ambitious line running below Princes Street and Calton Hill involving a tunnel extending from west of Princes Street station to London Road. This was to be a passenger-only railway.

The third major project announced in 1889 was for a branch line to the (then) country estate of Barnton north-west of Edinburgh. This had been suggested by the owner of the estate Sir James Gibson Maitland who intended to feu the land and thought a railway could attract potential developers. The branch was authorised in 1890 and opened in 1894.

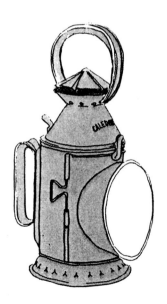

Station master's handlamp (with rotatable red or green lens) as used at Currie Station.
Courtesy A.J.C. Clark

Chapter Nine

The 1890s

The Exhibition Station

By 1890 the railway network in the Edinburgh area had been largely completed. Only a handful of lines remained to be built, to Barnton (1894), Gullane (1898), Gifford (1901), Lauder (1901), Corstorphine (1902) and Leith (the Caley completed a line to Leith eastern docks in 1903 and the North British a line to Leith Central in the same year).

No project was bigger than the Forth Bridge which was opened on 4th March, 1890 to be followed by a new line of railway giving access to it between Saughton and Dalmeny in June. William Arrol, whose first contract to make railway bridges had been the sub-contract from Charles Brand and Son on the Balerno branch in 1871, was knighted at the conclusion of the Forth Bridge opening ceremony.

This was a time of technical and scientific advances. There had been the first motor car in 1885; in 1888 cable-trams had begun operating in Edinburgh — initially there were two services between Hanover Street and Goldenacre and between Frederick Street and Stockbridge though later the system was developed throughout Edinburgh. The trams were operated by means of an underground cable to which they were hooked, the cable being driven from an engine house; the first was at Henderson Row but eventually there were four altogether including one at Tollcross.

The first electric underground train ran in London in 1890.

It was primarily to demonstrate progress in electrical science that a huge exhibition was opened on 1st May, 1890 at Slateford on land lying between the Caledonian main line and the Union Canal.

Both the Caley and the North British opened special temporary stations nearby to cater for the large crowds who flocked to see the exhibition throughout that summer. The Caley station was situated midway between Merchiston and Slateford, the North British station on the adjacent suburban railway which the NB had acquired in 1885.

The Caley's exhibition station was served by a half-hourly service of trains throughout the day, the first leaving Princes Street at 10.15 am. Return services left the exhibition station on the hour and the half-hour, the last train of the day arriving back at Princes Street at 11 pm.

Passengers travelling from stations on the Leith branch could purchase special tickets which included the price of admission to the exhibition.

The station was on a short purpose-built branch in effect, the use of which was strictly controlled by tablet working. When the exhibition closed after the summer the station was dismantled and the four block instruments sold off.

While the original idea behind the International Industrial Exhibition had been to illustrate progress in electrical science, by the time it opened its scope had been enlarged to include mechanical science and even fine arts. The main building faced the Union Canal and was 700 ft long and 250 ft wide, being divided into wings comprising nine courts each. In-between was a concert hall seating 3000 people complete with orchestra and organ.

To the east across the suburban railway – over which a pedestrian bridge was erected – was the machinery hall with a locomotive annexe. The buildings cost £50,000 in all and were electrically lit.

The exhibition was opened by the Duke and Duchess of Edinburgh whose procession travelled west along Dalry Road and up Ardmillan Terrace. As *The Scotsman* reported:

> At Ardmillan Terrace, where the Exhibition first bursts into view, the scene was indeed a gay one. The roadway at each side from Harrison Park to the Exhibition was lined with Venetian masts, from which were suspended bannerets and shields. At intervals bright-coloured rows of streamers were stretched across the road. The numerous flags on the Exhibition buildings and others on private houses in the vicinity fluttered gaily in the breeze, and the brilliant sunshine added greatly to the effectiveness of a very pretty scene.

While the exhibition lasted the Union Canal enjoyed an Indian summer; electrically powered boats conveyed visitors from the site to Slateford and back for a fare of one halfpenny!

Alarms and Excursions

Heavy excursion traffic on Saturdays on the Balerno branch sometimes taxed the little branch engines to the limit. As *The Scotsman* reported on Monday 12th May, 1890:

> A good deal of alarm was caused to many of the passengers by the 2.12 train from Edinburgh to Currie on Saturday afternoon, in consequence of the train coming to a stop in the tunnel at Colinton. It afterwards became apparent that the engine was not powerful enough to properly draw the train, which consisted of about fourteen carriages. After some delay the train was run backwards down the incline, and the steam having, it is presumed, been increased, another start onwards was made. To the relief of most of the passengers, the tunnel was this time passed through, though at a slow pace. The train, however, again came to a standstill several times at more distant points of the line, and ultimately in the vicinity of Juniper Green it was divided into two portions, and the journey to Currie was completed first with the one portion and next with the other. The afternoon train on Saturday fortnight also came to a stop between Juniper Green and Currie.

What the writer omitted to mention was the 1 in 50 gradient which made Colinton Dell and several other parts of the branch hard work at the best of times. A load of fourteen carriages was testimony to the popularity of the line with visitors but no doubt more than the tank engines had been originally designed to handle. The Caley were aware of the problem for before the decade was out a new engine had been specially designed for the branch. Twelve were built and became known as "Balerno Pugs."

The Caley lost some of its traffic on the Balerno branch in 1890 when Kates paper mill burnt down. Its owner David Chalmers was now an elderly man in failing health and the mill was not re-built. The siding from the railway across the river was consequently closed, as was the signal box. The cobbled track which enabled goods to be ferried between mill and siding is still there today.

There was more disruption to the Caley's local services when on 16th June, 1890 fire substantially destroyed Princes Street station. Ironically the contract for a new station had been already let just a month before, to Kinnear Moodie and Co. for £73,684; so in a way the fire only hastened the demolition process.

It broke out just before two o'clock as a train was arriving from Glasgow. Passengers got out quickly as the fire spread from the oil room at the south west of the station. The train left the station at once but three passenger vans and a carriage parked in the station's central track were destroyed in the fire.

"About three o'clock," noted *The Scotsman*, "it looked as if nothing but the total destruction of the shed could stop the fire. The south end was one mass of fire rising from platform to roof, the carriages were fiercely burning with a golden glare, and rising above them the sheets of flame, probably from paint and varnish, were of a deep rose pink colour, which had rather a fine effect against the lurid background of dull, yellowish smoke."

Various station fittings and furnishings were rescued before the fire could reach them, and "quite a heroic endeavour was successfully made by the junior members of the staff to save the automatic chocolate machines, which they placed upon a barrow and dragged in triumph to the outer yard."

For a time that afternoon incoming trains including those from Balerno were stopped at Merchiston, passengers being taken on from there in cabs. Outgoing travellers were advised to board trains either from the disused ticket platform at Grove Street or at Merchiston. Later trains used the goods station and the southernmost uncovered section of the Princes Street station platform. The following day it was announced that some of the Exhibition trains might not run but otherwise services would be as normal.

The demise of Princes Street station (which was completed within a short time, more conventionally, to make way for the new station) was not much regretted. It was described by *The Scotsman* as "by no means an ornamental structure" and more bluntly by another writer at the time as a "wooden shanty." However it was not alone in attracting criticism; Waverley station came in for even more. Both were in fact rebuilt in the 1890s.

The new Caley terminus came into use in 1894 and cost nearly £200,000 with another £60,000 spent acquiring land including properties in Rutland Square. The building was initially a one-storey structure; the present Caledonian hotel was then built over it, opening in 1903.

Of the three archways at the front of the building the left-hand was originally the entrance to a roadway for horse-carriages with an exit further along opposite King's Stables Road. When the hotel was added this became a hotel entrance; the carriageway was used to make the lounge and dining room. The centre archway was closed off, while that on the right continued to serve as the station entrance. Inside, the station was spaciously laid out with seven long, curving platforms under a fine bayed roof. The hotel was built to either side.

The 1890 Underground Bill

The Caley's controversial plan for a railway under Princes Street running to Leith was discussed in Parliament in June 1890. Among those giving evidence in its favour were two mill-masters from Juniper Green.

Alexander Corstorphine of Woodhall grain mill, today Inglis' mill, spoke for "the 31 principal traders and manufacturers in the Water of Leith valley" in approving the line as giving them better access to Leith. He himself had occasion to go there on business once- or twice-weekly and other mill-owners went daily. At present they had either to change trains at Princes Street station and reach the port via the roundabout Leith branch or take a tramcar on – and trams were often late or full up.

Mr Corstorphine was cross-examined by counsel for one of the many bodies opposing the plan, who dismissed his claim that many people travelled regularly from the Balerno branch to Leith; otherwise the Caley would already be providing a direct service for them via Slateford Junction and thence directly onto the present Leith branch.

Next, Henry Parker of Woodhall paper mill, who had succeeded Julius Beilby there, spoke for the owners of the "five or six" local paper mills who imported annually 26,000 tons of esparto and other materials at Leith east docks and exported paper to London from there. Improved access would also help the 30 residents or so who travelled to Leith daily, some being commuters who worked there but had feus for houses in the Juniper Green district.

Counsel was equally dismissive of Mr Parker. He pointed out that passenger traffic on the Balerno branch to Edinburgh – let alone to Leith – was small enough for the Caley to have recently considered withdrawing some services; and, secondly, that the planned underground line was intended for passengers only, so goods statistics were irrelevant to that particular debate.

Eventually the scheme, costed at £1 million in capital and borrowings, was partially authorised but the underground line, costed at £425,000 – nearly half the total – was thrown out. It had been fiercely resisted by among others the North British, on whose Waverley territory it would have impinged, and also public bodies worried that the line would pass just a few feet below Princes Street. The proposed line to the eastern docks from the existing Leith branch was authorised.

Less controversially the Caley arranged in November 1890 for a new goods yard to be built east of Slateford station. After it opened it became the starting and finishing point for goods services to and from the Balerno branch. It was known as Gorgie Yard.

Redhall Quarry next to Balerno Junction had by now ceased operating and in 1890 its contents including tramways were auctioned off. James Gowans had had little luck with working it, partly because the proximity of the Caley main line meant certain no-go areas had had to be observed (for which he received compensation which he saw as inadequate). He had latterly been bankrupted. The quarry was then used as a tip before being sold by Mr Inglis of Redhall in 1914 to Colinton Parish Council for use as a public park, which it remains today. The Parish Council also paid the Caley £40 for their interest in one acre while the Caley, astute as ever, insisted on reserving future mineral rights!

A National Strike

A bitter strike between December 1890 and February 1891 overshadowed

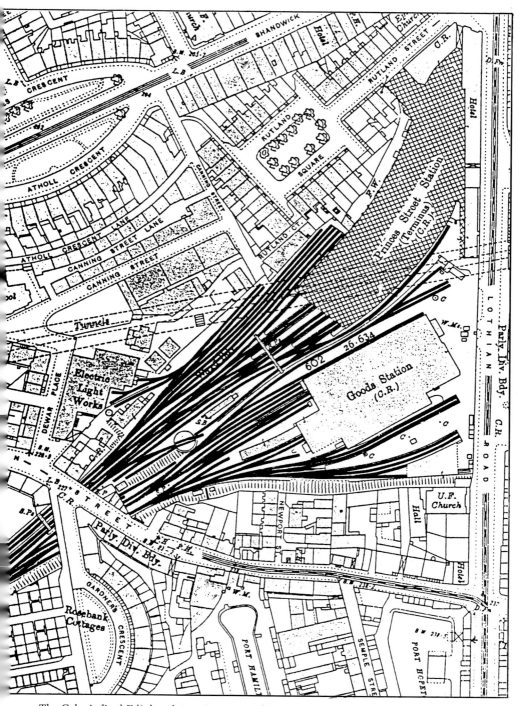

The Caley's final Edinburgh terminus opened in 1894. A hotel was added in 1903.
Reproduced from the 1914, 25″ Ordnance Survey Map

life in the three biggest Scottish railway companies that winter. It highlighted a grievance felt by all grades of railway worker about their excessive hours.

It started on the North British but was then taken up in sympathy by the men of the Caley and Glasgow & South Western, and then spread to ordinary factories. The companies retaliated by joining forces and employing new men as and where they could get them. At one point Caley strikers were evicted from their homes in Motherwell.

The strike left a legacy of bitterness among the defeated men. The companies were as yet all-powerful – indeed trade unions had only been legalised in 1871, when the first big railway union (the Amalgamated Society of Railway Servants) was formed. Not until 1911 was the real breakthrough achieved when a national strike was won at last. Before then railway employees had to accept hard conditions, long hours (often over 60 a week up to the end of the century) and low wages – an average was £1 but many got much less.

As an example of conditions, as late as 27th March, 1888 the Caley for the first time authorised waterproof coats and leggings to be issued to breaksmen, yardsmen, inspectors and messengers – men who worked outdoors in all weathers.

As a footnote to the 1891 strike the Caley paid tribute in April to their late locomotive superintendent, Hugh Smellie, for his "unremitting exertions during the recent strike, to which it is to be feared that his death may have been largely due."

The Barnton Branch

The Caley's Barnton branch which opened on 1st March, 1894 was their third and last Edinburgh passenger branch. It left the Leith line beyond Craigleith station to run to a terminus adjacent to Whitehouse Road behind the present Barnton Hotel.

There were two stations on the line, originally known as Barnton Gate and Cramond Brig but altered to Davidson's Mains and Barnton respectively in 1903.

The day before the branch opened to the public, a special train took 300 invited guests, mainly "architects, engineers, builders, house agents, and other gentlemen interested in feuing and building," to Barnton where they inspected the estate and were entertained to lunch by Sir James Gibson Maitland at Barnton House.

"The approach of the train was waited for with evident interest by the Davidson's Mains villagers, many of whom came to their doors and waved a welcome to it as it passed, while others – and in this group were evidently all the school children of the place – assembled at the station outside the railings and gave expression to their feelings in a hearty cheer." (*Scotsman*).

It has to be remembered that at this time Davidson's Mains was very much a country village well outside Edinburgh and had previously had to rely on a horse-bus service from Cramond for travel to the city.

At lunch Sir James Gibson Maitland told his guests that the contractors for the railway were now erecting the first fourteen villas on the new estate and that the branch would "provide for the people of Edinburgh in a very healthy suburban locality cheap sites for houses." An hourly service of trains would be operated.

The Caley's assistant general manager Mr Patrick thanked Sir James for his efforts in support of the Barnton branch which he hoped would be much appreciated: "He did not know if the citizens of Edinburgh were as anxious to live outside the bounds of the city as those of Glasgow, but if they were, the Barnton Railway, with its liberal service of trains, would enable them to get out to a pretty bit of country within easy distance of Edinburgh."

In 1895–96 the Caley planned to extend the Barnton branch in a rather curious way by making a semi-circular line south-east to Corstorphine. This would have involved passengers from that village taking a remarkably roundabout journey to reach the city. The scheme, however, fell through and Corstorphine was reached by a short North British line in 1902.

Expansion and Prosperity

Colinton and Juniper Green expanded considerably between 1891 and 1901 with land being feued and developed at a rapid rate as more and more people favoured the idea of living in the country and commuting to work in the city. The joint population of the two villages increased by a third during that time from 1797 to 2389.

The presence of the Balerno branch encouraged this growth in population. Services increased steadily on either side of the turn of the century to cater for the growing numbers of passengers. Traffic returns for the branch in 1896 showed a proportionately greater rise in passenger receipts than in goods receipts compared with those for 1883.

	Colinton	Juniper Green	Currie	Balerno	Total
Passengers booked	70,717	74,003	26,248	42,556	213,524
Passenger receipts	£1332	£1656	£623	£1171	£4782
Goods receipts	£2057	£1378	£3785	£4640	£11,860
Total receipts	£3389	£3034	£4408	£5811	£16,642

Goods receipts in 1883 had acounted for 77 per cent of revenue from the branch but were now 71 per cent; and in later years the proportion fell steadily to settle at around 60–65 per cent. (The lowest ratio in Caley days – up to 1923 – was for 1918 when goods receipts were just 51 per cent of the total.)

In July 1896 12 trains ran daily in each direction of which the first two in each direction served Midcalder. On Saturdays only, one of the weekday services to Balerno extended to Midcalder also and there was an extra afternoon train to Balerno. On Wednesdays only, the last up service of the day ran through to West Calder, this being a market train for farmers returning from the weekly Edinburgh market. It remained a regular feature of the Balerno timetable right up to World War II and was latterly the only passenger train using the Balerno–Ravelrig section.

Another feature of the branch timetable in these early years was the provision of "conditional trains" known as "C" trains which ran only when demand required. They were in effect a back-up service for other trains at

1896 TIMETABLE (WEEKDAYS ONLY)

	am	am	am	pm	pm	SO pm	pm	pm	pm	pm	pm	pm	WX pm	WO pm
Princes Street	6.10	7.33	9.50	12.20	2.07	2.25	3.25	4.27	5.40	6.40	8.30	9.35	11.00	11.00
Merchiston	6.14	7.37	9.54	12.24	2.11	2.29	3.29	4.31	5.44	6.44	8.34	9.39	11.04	11.04
Slateford	6.17	7.40	9.57	12.27	2.14	2.32	3.32	4.34	5.47	6.47	8.37	9.42	11.07	11.07
Colinton	6.24	7.47	10.04	12.34	2.21	2.39	3.39	4.41	5.54	6.54	8.44	9.49	11.14	11.14
Juniper Green	6.29	7.52	10.09	12.39	2.26	2.44	3.44	4.46	5.59	6.59	8.49	9.54	11.19	11.19
Currie	6.35	7.58	10.15	12.45	2.32	2.50	3.50	4.52	6.05	7.05	8.55	10.00	11.25	11.25
Balerno	6.41	8.04	10.21	12.51	2.38	2.56	3.56	4.58	6.11	7.11	9.01	10.06	11.31	11.31
Midcalder	6.51	8.15	–	–	2S55	–	–	–	–	–	–	–	–	11.42

S = Saturdays only

	am	am	am	am	pm	pm	pm	pm	pm	pm	pm	pm
Midcalder	7.40	8.18	–	–	–	–	–	–	–	–	–	–
Balerno	7.53	8.33	8.58	10.33	1.13	3.08	4.10	5.23	6.23	7.28	9.13	10.18
Currie	7.59	8.39	9.04	10.39	1.19	3.14	4.16	5.29	6.29	7.34	9.19	10.24
Juniper Green	8.05	8.45	9.10	10.45	1.25	3.20	4.22	5.35	6.35	7.40	9.25	10.30
Colinton	8.10	8.50	9.15	10.50	1.30	3.25	4.27	5.40	6.40	7.45	9.30	10.35
Slateford	8.17	8.57	9.22	10.57	1.37	3.32	4.34	5.47	6.47	7.52	9.37	10.42
Merchiston	8.21	9.01	9.26	11.01	1.41	3.36	4.38	5.51	6.51	7.56	9.41	10.46
Princes Street	8.25	9.05	9.30	11.05	1.45	3.40	4.42	5.55	6.55	8.00	9.45	10.50

Note: "C" trains (to run when required): leave Princes Street at 9.30, 10.07 am, 12.37 and 2.25 pm and leave Balerno at 6.58 and 7.41 pm.

Weekdays

Station	am	am	am	am	am	pm	pm	SO pm	pm	pm	pm	pm	pm	pm	pm	SX pm	SO pm	SO pm
Princes Street	5.50	7.30	8.07	9.26	10.45	12.45	1.40	2.10	3.00	4.30	5.05	5.45	6.35	7.20	8.30	9.30	9.40	10.45
Merchiston	5.54	7.34	8.11	9.30	10.49	12.49	1.45	2.14	3.04	4.34	5.09	5.49	6.39	7.24	8.34	9.34	9.44	10.49
Slateford	5.57	7.37	8.14	9.33	10.52	12.52	1.48	2.17	3.07	4.37	5.12	5.52	6.42	7.27	8.37	9.37	9.47	10.52
Colinton	6.04	7.44	8.21	9.40	10.59	12.59	1.54	2.23	3.14	4.44	5.19	5.59	6.49	7.34	8.44	9.44	9.54	10.59
Juniper Green	6.09	7.50	8.26	9.45	11.04	1.04	1.59	2.28	3.19	4.49	5.24	6.04	6.54	7.39	8.49	9.49	9.59	11.04
Currie	6.14	7.57	8.32	9.50	11.09	1.09	2.04	2.33	3.24	4.54	5.29	6.12	7.02	7.45	8.55	9.55	10.04	11.09
Balerno	6.21	8.03	8.40	9.56	11.15	1.16	2.12	2.40	3.30	5.01	5.36	6.18	7.09	7.52	9.02	10.02	10.11	11.16
Midcalder	–	–	–	–	–	–	–	2.51	–	–	–	–	–	–	–	10.12	–	11T27

T = Thursdays only

Station	am	am	am	am	am	am	pm	pm	pm	pm	pm	pm	SO pm	SX pm	SX pm	SO pm
Midcalder	–	–	–	–	–	–	–	–	–	–	–	–	–	–	10.17	–
Balerno	6.30	7.53	8.25	9.00	10.03	11.23	1.28	3.45	5.25	6.20	7.40	8.50	9.20	9.50	10.27	10.27
Currie	6.35	7.57	8.30	9.05	10.08	11.28	1.32	3.50	5.30	6.25	7.46	8.55	9.25	9.56	10.31	10.31
Juniper Green	6.42	8.03	8.37	9.12	10.15	11.35	1.38	3.56	5.37	6.31	7.53	9.03	9.32	10.03	10.37	10.37
Colinton	6.47	8.08	8.42	9.18	10.20	11.40	1.43	4.00	5.42	6.35	7.58	9.08	9.38	10.08	10.41	10.41
Slateford	6.54	8.15	8.49	9.25	10.27	11.47	1.49	4.07	5.51	6.42	8.05	9.15	9.46	10.15	10.47	10.47
Merchiston	6.56	8.17	8.51	9.27	10.29	11.49	1.51	4.09	5.54	6.44	8.07	9.17	9.48	10.17	10.49	10.49
Princes Street	7.02	8.22	8.56	9.32	10.34	11.54	1.56	4.14	6.00	6.49	8.12	9.22	9.54	10.22	10.55	10.55

Sundays

Station	pm	pm	pm	pm	pm	pm	pm	pm	pm
Princes Street	12.40	2.45	4.35	6.35	1.52	3.25	5.45	7.15	9.31
Merchiston	–	–	–	–	2.01	3.31	5.51	7.21	9.40
Slateford	12.46	2.51	4.41	6.41	2.06	3.37	5.57	7.27	9.46
Colinton	12.53	2.58	4.48	6.48	2.12	3.42	6.02	7.32	9.52
Juniper Green	12.58	3.03	4.53	6.53	2.17	3.49	6.09	7.39	9.57
Currie	1.03	3.08	4.58	6.58	2.24	–	–	–	10.04
Balerno	1.10	3.15	5.05	7.05	2.30	3.55	6.15	7.45	10.10
Midcalder	1.19	–	–	–	–	–	–	–	–

Station	pm
Midcalder	8.10
Balerno	–
Currie	8.16
Juniper Green	8.23
Colinton	8.28
Slateford	8.33
Merchiston	8.40
Princes Street	8.49

Notes:

(1) Hailes Platform: all up trains between 7.30 am and 5.45 pm call as required, and all down trains between 8.25 am and 6.20 pm. Up trains run 2 minutes later if calling, down trains 1 minute later.

(2) Services to/from West Calder: first and last Sunday trains (up and down), and the 10.45 pm (Thursday) up train.

potentially busy times of the day or week such as Saturday mornings and afternoons in the up direction and Saturday evenings in the down direction (conveying town-dwellers having a day out).

Thus in 1896 "C" trains were timed to leave Princes Street at 9.30, 10.07 am, 12.37, and 2.25 pm if required – they would then return from Balerno via the main line, empty. "C" trains from Balerno were timed at 6.58 and 7.41 pm and would travel out the same way, when needed.

The branch goods train still ran to a timetable similar to that of 1877 leaving Gorgie Yard now at 6.30 am, and operating between there and Ravelrig Junction for eleven hours of the day, finishing at 5.30 pm. Among its many duties it was detailed to supply wagons to Ravelrig Quarry in the early afternoon when required; and to shunt at Slateford station and take empty wagons to Balerno Junction sidings (also in the afternoon). The junction sidings both there and at Ravelrig were used to stage traffic to and from the Balerno branch, with wagons being temporarily dropped there for later collection.

The goods train was required to adhere to a strict timetable during the late afternoon when returning to Edinburgh. Just 32 minutes were allowed for the trip from Currie to Balerno Junction, including visits to Kinleith siding, Juniper Green and Colinton, so as not to hold up the down passenger train which was scheduled to leave Currie at 5.24 pm. If time was pressing, the goods train was to omit as many stops as necessary and it was noted:

> Should any traffic not have been lifted at any of the stations or sidings in consequence, the agent or person in charge thereat must wire Inspector McMillan to that effect, so that he may make arrangements for having the traffic brought forward.

By this time the passenger services on the Balerno branch were in the charge of the '171' class 0–4–4 tanks described earlier, having superseded the older Neilson tanks. These efficient Drummond engines continued on the branch until the introduction of new purpose-built 0–4–4 tanks in 1899, designed by the Caley's locomotive superintendent J.F. McIntosh, who succeeded to that post in 1895 after the short tenures of Hugh Smellie (1890–91) and John Lambie (1891–95). At the introduction of the 1899 engines, Nos. 171 and 172 of the '171' class were working the branch.

The Railway and the Landscape

By the mid-1890s a generation had grown up for whom their local railway line, the Balerno branch, was simply part of day-to-day life. Even for those who did not travel on the line, or work on it, there was no doubting its importance: mill-workers, farmers, housewives all used supplies which came by rail, none more important than coal; and the mill-workers saw their finished products being sent away from siding or station.

The men who worked on the line were a substantial body, many of them no doubt already well-respected figures, such as John Kerr and George Melrose, the Colinton and Currie station masters.

Three of the villages – Colinton, Juniper Green and Currie – now had their Railway Inn. (Juniper Green still does.)

The railway fulfilled a curious function in 1896 when it assisted indirectly in improving the amenity of the district; part of its route was used to facilitate the laying of sewerage pipes by the Water of Leith Sewerage and Purification Commission, recently established to combat among other problems the pollution of the river by paper mills. That year, the commission paid the Caley £269 for wayleaves in regard to the branch. (The commissioners comprised members of parishes adjoining the river and also two mill-masters; they remained in office until 1920 when their task was taken over by local councils.)

In 1896 an interesting descriptive account of the countryside bordering the Water of Leith was published, in which a contemporary view of the Balerno branch in its setting of river and trees, mills large and quaint, and contrasting villages, was recorded. The pictures painted by John Geddie in *The Water of Leith from Source to Sea* are worth quoting; unfortunately, though understandably, he did not bother with details of the working of the railway very much – this being a time when railways were too new to be of great interest!

Geddie followed the river from the moorland by its source down to Balerno from where he briefly explored the surrounding district. On Ravelrig Hill, where he went in search of the Roman camp whose remains had once been visible before quarrying obliterated all trace of them,

A pleasant pathway leads over the ridge, winding among the rocks and furze and crossing the rails that convey the whinstone of Ravelrig down the steep slopes to the northward, to the level of the main Caledonian line.

This was the tramway serving Hannahfield quarry; had Geddie followed it down he would of course have found it stopped at the branch, not the main line.

He noted with appreciation that

. . . the pretty Water of Leith Valley Railway to Balerno gives easy access to this charming district, neighbour to the hills, yet sheltered from the rougher winds by its trees and braes; and men who labour hard at the drudgery of commerce, law and journalism find here a delightful place of sojourn in the holiday months of summer and autumn, and an agreeable retreat all the year round from the course of the week.

At Currie the railway presented Geddie with a pleasing picture,

. . . you look directly down into the bed of the Water, where the little Balerno line twists and shifts from bank to bank, seeking, as would seem, for firmer foothold, its rails not very much above the level of the retaining walls of the lades, and overshadowed by trees, gardens, mills and dwellings.

Lower down the valley the sheer bulk of Kinleith paper mill impressed Geddie; but then his eye was taken with a much smaller building where the railway prepared to re-cross the river:

The old snuff mill is tilted quaintly over the stream; and out of the open casement with its diamond panes comes a whiff of pungent tobacco dust that sets your eyes watering. It leans towards the rock-work garden that crowns the vaulted basement of the ruined grain mill across the river – its partner in business in other days, when they shared by turns the same head of water, as barley or snuff happened to be in demand.

This picturesque old mill would survive another few years until, in 1920, finally ceasing production of snuff after more than 170 years.

Continuing his journey Geddie saw Juniper Green as

> . . . a new and enlarged edition of Currie; and, like other later editions, it is of less interest to the antiquary but is in fresher repair.

Here there was a marked contrast between life up on the Lanark Road and down in the narrow glen below, with the mills churning away:

> The main points of contact are the railway stations; the line follows, mostly hidden under the steep wooded banks, all the crooks and twists of the stream, and is the spinal cord of the valley.

Colinton struck John Geddie as being two villages in one; the old being tucked away beside the kirk and the brig, the newer version having grown up further west.

> The casual visitor to Colinton might land a score of times on the station platform and take his way across the new bridge and through the upper village without once suspecting what is hidden down under the trees and round the bend of the stream.

Kates mill stood in ruins, "a howling wilderness of shattered walls and rusting machinery, memorials of the day when, in 1890, the Dell was lighted up by its blaze." But Boag's mill was still busily turning out peasemeal and pot barley as well as more exotic spices. As Geddie passed by he savoured "the pungent flavour of pepper, curry and ginger, and the sweet odours of cinnamon, mace and cassia."

Slateford village, where he emerged from the dell, was then very much an industrial community; the two great bridges overshadowed "the rather shabby little streets inhabited by carters, quarrymen, dyers and farm labourers. The barges sail in summer time, and the skaters skate in winter, high above the chimneys of Slateford, and, but for its reek, take no note of its presence."

The Slateford of today is still overshadowed by the bridges but John Geddie would otherwise hardly recognise it. It remained much the same until after his death in 1937 but since then the little houses that lined Inglis Green Road have been cleared away, the dye works has closed, the church became disused in the 1950s and the population has dwindled. In 1871, 647 people lived here, only 70 fewer than in Juniper Green, and many more than in Colinton, Currie or Balerno.

Balerno Engine Loop

In 1896 the extension of the city boundary from Polwarth Terrace out to Craiglockhart, near the top of Craiglockhart Avenue, led to a similar extension of the local tram service. On this route horse-drawn trams continued to operate. The new service stopped just short of the Craiglockhart Hydropathic which had opened in 1880 (today part of Napier College).

The city boundary now also ran to just east of Slateford.

In July 1897 fares on the Balerno branch were reduced in response to a petition from those who travelled on it. Other lines were unaffected. The new rates were:

	3rd single	1st single	3rd return	1st return
Colinton–Edinburgh	3d.	5d.	5d.	8d.
Juniper Green–Edinburgh	4d.	6d.	7d.	11d.
Currie–Edinburgh	5d.	8d.	8d.	1s. 2d.
Balerno–Edinburgh	6d.	10d.	10d.	1s. 5d.

These fares were to remain in operation until after World War I, but they were by no means the lowest ever – despite the increases which were to come in 1919 and 1920.

For over twenty years now the Caley had been unable to turn trains round at Balerno passenger station; there had been no alternative to running them down to Ravelrig Junction and back, with the engine using the junction sidings to run round its carriages. This was a time-consuming manoeuvre, expensive in fuel and lost operating time.

Evidently the Caley were loath to take advantage of the space in the goods station to install a turntable and run passenger services in there, now that most trains terminated at Balerno instead of continuing along the Ravelrig section to Midcalder. No doubt they did not want to interfere with the valuable goods operations in the yard.

Nor was there room for a turntable at the passenger station. Eventually it was resolved on 19th October, 1897 to construct a "loop to allow of engines getting round their trains" at the station. This involved putting down a new section of track some 100 yards long. The required land was purchased for £120 plus £15 to the local farm tenants, Messrs Laing and Dow.

In June 1898 a plan was submitted, and approved by the Board of Trade. The completed loop was inspected in early 1899. Colonel Yorke reported:

> It is now desired that certain trains shall end their journeys here, and the loop line has been laid in to enable engines to run round their trains. The existing signal box has been enlarged and it now contains 16 levers in use, four spaces, and four spare levers. There is also a ground frame at the west end of the station, containing three levers bolted from the main signal box, and the interlocking is correct.
>
> The place is awkwardly arranged, and the position of the signal box is very inconvenient [in fact it was on the other side of the Lanark Road from the station, out of sight] and I can only recommend the Board of Trade to sanction the use of the new loop, on the condition that the station is not to be used to enable any two trains to pass each other, the loop being solely employed for engines to run round their trains.

Colonel Yorke was also unhappy that the staging by the junction, where the goods line branched off, lacked a railing; it was here that the signalman stood to exchange tablets with the engine drivers and Yorke felt it was unsafe. On 20th April, 1899 the Caley informed the Board that a special tablet platform with a railing had been erected.

Other improvements were made at Balerno station at this time. In 1896 a piped water supply was provided to replace the well specially dug in 1875.

And on 20th September, 1898 the first telephone on the branch was authorised to connect the passenger station with the goods station: £20 was allocated. (This was also one of the first telephones in the entire district.) Later
in 1906 Currie and Kinleith signal box were similarly linked.

The Malleny Light Railway Scheme

High above Currie at over 900 ft were Malleny rifle ranges, erected in the
1880s by the 4th/5th Royal Scots Queen's Edinburgh Rifles. Over the years
the Pentlands became dotted with such ranges; there were others at Dreg-
horn further east and Castlelaw to the south.

The Malleny ranges were about two miles walk from Currie, adding
considerably to the journey time of Volunteers coming to practise, who
would leave Balerno branch trains at Currie. In January 1899 therefore an
enterprising officer, General Chapman, suggested that the Caley might consider building a light railway from the station to the ranges.

Light railways were a new concept. An Act of 1896 had authorised
companies to build lines without having to observe all the previous safety
requirements such as chairs holding rails to sleepers, and fencing; the
purpose being to simplify and encourage construction of new branches. The
lines to Lauder and Gifford opened by the North British in 1901 were light
railways.

RHP 29794 is the reference number for the detailed plan drawn up by the
Caley for the Malleny Light Railway and still held by the Scottish Record
Office in Edinburgh. Though it was never built, the line was carefully
surveyed; and the project must have been seriously considered before it was
finally rejected.

The plan, drawn up by the south-east area Engineer Mr Paterson, actually
included two branches. For in addition to the main line to the ranges – 2¼
miles long – there was to have been a sub-branch to Hill Craig and Co's
Balerno Bank paper mill over a quarter of a mile long.

The line was to leave the Balerno branch close to Balerno goods junction,
cross the river, and climb at successive gradients of 1 in 24 (to 642 feet),
1 in 25½ (to 774 feet), 1 in 33 (to 829 feet) and 1 in 68 (to 860 feet, the
summit level) before running on a further 250 yds to nearby the ranges. The
total rise in the line was 360 ft. Three roads were to be crossed, the Lymphoy
road, Harlaw road, and the road from Harlaw to the reservoir. The paper mill
branch was to leave the main line not far above the Water of Leith and reach
the mill by a bridge over the Bavelaw burn.

Had the project been carried through it would surely have been a tourist
attraction, not just of use to the shooters for whom it was proposed. Whether
because it was feared to be too steep or too expensive, the scheme unfortunately remained on the drawing board.

The "Balerno Pugs"

It was rare enough for special engines to be designed and built to operate a
particular branch railway or indeed any railway. So when in 1899 a new
class of tank engine was constructed for the Balerno branch for the *second*

The Caledonian Railway Company's most enduring relic in Edinburgh is the Caledonian Hotel. The station came first in 1894 and the three archways originally opened into it. With the addition of the hotel (built 1899–1903), the right hand archway alone was retained as a station entrance.   *Author*

The station which it replaced. In 1870 this humble structure had in turn replaced the Caley's original Lothian Road terminus (just visible, top right). Lothian Road is seen on the left.   *Dr. N.R. Ferguson*

The web of lines running into Princes Street station. The goods station (formerly the passenger station too) can be just seen on the right. *Lens of Sutton*

Until recent years this old fragment of the original 1848 Caley station at Lothian Road was preserved. Trains could initially pass through the three (now) blocked-up arches, which stood just a few yards short of Lothian Road. The station became a goods station in 1870 when another terminus for passengers was erected by Princes Street, just a quarter of a mile north. Most of the 1848 station was destroyed by fire in 1939.
Royal Commission on Ancient Monuments, Scotland

A row of brand-new carriages built specifically in 1920 for the Balerno branch as the lettering on the first coach indicates. There were 39 built. These were electrically lit and to a modern standard of comfort, yet still only 4-wheeled, due to the CR requirement that only 4-wheelers could work the branch, due to the tight curves.

Historical Model Railway Society Collection

A Caley Glasgow to Edinburgh train, hauled by 4−6−0 locomotive No. 51, seen here in pristine condition. *L.G.R.P., courtesy David and Charles*

An 0–4–2, LMS No. 17020 (originally CR No. 717, built 1881) seen here at Slateford Yard, Edinburgh on the 12th March, 1927. Note the 4-wheeled tender, small enough to be suitable for the curves on the Balerno Branch. The engine was withdrawn in 1932.

W.E. Boyd, Scottish Record Office

CR, 0–4–4WT, No. 1167 – previously No. 488 then No. 167 – was the first of the four engines of its class, built in 1872 with the opening of the Balerno branch in mind.

Real Photographs

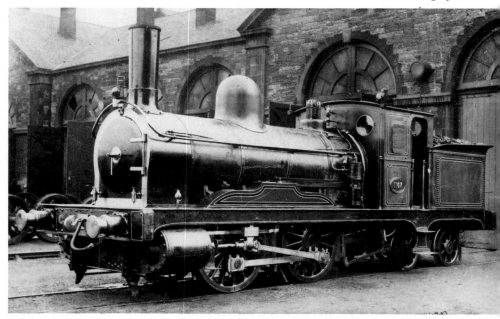

The original Balerno branch locomotive, 0−4−4T, No. 488 (soon re-numbered 167 in 1881). It was ordered as one of a pair in 1872 and built in 1873. No. 170, one of the second pair (ordered in 1873) often worked the Balerno branch.
Mitchell Library, Glasgow, North British Locomotive Co. Collection

This view of the same engine, bearing yet another number (No. 1350), which it briefly carried in 1899−1900, shows the engine crew proudly posing for their picture.
L.G.R.P., courtesy David and Charles

CR, 4-2-2, No. 123 – the engine which hauled the Caley trains to Edinburgh in the races of 1888, now preserved.   *L.G.R.P., courtesy David and Charles*

CR, 2-2-2, No. 115. A single-driver locomotive built by Benjamin Conner. The driving wheel size was 8 ft 2 in. (*see page 34*).   *Real Photographs*

CR 0−4−4, No. 193 of the 171 class, designed and built by Dugald Drummond and which worked the Balerno branch in the 1890s. There were 24 tank engines in this class (built 1884 to 1891 in four batches). No. 193 was built in 1891.

L.G.R.P., courtesy David and Charles

A 'Balerno Pug', LMS No. 15151, standing on the engine loop at Balerno station on the 14th April, 1925. In Caley days it carried the number 108.

W.E. Boyd, Scottish Record Office

CR, 0−4−2, No. 391 (rebuilt in 1871) after being built by Dübs and Co. in 1866. One of the original goods engine class to work the Balerno branch, its sister engine, No. 393, was damaged at Balerno in 1875. *Real Photographs*

A goods train leaving Colinton station for Juniper Green on the 30th October, 1953. This 0−4−4T, No. 55210, was formerly a Caley-built standard passenger tank. *W.S. Sellar*

General Arrangement drawing of the Balerno Pug.

Courtesy British Rail

time in 26 years it was testimony to the unusual demands which the line made.

J.F. McIntosh, the Caley's locomotive superintendent since 1895, designed the new engine with three requirements in mind. It had to be powerful enough to handle the severe gradients on the branch, which had proved too much for the engine involved in the 1890 incident. It had to be manoeuvrable enough to deal with the very sharp curves in the line; and it had to be capable of quick acceleration away from the closely-spaced stations on the branch.

The new class of twelve engines which became afterwards known to Caley men as the "Balerno Pugs" was designed also to operate on a branch of similar lay-out, the Cathcart Circle in Glasgow which had opened in 1894.

McIntosh's design derived in essence from Dugald Drummond's earlier '171' tank-engine design. Indeed McIntosh, unlike Drummond, was not an engineer by profession; he was a former driver who had joined the Scottish and North Eastern Railway in 1860 aged 14 (before it merged with the Caley) and worked his way up through the ranks from engine cleaner to his present position. Early in his career he had lost his right arm in an accident and had to learn to write left-handed. In his successful career as locomotive superintendent his *forte* proved to be in adapting and extending Drummond's innovative designs.

His most famous engines were the 4−4−0 "Dunalastairs", main-line passenger engines. Just as successful were the standard passenger tanks which he constructed in a long series starting in 1900.

The "Balerno Pugs", officially the '104' class, were in fact a slightly smaller version of the standard passenger tanks, many of their dimensions being the same. The following list of their respective main measurements shows the similarities and differences:

	"Balerno Pug"	*Standard Passenger Tank*
Cylinders:	17 in. x 24 in.	18 in. x 26 in.
Coupled wheels:	4 ft 6 in. dia.	5 ft 9 in. dia.
Bogie wheels:	2 ft 6 in. dia.	2 ft 6 in. dia.
Wheelbase: − leading driving:	7 ft 6 in.	7 ft 6 in.
− overall:	20 ft 6 in.	22 ft
length over buffers:	31 ft 7¼ in.	33 ft 11¼ in.
Boiler pressure:	150 lb./sq.in.	160 lb./sq.in.
Boiler diameter:	4 ft 4⅛ in.	4 ft 4⅛ in.
Height of boiler centre:	7 ft 3 in.	7 ft 3 in.
Water capacity:	1000 gal.	1270 gal.
Coal capacity:	2¼ tons	2½ tons
Heating surface: − tubes:	975 sq.ft.	975 sq.ft.
− firebox:	110.9 sq.ft.	110.9 sq.ft.
− Total:	1085.9 sq.ft.	1085.9 sq.ft.
Grate area:	17 sq.ft.	17 sq.ft.
Weight of engine:	51 t. 2½ cwt.	57 t. 7 cwt.
Adhesion weight:	32 t.	34 t. 17 cwt
Tractive force (at 85% b.p.):	16,376 lb.	16,603 lb.

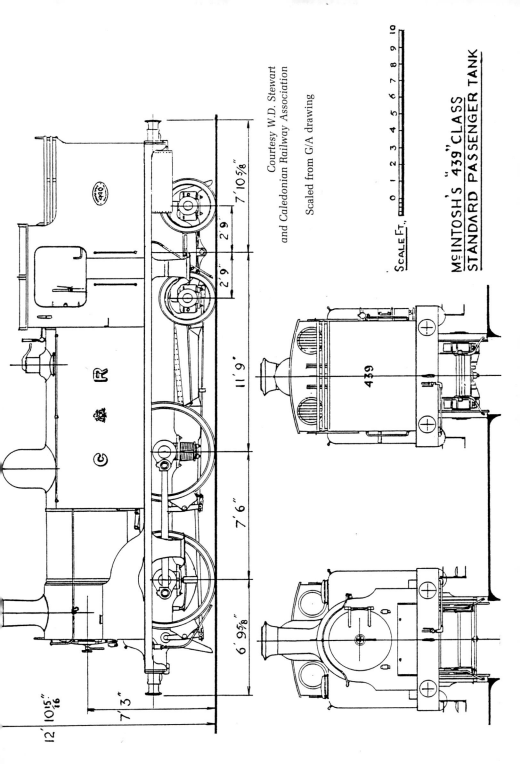

12' 10 15/16"

7' 3"

7' 10 5/8"   2' 9"   2' 9"   11' 9"   7' 6"   6' 9 5/8"

C R

439

Courtesy W.D. Stewart
and Caledonian Railway Association

Scaled from G/A drawing

SCALE FT.,   0 1 2 3 4 5 6 7 8 9 10

McINTOSH'S "439" CLASS
STANDARD PASSENGER TANK

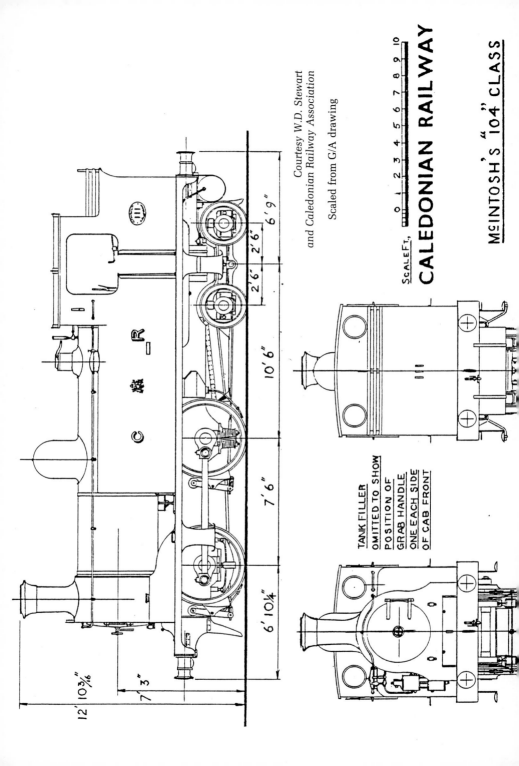

Courtesy W.D. Stewart
and Caledonian Railway Association

Scaled from G/A drawing

TANK FILLER
OMITTED TO SHOW
POSITION OF
GRAB HANDLE
ONE EACH SIDE
OF CAB FRONT

ScaleFt.

0 1 2 3 4 5 6 7 8 9 10

CALEDONIAN RAILWAY

McINTOSH'S "104" CLASS

12' 10 3/16"

7' 3"

6' 10 1/4"   7' 6"   10' 6"   2'6"   2'6"   6' 9"

C   R

The class were all built at St Rollox in 1899 and cost £1719 each. They were numbered 104–111 and 167–170, with Nos. 106–109 and 167–170 being sent to Dalry Road shed in Edinburgh to take over the working of the Balerno and Barnton services in particular. The engines were turned out in the normal blue livery of passenger engines, being all Westinghouse-braked. They were not equipped with steam carriage-heating apparatus as yet, though that was to be fitted eventually, in the early 1920s.

The "Balerno Pugs" would remain in charge of the Balerno branch passenger service until well into the 1930s (when they gave way to the larger standard tanks) and in due course earned their nickname by association with the line. Nicknames were a rarity on the Caley, so this was something of a distinction; Drummond's "Jumbos" and "Jubilee Pugs" were two other cases, while the only other engines associated with a particular line were the "Dundee Bogies", "Oban Bogies" (the latter in two different vintages), and "Gourock Bogies".

With the arrival of the 1899 tanks on the Balerno branch, the earlier tanks of the '171' class moved on to other duties from the line – Nos. 171 and 172 had been working it. The class were always synonymous with rural branches, and it was in corners of Perthshire, Angus and the south-west that they were often to be found. The first was scrapped in 1917; fifteen out of 24 lasted into LMS days in 1923, when they were re-numbered as Nos. 15100–15114; and, though only three survived after 1925, one of those carried on until 1944, working the Lybster branch (ex-Highland Railway) by that time.

The "Balerno Pugs" also had an effect on the original branch tank engines in 1899, in that Nos. 167–170 took over the numbers of the 1873–74 Neilson engines. These became, in quick succession, 167A–170A, then 1350–1353, and then (after No. 1353, formerly No. 170, was withdrawn in 1900) Nos. 1167–1169. The reasons for these changes were the Caley's alterations to their duplicate listings; until 1899, when new engines took over existing numbers the previous holders had "A" added to the end; then briefly a new series was started at 1200; before it was decided to add 1000 to old numbers.

After the withdrawal of Neilson engine No. 1353 in 1900, the other three followed in 1902 (1169), 1907 (1168) and 1913 (1167).

BALERNO BRANCH.

SPEED OF TRAINS; NUMBER OF VEHICLES AND POSITION OF BRAKES ON PASSENGER TRAINS:—

No Train or Engine must run over the Balerno Branch at a greater speed than 15 miles an hour.

No Passenger Train to or from the Balerno Branch must exceed 12 Vehicles, and Trains requiring accommodation in excess of 12 Vehicles must be run in duplicate.

A Brake Van or Brake Carriage must be marshalled at the front and rear of every Passenger Train run on this Branch. Only four-wheeled Carriages must be run on Trains on this Branch.

Horse Boxes and Carriage Trucks are not conveyed to or from Balerno Branch Stations.

JUNIPER GREEN GOODS SIDING.—KINLEITH GOODS SIDING.—KATE'S MILL SIDING.—SIDINGS AT COLINTON.—The Traffic into these Sidings may now be worked by Trains from Edinburgh as well as by Trains to Edinburgh; but when worked by Trains from Edinburgh, the load of such Trains must in no case exceed 20 wagons.

The Bridge over the Water of Leith, at the far end of the Paper Mill Sidings at Colinton, is not sufficiently strong to carry an Engine. Under no circumstances, therefore, must an Engine go upon it.

BALERNO STATION.—Working of Points Locking-Frame.—When the Loop requires to be used, No. 1 Lever must be drawn over in the Frame, when No. 2 Lever, which works the Points, can be worked as required. No. 3 Lever can then be drawn to operate the Signal from the Loop. The Frame is controlled by Rod Lock from the Signal Box.

Extract from the Caley's 1902 service timetable.

JULY 1909.

BALERNO BRANCH

SINGLE LINE—BALERNO JUNCTION TO RAVELRIG JUNCTION.—Tablet Stations—
Balerno Junction, Juniper Green, Currie, Balerno, and Ravelrig Junction.

UP.

Distance from Edinburgh.		Stations and Sidings.	1 Pas.	2 GOODS	3 Pas.	4 Pas.	5 Pass.	6 Pass.	7 GOODS	8 Pas.	9 Pas.	10 Pas.	11 Pas.	12 Pass.	13 Pas.	14 Pas.	15 Pas.	16 Pas.	17 Pas.	18 Pass.
Mls.	Chs.		a.m.	a.m.	a.m.	a.m.	a.m.	p.m.	p.m.	p.m.	p.m.	p.m.	p.m.	p.m.	p.m.	p.m.	p.m.	p.m.	p.m.	p.m.
—	16	Edinburgh (Prin. St.) dep.	6 15		7 10	9 25	10 30	12 30		1 35	2 10	2 30	3 30	4 30	5 30	6 30	7 30	8 30	9 30	11 0
1	16	Merchiston .... ,,	6 19		7 14	9 29	10 34	12 34		1 39	2 14	2 34	3 34	4 34	5 34	6 34	7 34	8 34	9 34	11 4
2	16	Gorgie ,,			6 50					1 10										
2	31	Slateford .... ,,	5 22		7 17	9 32	10 37	12 37		1 25	1 42	2 37	3 37	4 37	5 37	6 37	7 37	8 37	9 37	11 7
		Hailes Platform......... ,,	5 43	6 45	7 19	9 33	10 38	12 38		1 50	1 43	2 38	3 38	4 38	5 38	6 38	7 38	8 38	9 38	11 8
3	56	Colinton .... ,,	6 29	7 10	7 44	9 39	10 44	12 44		2 2	1 49	2 24	2 44	3 44	4 44	5 44	6 44	7 44	8 44	9 44	11 14
4	63	Juniper Green .... ,,	6 34	7 25	7 49	9 44	10 49	12 49		2 14	1 54	2 29	2 49	3 49	4 49	5 49	6 49	7 49	8 49	9 49	11 19
5	31	Kinleith Siding . . . ,,		7 35											4 54			6 54	7 54	8 54	
6	1	Currie .... {arr.		7 54																	
		Currie .... {dep.	5 40	7 45	7 53	9 50	10 55	12 55		2 25	2 0	2 35	2 55	3 55	4 55	5 55	6 55	7 55	8 55	9 55	11 25
7	15	Balerno . . . . . . ,,	6 46	8 45	8 49	9 56	11 1	1 1		2 50	2 18	2 41	3 1	4 1	5 1	6 1	7 1	8 1	9 1	10 1	11 31
8	33	Ravelrig Junction ... arr.		8 50						2 55	2 23										11 42
11	7	Midcalder .... ,,									2 52										

No 2—Crosses No. 1 Down at Balerno.
No. 3—Crosses No. 1 Down at Currie.
No. 7—Supplies Empty Wagons to Ravelrig Quarry when required. Shunts Slateford Station, taking Empties to Balerno Junction. Leaves Gorgie at 1.20 p.m. on Saturdays and runs to Ravelrig Junction, via Main Line, on that day.
No. 8—Returns No. 48, page 108.
No. 9—Returns No. 50, page 108.
No. 12—Crosses No. 10 Down at Juniper Green.
No. 13—Crosses No. 12 Down at Juniper Green.
No. 18—† Runs to Westcalder on Thursdays. Empty Carriages to be returned to Edinburgh, via Main Line, at 11.31 p.m
Trains calling at Hailes Platform will run 2 minutes later from Colinton to Balerno.

DOWN.

Distance w/from Midcalder.		Stations and Sidings.	1 Pas.	2 Pas.	3 Pas.	4 Pass.	5 GOODS	6 Pass.	7 GOODS	8 Pas.	9 Pas.	10 GOODS	11 Pas.	12 Pass.	13 Pas.	14 Pas.	15 Pas.	16 Pas.	17 Pas.	18 Pass.
Mls.	Chs.		a.m.	a.m.	a.m.	a.m.	a.m.	a.m.	a.m.	p.m.	p.m.	p.m.	p.m.	p.m.	p.m.	p.m.	p.m.	p.m.	p.m.	p.m.
3	54	Midcalder . . . . dep.		8 58				19 5			8 50		5 50								
2	72	Ravelrig Junction ... ,,				10 55		11 8			8 56		6 25								
5	6	Currie .... {arr.	7 53	8 28	5 10	8 11	2 11	8 12	13 1	8 8	8	2 4	8	5 . 2	5	10 4	15 7	8 8	8 9	3 10	8
5	6	Currie .... {dep.	7 58			10 18	11	7 11	13 1	12 18	18 3	13	4 7		5 7						
5	56	Kinleith Siding .... ,,					11 35						4 20		5 20						
6	24	Juniper Green .... ,,	8 5	8 35	9 18	10 20	11 50	11 20	12 25	20 3	20	4 50	20	5 50	5 22	6 25	7 20	8 20	9 15	10 20
7	31	Colinton .... ,,	8 10	8 40	9 28	10 25	12 15	11 25	12 30	25 5	25	5 10	25	6 10	5 27	6 30	7 25	8 25	9 20	10 25
—	—	Hailes Platform......... ,,																		
3	56	Balerno Junction ...... ,,	8 18	8 48	9 33	10 32		11 33	12 37	33 8	33	17	4 32		5 34	5 37	8 25	8 29	9 27	10 32
8	71	Slateford . . . . . . ,,	8 17	8 47	9 30	10 32		11 32	12 37	32 3	32		4 32		5 34	5 37	8 28	8 32	9 27	10 32
		Gorgie .... ,,				12 30							5 20		6 20					
9	71	Merchiston ...... {arr.	8 19	8 49	9 32	10 34		11 34	12 39	34 3	34		4 34		5 36	6 39	8 48	8 49	9 29	10 34
		Merchiston ...... {dep.	8 21	8 51	9 34	10 36		11 36	12 41	36 5	36		4 36		5 51	6 49	8 49	8 49	9 30	10 36
11	7	Edinburgh (Prin. St.) arr.	8 25	8 55	9 38	10 40		11 40	12 45	40 3	40		4 40		5 42	6 45	7 49	8 40	9 35	10 40

No. 1—Crosses No. 2 Up at Balerno and No. 3 Up at Currie.
No. 5—Crosses No. 6 Down at Currie.
No. 3—Carriages go out via Main Line at 8 80 a.m.
No. 7—Empty Carriages to leave Edinburgh for Balerno, via Main Line and Ravelrig Junction, at 11.45 a.m.
No. 10—Crosses No. 12 Up at Juniper Green.
No. 12—Crosses No. 13 Up at Juniper Green.

Hailes Platform.—This Platform has been erected for the use of the Members and Employees of the Kingsknowe Golf Club, and was opened on 16th November, 1903.
The following Trains call at Hailes Platform, viz. :—
Up.—All Up Trains between 6.15 a.m and 8.30 p.m. inclusive, on notice being given to the Station Masters at Edinburgh or Merchiston.
Down.—All Down Trains between 11.8 a.m. and 10.8 p.m. inclusive.
The 10.8 a.m. Train from Balerno will also call conditionally to set down Golfers on notice being given to any of the Station Masters on the Branch.
The Station Masters to instruct Drivers and Guards of Trains requiring to call at the Platform.
Trains calling at Hailes Platform will run 1 minute later from Slateford to Edinburgh.
Special Golfers' Return Tickets available between Edinburgh (Princes Street) and Hailes Platform or Kingsknowe Station are issued to the Secretary of the Club for the use of Members and Officials, and Ordinary Fares have also been put in operation from Edinburgh (Princes Street), Merchiston, Slateford, and from Stations on the Balerno Branch to Hailes Platform.
The temporary arrangement under which the Special Golfers' Tickets were recognised as available to Colinton, has now been discontinued.
The Guards of the Trains, in both directions, collect the Tickets, and any Excess Fares from Passengers without Tickets alighting at the Platform, and hand the same over to the Station Master at Colinton in the case of Passengers travelling from the East, and to the Station Master at Merchiston in the opposite direction, who will grant to the Guards an Excess Voucher for the amount, the Guards to hand such Vouchers to the Station Superintendent at Edinburgh (Princes Street), who will forward them to Audit Office daily.
The Station Master at Colinton to arrange for the cleaning and lighting of the Lamps at the Platform, and the Guard of the last stopping Train must extinguish them.

Only Four-Wheeled Carriages must be used on this Branch. Horse Boxes and Carriage Trucks are not conveyed to or from Stations on the Balerno Branch.

The branch timetable of July 1909 as discussed in The Colinton Tramways Inquiry proceedings.

Chapter Ten

The Balerno Branch at the Turn of the Century

Juniper Green station was authorised to be equipped with tablet instruments in May 1898, thereby splitting the long Balerno Junction–Currie section into two shorter ones. The work was held up, though, and the new arrangement did not come into operation until 1901.

The tablet instruments were installed in the station booking office; the old signal box, a little to the east of the station, was closed. Two ground frames were provided: one was in the station and worked the signals, also unlocking the second frame, which worked the points of the station sidings. (The same arrangement was used at Colinton.) The conversion cost around £300.

The work was done to enable a branch passenger train to cross or pass the goods train at Juniper Green – this involved the goods train standing at the station sidings – although there was still no way for two passenger trains to meet there.

At about this time Kinleith siding was converted to be worked by a ground frame also, and the signal box became disused. The procedure was as for Colinton paper mill siding, described earlier, the local section tablet being used to unlock the frame (a special locking device had been invented by the Caley's signal superintendent, J. Steven), before the levers controlling the points could be manually operated.

There was more work on the branch tablet system to come. About 1910 the existing instruments were changed from Tyer's No. 2 (patented 1888) to Tyer's No. 7, an improved version. Then in 1921 modifications were made at Juniper Green to allow the station to be switched out of tablet working when required and enable long-section working between Balerno Junction and Currie to resume. This was to avoid the unnecessary exchange of tablets at those times when the goods train was not on the branch. In April 1921 it was ordered that the tablet instruments be "transferred from the booking office to the signal box", but it seems that the old signal-box remained disused, for a new lever frame was installed at the station subsequently. Switching-out came into effect on 17th November, 1921. The tablet instruments used were another variation, Tyer's No. 6.

The turn of the century saw more gradual developments and alterations on the Balerno branch. New sidings were provided at Colinton (1891) and at Kinleith mill (1899); and at Kinleith in 1901 a most unusual sight appeared, in the shape of an electric shunting locomotive which Henry Bruce and Sons had bought for use at the works. It was a good investment, for it was still being used in 1965!

The use of electricity was at this time under scrutiny by the Caley; in 1896 an experimental lighting of a seven coach train had proved successful. Meantime, however, on the Balerno branch trains continued to be gas- or oil-lit; and stations were also lit by oil lamps until 1908, when gas lamps were installed at Colinton and Juniper Green, and 1913 when they were installed at Currie and Balerno.

Stations And Staff

The four stations of Colinton, Juniper Green, Currie and Balerno were the focal points of the line. Each was similar in having the typical Caley design of wooden booking office; yet each was quite different from the others.

Colinton station was detached from the village by the river and out of sight behind the trees lining the water. Similarly both Currie and Balerno stations were across the river from their villages; but while Currie at least commanded an open view of the surrounding country, Colinton station was more enclosed, tucked up against a bank and with the road bridge obscuring the view to the west.

At the eastern end of the station between the booking office and the tunnel mouth was the path known as Jacob's Ladder which led up to Spylaw Bank Road. At the very top was the station master's cottage, home from 1874 on to John Kerr and his wife.

Mr Kerr was something of an institution. This was not in itself unusual for a village station master, the job being one of responsibility and stress which often showed up in a quick temper. For John Kerr as for the other station masters along the line there were goods and passenger trains to be supervised, stores to be ordered, takings to be checked, instructions to be given, and the image of the Caley to be upheld.

W.B. Robertson recalled him: "Slight of frame, with a short beard surmounted by a somewhat highly coloured complexion, he possessed a raucous voice which a sergeant-major might have envied. His peppery temper was never far below the surface, due no doubt, to long drawn out working hours throughout a six day week."

John Kerr kept a chicken run behind the booking office. Among his talents was an expert ability with a sling with which he controlled the numbers of rats around the station and in particular perhaps his chicken run!

By contrast with Colinton, Juniper Green station lay immediately below the village main street. The steep and winding station brae led up to the street; at its top was the station master's house, formerly the north lodge of the Woodhall estate.

Woodhall House in fact stood directly across the river from the station, high above the bank. A footbridge ran over the river to the estate, but access to it by road was only from the east or west. The station was squeezed in beside three mills. On the west, and reached via the station brae and then a track with a level crossing over the railway, was Woodhall paper mill. (Before the branch was built it had been reached by a track from the other direction.) Behind the station and to the east were Wright's meal mill and Watt's snuff mill, two quaint old mills both served by the same lade which ran behind the station. Archibald Walker operated the meal mill until the turn of the century when it closed; the snuff mill remained open until 1940.

Currie station was completely different again. Wide open to the gently sloping fields of the Pentland foothills to the south and looking north over the Water of Leith to the village, with the kirk and old school buildings adjacent, its setting was truly pastoral. Directly below the line, between it and the river, was station field where farm animals were pastured before or after being transported on the branch.

At the west of the station, between the branch proper and the sidings running to the goods yard, was the solitary water tank on the line. The station was presided over by George Melrose who, together with his willing staff, enjoyed keeping it as attractive as possible. As John Tweedie, his grandson and historian of the area, recalled, it was "a station of beauty in its day, with its rambler roses, rustic arches, rockeries and floral baskets. This was due to the enthusiasm of Mr George Melrose, the station master, and the wholehearted cooperation of the porters and staff – even the goods yard was a picture with its rockeries, bushes, and weeping ash. When on duty, Mr Melrose wore a flower in his buttonhole." Mr Melrose lived in a house nearby, again dating back before the railway's day as evidenced by the cowstalls in its basement!

Little Balerno station, cut off from its goods yard by the Lanark Road and even from its signal box, nestled in a man-made hollow almost in the middle of nowhere until, early this century, nearby houses began to be built. At the turn of the century it still had only Newmills mill and farm plus a few cottages for company. Guarding the stairs leading down to the platform was the station master's and porter's house, two cottages rolled into one in an L-shaped design and nowadays a chartered surveyor's office.

Balerno was not only the end of the line (for most trains) – it was also the top of the line. Either way the rails leading past the ends of the platforms descended; east, 1 in 60 towards Currie, west, 1 in 70 to Ravelrig. Balerno too had its flower-beds framing the long platform. Early this century John Poyner took over here after being several years at Juniper Green.

For the many staff along the line, from the signalmen who had time to relax between trains and helped out at stations as required but whose jobs held great responsibility, to the porters and those like the surfacemen working on the actual line, life was less careworn than for the station masters. A few lived in railway-built accommodation by the main-line junctions: Balerno Junction cottages and Ravelrig Junction cottages. The latter were fairly remote, with only the quarrymen working in Ravelrig quarry for company.

There were other workers who did not live locally, but who were familiar faces on the branch. These were the drivers, firemen and guards who brought the trains through. Drivers would divide their time between the three local branches. In 1924 Robert Lindsay was reported as retiring after 55 years' service in the Caley (latterly the LMS) of which 28 had been spent working the Balerno, Leith and Barnton lines. At the same time Alexander Hall retired after a similar record.

Kinauld Siding

The Caley made several improvements to their Edinburgh system in the first years of the 20th century. In 1900 Dalry Road station opened next to the engine shed and appeared in all Leith and Barnton services. In 1902 a new service was begun when the Caley agreed to provide workmen's trains (for 21s. each) to Granton Gas Works, running to a station specially constructed by the Edinburgh and Leith Gas Commissioners. The service was to continue until 1942 and was in fact the only passenger service the Granton branch ever saw.

Of more importance to the Caley was the opening of their new goods line to Leith eastern docks on 1st August, 1903. Planned as far back as 1889 along with the ill-fated underground scheme, the new line was built at huge expense but gave the Caley access to a vital market.

The branch was in fact laid out to handle passenger services as well as goods, with platforms erected at Newhaven, Bonnington (Ferry Road) and Leith Walk. However the Caley contented themselves after all with handling goods traffic only. (Leith was already very well served by train services, especially after the opening of the North British line to Leith Central in 1903; this was additional to the established Caley and NB branches to Leith North and North Leith respectively.)

At the eastern end of the Caley's new line a large yard was laid out complete with an engine shed; at this end of the branch Caley trains briefly passed over North British track.

The two stations on the Barnton branch were re-christened Davidson's Mains and Barnton in 1903. By now a sort of pecking order had been established on the Caley's three local Edinburgh lines, whereby the Leith branch had most services, followed by the Barnton and then the Balerno branches; this pattern remained constant over the years.

The great Caledonian Hotel opened in December 1903 above Princes Street station. Work was also completed about this time on a large parcels office to the south of the station (by Lothian Road) while yet another new building was the laundry east of Slateford which serviced both the Glasgow and Edinburgh station hotels.

Princes Street station was by now an increasingly busy station, with its services to Carstairs and England, Glasgow and the west coast, Lanark and Ayr, Moffat, Peebles, Oban, Stirling, Dundee and the north, as well as the three local branch services.

The station was laid out to accommodate large numbers of passengers, with seven long platforms curving away from the spacious entrance area. In July 1901 a *Railway Magazine* article noted:

> The arrangements connected with the terminal buildings have been conceived and executed in a generous spirit, and embrace extensive office etc. accomodation for the station superintendent and his staff generally; very complete refreshment and dining rooms; spacious and well-furnished first and third class ladies' waiting room; a first-class gentlemen's waiting room; a general waiting room; telegraph office; excess luggage office; cloak room; and lost property office.

The station booking office was an oval room standing in the centre of the circulating area, with eight ticket windows. Another feature of note in the station lay-out was the three-faced clock on the east side and, next to it, the station master's private office with its projecting windows overlooking the concourse. On the opposite side was a cab entrance opening onto Rutland Street.

The parcels office, beside platform 7 on the Lothian Road side, had its own large staff who took in parcels from 39 receiving offices in Edinburgh, and made five deliveries daily from incoming trains.

Princes Street station was provided with electricity by its own light engine room, to the immediate west; while a "complete system of telephonic communication" connected the station master's office with the goods station, signal cabin, and other important installations. The main signal cabin had no fewer than 152 levers, with the signals being displayed on a wide gantry stretching across the rails near Morrison Street bridge.

Of the seven platforms, 1 and 2 were usually reserved for main line expresses, while those at the Lothian Road side catered for branch services.

One distinctive and enduring feature of Caley passenger services was the semaphore route-indicator which every train carried (and it was a feature which survived on former Caley lines even after the company had ceased to exist). Indicators were displayed at the head of each engine, and the local Edinburgh codes were as follows.

Balerno branch:	Glasgow line:	Dalry shed:
Barnton branch:	Carstairs line:	Empty coaches:
Leith branch:	Lines to north:	

The semaphore indicators could be seen not only on LMS trains after 1923 but in the days of British Railways after 1948.

With the 20th century came new ideas. The Caley's locomotive and stores committee decided on 16th July, 1901 to purchase two motor lorries on trial, which proved satisfactory and were bought, the first being a two-ton lorry for use in parcels traffic; it cost £550 from Milnes and Co. Ltd. It seems ironic that the Caley should thus early have encouraged road transport (and indeed they even began operating a motor-bus service between Clarkston and Eaglesham in 1904) but in those days it would have needed great foresight to predict how road transport would one day threaten much of the rail network.

In late 1904 another private works siding was opened on the Balerno branch to serve a glue and gelatine-making factory recently erected at Kinauld midway between Currie and Balerno. The new works stood on the site of the former Balerno paper mill which had fallen into ruin after closing in 1882.

The siding was constructed only after much delay. In January 1903 the works manager Colin Macandrew had sounded out the Caley about having the work done and the company had agreed to instal a short length of track (for there was little room for manoeuvre) running east from the branch, at a cost of £310 of which Macandrew was to contribute £175. It was to be worked by a ground frame located at the siding junction, with two levers, to be operated by the Currie–Balerno section tablet.

However, the Board of Trade refused to approve the plan. The problem was that at the siding junction both the branch proper and the siding sloped down to the east, towards Currie, and, although the siding then continued on a rising gradient, this worried the Board's inspector Colonel Yorke. He asked that the Caley agree to operate the siding only with the engine at the lower (east) end of its train so as to guard against wagons breaking away.

But the Caley felt this was impractical; the siding being rather short to begin with, they did not want to have an engine pulling wagons onto it as this would restrict the space available for the loading and unloading of goods. They therefore asked if the Board of Trade would allow the engine to be at the upper end of its train as long as this consisted of no more than ten wagons. The Board refused, arguing that even a breakaway of ten wagons or less would still be dangerous.

Yet again the problem of the gradients on the Balerno branch had caused a hold-up in work. The question of the proposed siding then in fact lapsed for ten months from April 1903 until February 1904. On 10th February the Caley submitted a revised plan, this time for a siding running west from the branch immediately beyond the bridge over the Water of Leith. Although less convenient for the mill in that it faced away from it rather than towards it, this siding made it practical for the engine of a train to be at the lower (east) end; and the Board of Trade duly approved.

The completed siding was inspected by Colonel von Donop in September 1904 and sanctioned. The method of working was by a ground frame controlled by the section tablet, with a limit of sixteen wagons per train imposed – due to lack of space. The Caley subesquently issued instructions to drivers as follows:

> McAndrews siding Kinauld (between Currie and Balerno). Traffic to and from this siding must only be worked by trains proceeding from Balerno. Wagons for the siding must be marshalled next the brake van, so that when they are detached on arrival at the siding there will be nothing hanging on the van – the brake of which must be put hard on before detachment.
>
> Trains which work the siding must not consist of more wagons when leaving Balerno than together with those to be dealt with at the siding will amount to sixteen wagons. The engine must always be on the lower end of the wagons.

In 1913 the siding and works at Kinauld passed into the hands of the present owners, J. Hewit and Son, who converted the building into a leather works and tannery.

Hailes Platform

The Balerno branch was a factor in the opening of a golf course on Torphin Hill above Juniper Green in April 1903. The Edinburgh Estabishment Golf Club Federation were a group of clubs attached to printing companies in the city and dating from 1895, since when they had played over the Braid Hills public course. However, finding that play had become too slow there as the game grew in popularity, the federation decided in 1902 to look for ground on which to lay a course of their own.

Landowners at Bonaly and Torphin (above Colinton and Juniper Green) and Craigenterrie (above Currie) were approached and the Torphin site was chosen when the owner, Mr Hunter of Woodhall farm and grain mill, offered the best terms. The presence of the Balerno branch close by, with the station at Juniper Green, also influenced the choice of location. The club history recalled:

> Travel to the course was mainly by train to Juniper Green station, followed by a twelve minute walk uphill to the clubhouse. This walk gave the younger and fitter members a considerable advantage, and they invariably were first off the tee. After complaints by those not so fit, it was arranged that, on the arrival of each train, names would be put in a ballot and drawn for order of play.

Torphin Hill clubhouse was in those days situated further west than at present and almost directly above the railway station; it was re-located in 1934 after Torphin quarry had begun to encroach too close for safety.

Torphin Hill Golf Club (as it became known from 1905) was not the first to be set up locally; in 1893 the Baberton club on the other side of Juniper Green had been founded to replace a nine-hole course opened at Bonaly in 1890. Then in 1907 a new course was built at Kingsknowe on land rented from the Hailes Estate and Quarry Company, with the clubhouse adjacent to the Lanark Road a short way below Hailes House.

The new course was at the time somewhat remote and for most members the quickest way to reach it was by train to Kingsknowe station a quarter of a mile to the north or Colinton station half-a-mile south-west.

However, the Balerno branch railway passed close by the course at a point just west of the disused Kates mill siding, where it came within a few yards of the Lanark Road and only 200 yards from the clubhouse. Consequently in 1908 the club management approached the Caley to ask whether a platform might be erected at the spot, offering in return to guarantee an annual income in fares of £50. The Caley at first rejected the proposal but on being approached again relented and agreed to provide a platform subject to a guaranteed annual income from it of £75 for ten years. The club accepted.

On 16th November, 1908 Hailes Platform opened, being built at a cost of £475. Ten of the fifteen up trains and seven of the fifteen down trains called at the platform on request. Passengers travelling from town were required to notify the station masters at either Princes Street or Merchiston that they wished to alight at Hailes in which case the station master then informed the driver or the guard of the train. Passengers coming from the west could give notice at any of the stations on the Balerno branch.

Though the platform was primarily intended for the use of golfers and was not listed in public timetables until the mid-1920s, local residents were also allowed to use it. Both ordinary fares and "special golfers' return tickets" were available to and from Hailes Platform. (Before the platform opened special return tickets were also available for travel to and from Colinton station, and also to and from Kingsknowe; they continued to be valid at Kingsknowe.)

One local resident remembers travelling to school from Hailes Platform during World War I while his father regularly used the branch trains to travel to work. Season tickets were issued by the station master at Kingsknowe. The platform itself, however, was the responsibility of the Colinton station master, who had to arrange for the lamps to be lit each day and also cleaned. The guard of the last train to call, the 6.30 pm down, was required to extinguish the lamps.

Sometimes the drivers of trains not scheduled to call at the platform could be induced to stop. The same gentleman recalled: "If we had been to a show in Edinburgh we asked the driver if he would stop at Hailes; some were quite agreeable while others said no, so it was a matter of walking up from Slateford or walking back from Colinton."

In 1913 a shelter was erected at the platform after the captain of the golf club had complained about its "exposed condition". Whereas the Caley owned the actual platform, Kingsknowe Golf Club owned the path leading between it and the Lanark Road; in later years a number of residents of new houses whose gardens backed onto the path were allowed to make gateways giving access to it for a token rent.

Hailes Platform in due course became Hailes Halt. Ultimately there was a halt on each of the three Caley branches in the Edinburgh area following the opening of East Pilton Halt on the Leith branch in 1934 and House o'Hill Halt on the Barnton branch in 1937.

The siding serving the West paper mill at Colinton became disused for a time early this century when the tenant, John Plummer, closed the mill down. It was offered for sale in 1906 and bought by A. & R. Scott Ltd, millers and makers of porridge oats, who already owned the neighbouring grain mill, having bought it from Messrs King in 1900.

The siding re-opened on 26th April, 1909, the Caley once again instructing that engines should on no account go onto the bridge over the river.

Later Scott's erected an imposing building directly over their siding through which wagons actually passed on their way into and out of the mill. (A. & R. Scott Ltd were not to be confused with Andrew Scott and Co. who made brown paper at nearby Mossy mill for over a century until 1972.)

When paper-making ceased at Plummer's mill just four paper mills remained along the valley. One of them, Balerno Bank mill, burnt down in 1909 but was later re-built. It was much the biggest mill in the district never to have a railway siding of its own, although one was planned under the Malleny Light Railway scheme. Hill Craig and Co. and their successors John Galloway and Co. Ltd had to make do with carting goods to and from Balerno goods station via the steep main street of the village.

The Colinton Tramways Inquiry

In the early 1900s buses and trams gradually began to approach within easy walking distance of the four villages, though not as yet offering any realistic competition to the Balerno branch railway.

On 14th April, 1908 the Craiglockhart tram service re-opened using cable traction, replacing the horse-drawn service which had been withdrawn the previous year to allow conversion work to be carried out. This had been Edinburgh's last horse-drawn tram route.

Cable trams ran every six minutes to Canonmills. Another cable tram service nearby operated to the foot of Ardmillan Terrace along Dalry Road. There were also rail-less horse buses between Slateford Road and Tollcross or the Tron.

By 1909 a motor bus service was running along the Calder Road to the north of Juniper Green, Currie and Balerno between Edinburgh and West Calder or Pumpherston. The service was operated by the Scottish Motor Traction Company, better known as the SMT, and involved five buses each way daily with ten on Saturdays and eight on Sundays.

The SMT had been formed in 1905, and their first service had been between the Mound and Corstorphine from 1906 on. They originally planned to run buses out to Juniper Green; but it was in fact 1920 before that village received a service, and it was then provided by Edinburgh Corporation.

In 1909 the Colinton Tramways Company announced that they planned to construct an electric tramway from the foot of Westgarth Avenue in Colinton to the cable tram terminus at Craiglockhart. The main stimulus for the project was Redford Barracks, which the War Department were about to build east of the village. There was also to be a tramway down Craiglockhart Avenue (then just a country lane) from Craiglockhart to Slateford with a spur to the Union Canal and another to Slateford station.

At Slateford it was hoped that the branch would connect eventually with another proposed tram service from Gorgie which had already been authorised to run to new cattle markets and slaughter-houses, soon to be built at Slateford.

The Colinton Tramways were to be worked by electric trams. Though the Edinburgh system was cable-operated, there were already electric trams running on overhead wires in Leith and Musselburgh.

The whole scheme was discussed at an inquiry in July 1909 in Edinburgh. (Since 1899 it had been possible for such projects to be passed by local Provisional Order rather than a Parliamentary Act.)

Prior to the inquiry the Caley withdrew their initial opposition; they had been worried that it was planned to carry goods on the trams, mainly for the barracks, and also that the line might later be extended beyond Colinton and threaten their Balerno branch services. But Mr Tait, the tramways engineer, reassured them, pointing out that any goods would be brought in via Slateford station – useful to the Caley – and no extension was planned.

Of those who spoke at the proceedings, several mentioned Balerno branch train services; some critically, arguing that trams were needed as well.

A spokesman for the War Department who planned to use the tramway to supply materials to the barracks while they were being built and who were to contribute to its cost stated that the trams would be of use in taking officers and men to recreation in the town; the men would wish to go to "the theatres and so on", and "officers will naturally make for the residential part of Edinburgh, to Murrayfield and to the polo ground."

Of the Balerno branch he added: "The railway accommodation we don't want to say anything serious against, but there is only one train per hour, and indeed there is not that. It would be an exaggeration to put it that there is a train an hour, and there is inconvenience felt at present in the district."

Alexander Fairgrieve, who managed Spylaw board mill by Colinton kirk, felt the same way. He believed that the Balerno branch service, which now involved fifteen trains each way daily, was "as satisfactory as the railway can possibly make it" but still left a need for more transport.

"We have only a single line, and there is heavy goods traffic. The passenger train service has to be regulated along with the goods traffic, with the result that we only get trains once every hour. There is a space from half-past one till half-past three when there are no trains at all into town." He also regretted that the earliest train to town was after 8 am. He had appealed without success for an earlier service.

He said that a considerable number of villagers at present walked down to the tram terminus at Craiglockhart to get to town – an inconvenient walk. The new tramway would assist them and also the many people who visited the district at weekends.

Mr Fairgrieve under cross-examination was asked: "Would not that discourage the progress of Colinton?" "No," he replied. He was asked: "I thought it depended very much on its seclusion and quietude?"

"Some people would like to make it that way," replied Mr Fairgrieve.

By contrast James Moncur, a resident in Westgarth Avenue, strongly objected to the proposed tramway and deplored any possible influx of visitors.

Speaking in support of the tramway its engineer, Mr Tait, criticised the Balerno branch service. He had seen the population of Colinton grow steadily for fifteen years during which time he had "laid any amount of water pipes in the neighbourhood for new houses" in his capacity as engineer to the Edinburgh and District Water Trust.

"One train per hour is no use to develop a district, and sometimes there is an interval; they miss an hour altogether." His counsel put it to him: "Life needs to be leisurely for that sort of treatment?" "Yes," agreed Mr Tait.

But the laird of Colinton House, Colonel Trotter, would have none of this. The Balerno branch, he said, gave a perfectly adequate service. Businessmen and schoolchildren could get to town in the morning quite well; as to the need of an earlier train, it had been tried before but had been taken off from lack of business. Villagers could also visit the town in the evening and return at eleven o'clock, after the theatre for instance. The railway was ideal for residents of the villas which had been built since it opened. Colonel Trotter reckoned the train return fare of 5d. good value; though, this being the third class fare, one imagines he may himself have paid the extra 3d. to travel first class.

Despite Colonel Trotter's misgivings the inquiry found in favour of the tramway to Colinton; in fact most of the opposition was focused on the proposed line to Slateford which many thought unnecessary and which was to involve a long walk for passengers changing trams to use the proposed service from Slateford to Gorgie.

Yet Messrs Trotter and Moncur need not have worried, for the Colinton Tramways Company never made their line to Colinton. All that was built was a tramway from Slateford up to the site of the barracks, along which the War Office carried materials until the works were complete in 1913. This tramway, which crossed the Union Canal by a small bridge still in existence at the top of Allan Park Road (and over which a conduit now runs), then became disused.

The Tramways Company continued to exist, in name only, until 1920 when, following the extension of the city boundary to take in Colinton and Juniper Green, it was acquired by Edinburgh Corporation. It was the Corporation which finally brought trams to Colinton in 1926; and which before that also introduced the first local motor bus service – this ran between Juniper Green, Colinton and the Craiglockhart tram terminus from 1920 to 1926.

Edinburgh's first electric trams duly began running to Slateford in 1910 after the new markets opened there; the service operated from the foot of Ardmillan Terrace at Gorgie Road, where there was an existing cable tram route.

Chapter Eleven

1910–1923: Years of Change

The Pre-War Years

The Caley minute books for the years leading up to World War I give many insights into how times were changing. In August 1912 the Caley agreed to lease part of their land at Morrison Street goods yard for the erection of a picture-house – one of the first in Edinburgh.

There were also industrial troubles at this time. Trade Unions were beginning to assert their influence, and in 1911 a national railwaymen's strike involving the two big unions, ASLEF and the Amalgamated Society of Railway Servants, achieved a major victory. In 1912 a miners' strike in the spring reduced supplies of coal, which affected train services.

That year Dalry Road engine shed in Edinburgh was enlarged and modernised. Until then the site had comprised two small sheds, each served by two sidings, with nine outside sidings and a turntable. Now, with £5190 allocated to improvements in July 1911, a large new shed was added on the north side as well as extra siding accommodation; the turntable was removed. The engine shed remained a compact affair, hemmed in as it was by the main line on the south side and the line of the Wester Dalry Branch and Granton loop on the north. Still, it managed to cope with an allocation of 61 locomotives in 1921!

New signal boxes were erected at the junctions of the Balerno branch with the main line in 1912 (Ravelrig Junction) and 1914 (Balerno Junction). At both sites this involved the signal boxes being re-located from the north side of the main line to a position between the main and branch lines; at Ravelrig Junction this was described as being "to obviate the signalman having to cross the main lines to exchange tablets with the enginemen on the branch line."

The Ravelrig Junction signal box opened on 3rd September, 1912, having been authorised on 20th February at a cost of £770; the Balerno Junction box opened on 29th October, 1914, a year after being authorised on 14th October, 1913, for £730.

These years leading up to World War I are generally thought of as the heyday of the railway system in Britain – and of the Caley, which now boasted an impressive fleet of engines including the mighty "Cardean" express locomotive and the successful 4–4–0 "Dunalastairs". The company even owned a fleet of ships, through the subsidiary Caledonian Steam Packet Company, which operated on the Clyde in connection with the trains to Gourock, Wemyss Bay and Ardrossan. Services were at their most extensive; crack residential trains ran daily between Glasgow and Edinburgh; between those cities and Moffat and Peebles; between Glasgow and Crieff. Pullman coaches were introduced in 1914.

Yet even before the war there were ominous signs for the railways' future. Bus mileage was already growing rapidly; the mileage of the SMT rose between 1906 and 1914 from 161,200 to 728,000. Railways were prevented by law from competing as they would wish with other transport for they were handicapped, when their costs increased, by not being allowed to raise

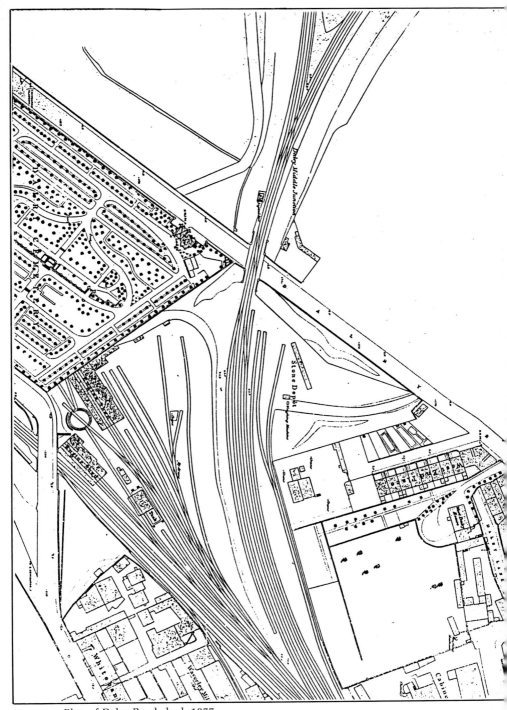

Plan of Dalry Road shed, 1877.

Reproduced from the 1877, 25″ Ordnance Survey Map

fares and rates. Indeed right up to the 1930s the railways were controlled by legislation as though they had still a monopoly of transport while road competition was, in effect, allowed to progress unchecked and develop enormously. By 1928 SMT mileage was 10,500,000.

On the Balerno branch it was the bus competition provided by the SMT that led to the starting of a Sunday service on the line for the first time in 1913.

On 21st January the traffic committee considered a proposal from the general manager Mr Matheson to "run trains between Edinburgh and West Calder via the Balerno Branch on Sundays in opposition to the road motor service." In fact the SMT service had been running for several years already.

From the figure given for estimated weekly mileage, 164, it would appear that five trains each way to and from West Calder were initially proposed (wages to be £5 13s. 0d.). However when the service began in March three of the five trains terminated at Balerno; only the first and last ran to and from West Calder. None of the trains called at Merchiston station.

Trains continued to run on the branch on Sunday at this level until the end of 1916, when the need to cut costs for the war effort led to their withdrawal along with many of the weekday services, in line with simultaneous reductions everywhere.

Traffic on the Balerno branch by 1914 had developed to the extent that there were three engines regularly working the passenger services. Trains usually comprised eight carriages; four third class, two brake thirds and two first class. Each of the three sets was increased to thirteen carriages on Saturdays.

These gas-lit four-wheeled carriages, 28 ft 6 in. long and of Drummond design, were painted an all-over purple-lake colour. (The cream bands along the upper panels which the Caley rolling stock originally carried and which had been removed in 1873 had been restored on main line coaches in the 1890s but not on local service coaches in Central Scotland.) (See page 112.)

The last of the tank-engines built for the opening of the Balerno branch in 1873 by Neilson and Co. was scrapped in 1913. Neilson and Co. by now no longer even existed, having amalgamated (as Neilson, Reid and Co.) with the two other Glasgow locomotive builders in 1903 to form the North British Locomotive Company – which had no connection with the Caley's Edinburgh rivals.

Goods traffic on the Balerno branch peaked in Caley days between 1908 and 1915, as follows:

Goods sent:	most in 1915 – 20,747 tons.
Goods received:	most in 1912 – 38,008 tons.
Minerals sent:	most in 1908 – 61,914 tons (mainly stone).
Minerals received:	most in 1913 – 71,085 tons (mainly coal).

The figure for goods received was always higher than that for goods sent, despite the amount of paper dispatched from the mills. The figure for minerals sent was almost entirely contributed by Balerno, being the stone from Ravelrig and Kaimes quarries. The two remaining quarries at Ravelrig were now in the hands of the Lothians Quarry Company.

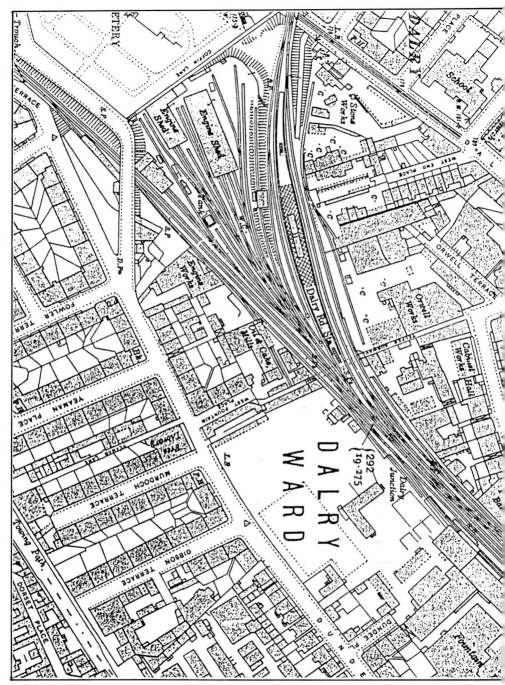

Dalry Road shed in 1914 after being enlarged.
Reproduced from the 1914, 25″ Ordnance Survey Map

World War I and its Aftermath

When World War I broke out on 4th August, 1914 a special Railway Executive Committee took control of all Britain's railways. This had been set up under the 1871 Regulation of the Forces Act, so that railways should be used in the best interests of the war effort, and to stop private profiteering.

The various companies including the Caley continued to operate, but were no longer fully masters of their own affairs.

As the war dragged on the Caley found themselves with a severe shortage of manpower; 184,475 British railway workers served in the war, 40,000 of them with the railway troops who laid over 2000 miles of track on the continent. (The track was taken from branches in Britain which were meantime closed.)

The Caley took women on to work in certain jobs. Thus on 28th November, 1916 they decided to fit up two rooms for "women learners training for the duties of signalmen, guards and telegraphists." Men nearing retirement age were also retained including the long-serving Colinton station master John Kerr who was asked to stay on for an extra year in early 1917.

At the same time services were cut and stations closed. On the Balerno branch in early 1916 there were 17 up and 16 down trains; by December there were 16 up and 14 down trains; and on 1st January, 1917 frequencies were cut to just 12 up and 11 down trains with an extra up train on Saturdays. All Sunday services were withdrawn.

Many stations in the Edinburgh area closed, but most of these were on the North British; Kingsknowe however also closed. Most of these stations, including Kingsknowe, re-opened in 1919.

In 1916 Slateford station was reconstructed at a cost of about £4,000.

There were more cuts in services at the end of the war in November 1918. On the Balerno branch there were now just nine up and eight down trains. However these reductions were reversed three months later. But it would be the late 1920s before the frequencies achieved in 1916 were restored on the branch.

The Caley, like other companies, suffered during the war from not being allowed to raise fares and rates as costs of materials and labour rose sharply. A fare increase was at last authorised long after the war ended in June 1919 and again in September 1920. This meant fares on the Balerno branch were now as follows:

	3rd sin.	1st sin.	3rd ret.	1st ret.	Weekly 3rd	1st
Colinton–Edinburgh	5d.	9d.	9d.	1s. 2d.	2s. 9d.	4s. 0d.
Juniper Green–Edinburgh	7d.	10½d.	1s. 0½d.	1s. 7½d.	3s. 3d.	4s. 10d.
Currie–Edinburgh	9d.	1s. 2d.	1s. 2d.	2s. 0½d.	4s. 0d.	5s. 6d.
Balerno–Edinburgh	10½d.	1s. 5½d.	1s. 5½d.	2s. 6d.	4s. 0d.	5s. 6d.

Price inflation during the war led to the unusual practice of the Caley using two scales of cost whenever they carried out work on the railway. There was the cost "at present prices" and the cost "at pre-war prices", "the difference being a special charge against the Government" and which was noted with a view to future compensation. Long after the war ended, in 1922 and 1923 the Government in fact paid out £10 million in compensation to the Scottish railways, of which the Caley received £1.8 million for their "abnormal expenditure in wages, hours of duty, and other conditions of service." (The Caley however were not happy about this payment and calculated that they had been badly short-changed.)

An example of the extent of inflation was the estimate for work at Juniper Green in 1921 when the tablet apparatus was converted so that the station could be switched out as required. The "pre-war" cost was £250 and the "present" cost £790.

After the war the Railway Executive Committee, by previous agreement, remained in charge until 15th August, 1921. It would have been impractical for the private companies to resume immediate control of their affairs. It was the Executive Committee who conceded the eight hour day in February 1919, which required the companies to take on and pay for thousands more staff as a result – without being able to raise fares and rates; and the Committee who conceded a minimum wage to men in the autumn of 1919 following a national strike, which again affected company coffers.

The Pickersgill Four-Wheelers

1920 was a boom year for the railways in terms of the volume of traffic handled. This was reflected in the returns for the Balerno branch. The following table shows how traffic grew between 1914 and 1920:

	Colinton	Juniper Green	Currie	Balerno	Total
1914: Passengers booked	175,944	166,653	53,130	84,312	480,039
Passenger receipts	£2623	£2606	£980	£1816	£8025
Goods receipts	£2242	£1304	£5590	£4168	£13,304
Total receipts	£4865	£3910	£6570	£5984	£21,329
1920: Passengers booked	255,672	207,466	64,699	114,080	641,917
Passenger receipts	£4854	£4033	£1683	£3426	£13,996
Goods receipts	£7494	£2860	£11,159	£18,098	£39,611
Total receipts	£12,348	£6893	£12,842	£21,524	£53,607

The size of the 1920 receipts was however due in part to inflation. The rise in costs of labour during the same period is illustrated by the following table:

	1914 wages	1920 wages
Engine-drivers:	36s. 4d.	95s. 6d.
Telegraph linemen:	31s. 6d.	81s. 2d.
Guards (passenger/goods):	28s. 6d.	74s. 3d.
Gangers:	25s. 2d.	71s. 11d.
Signalmen:	24s. 9d.	70s. 4d.
Firemen:	23s. 1d.	69s. 9d.
Goods porters:	22s. 0d.	67s. 2d.
Surfacemen:	20s. 3d.	66s. 8d.
Passenger porters:	18s. 6d.	62s. 4d.

(Different grades of drivers received slightly varying amounts.)

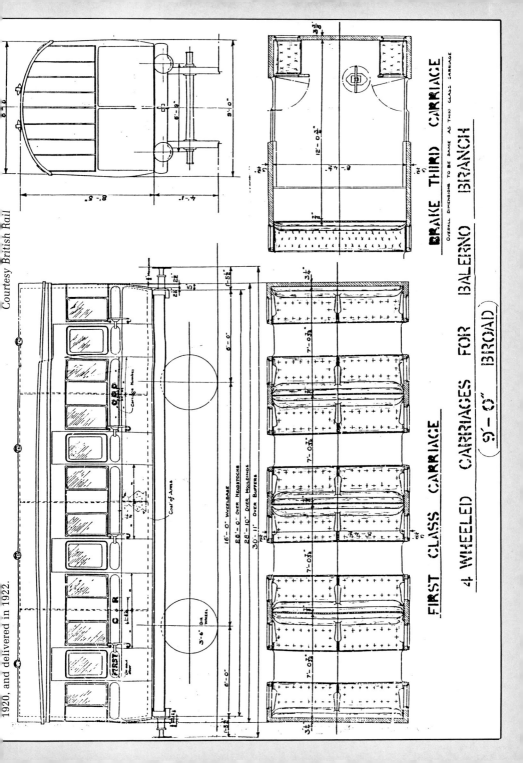

Courtesy British Rail

1920, and delivered in 1922.

FIRST CLASS CARRIAGE

BRAKE THIRD CARRIAGE

OVERALL DIMENSIONS TO BE SAME AS THIRD CLASS CARRIAGE

4 WHEELED CARRIAGES FOR BALERNO BRANCH

(9'-0" BROAD)

Thanks to the shorter working day there were now more men to pay these increased wages to, so the boom in trade was not reflected in profits.

Meantime the Government had been weighing up the advantages of a rationalised rail network, having seen its benefits in the war. In 1919 the Ministry of Transport was set up and considered how to achieve this. Nationalisation was rejected in favour of a scheme to create four large groups of companies.

Each group was to comprise in theory several financially strong companies plus a number of weaker ones. An all-Scottish group was mooted but rejected as being too weak a unit.

Eventually the largest group to emerge was the London, Midland and Scottish (the LMS) whose main constituents were the London and North Western, the Midland, the Lancashire and Yorkshire, the Caley and the Caley's bitterest rivals, the Glasgow and South Western. The Highland Railway was also included.

The Act to set up the four groups was passed in August 1921 just days after the Railway Executive Committee had handed back control of the railways to the private companies on 15th August. The date scheduled for the groups to take over was 1st January, 1923, though the Caley in fact did not join the LMS until 1st July, 1923.

On the Balerno branch meantime there were several developments which only such an unusual line could throw up. Two of them, indeed, were earthshattering – at least literally! For in 1918 a landslip occurred near Upper Spylaw between Colinton and Juniper Green at a point where the branch ran under a steep wooded bank; and in 1921 another landslip, this time in Colinton Dell a little to the east of the tunnel, also affected the line. In each case the Caley's district engineer made detailed inspections of the site and arranged for shoring-up work. However, landslips were to recur in later years.

A more conventional problem facing the trains on the Balerno branch was that of negotiating its sharp curves. Rolling stock was still limited to four-wheelers; and when, in 1920, the Caley's locomotive, carriage and wagon superintendent William Pickersgill designed new coaches for use on the line, they were still four-wheeled – despite being fitted to modern standards of comfort and electrically lit.

39 coaches were ordered from the works of R.Y. Pickering and Co. Ltd of Wishaw, and introduced to service in 1922; 22 were third class, with 10 brake thirds and 7 first class. The third class stock were two feet longer than the first class, the respective dimensions being as follows:

	Third class	First class
Length over buffers:	32 ft 11 in.	30 ft 11 in.
Length over mouldings:	30 ft 10 in.	28 ft 10 in.
Wheelbase:	16 ft 8 in.	16 ft 0 in.
Wheel diameter:	3 ft 6 in.	3 ft 6 in.
Height above rails:	8 ft 5 in.	8 ft 5 in.
Width:	9 ft 0 in.	9 ft 0 in.
Weight:	13 t 9 cwt	13 t 16 cwt

Note: the Brake Third weighed 14 t 7 cwt

At a time when twelve-wheeled coaches over 70 ft long were in use on the main line services, these new four-wheelers made a striking contrast!

Third class coaches had five compartments, brake thirds three, and first class four, the latter being a foot wider than on third class stock. A notable feature of all the carriages was the high curved roof.

The carriages were not confined to the Balerno branch, being used also on the Barnton branch and occasionally the Leith branch too. On the Balerno branch they were the only stock used until, in 1929, the LMS decided to permit standard 57 ft bogie coaches to work the line for the first time; but even then the four-wheelers remained the usual composition of trains.

The coaches were turned out in 1922 in "main line" livery, namely lake-and-white; previously the branch had been worked by coaches in the all-over crimson-lake colour associated with the Caley's lowland branches, but now the upper panels of the new four-wheelers were painted white. Each coach carried the Caley coat of arms halfway along the side.

A peculiarity of the new stock was that the wheelbase of each coach was almost exactly equal to the distance between the wheels of successive coaches, resulting in the effect of a regular beat as trains passed over joints in the rails of the branch – an unusual but rather entrancing sound!

In 1920 a new siding was put in at Balerno goods station to serve Balerno Bank paper mill, for whom a shed was also erected for the storage of wood pulp. The following year Curriehill station burnt down, but was quickly rebuilt; that year was notable for a severe slump in trade, worsened by a miners' strike.

1922 was the last year of the old railway companies, during which the Caley registered 495,283 people booking tickets on the Balerno branch (out of 32,457,705 altogether), and handled 143,000 tons of freight on the line (out of 21,700,000 tons in total). The Caley operated at the finish a network extending to 1114 route miles, roughly comparable in size to that of the rival North British Railway Company, which became part of another group, the London and North Eastern Railway (the LNER). The Caley also handed over the small matter of 1070 engines, 3040 carriages and 51,536 wagons!

The Coming of the Motor Bus

Until 1920 the Balerno branch train service continued to monopolise the market in passenger travel to and from the villages of Colinton, Juniper Green, Currie and Balerno. Within two years, however, buses were running through each community and for the first time the railway faced competition at all points.

Buses first reached Colinton and Juniper Green in 1920, when a service was introduced by Edinburgh Corporation Motors (the two villages were absorbed into Edinburgh that year) connecting with the cable tram terminus at Craiglockhart. The service initially operated only to and from Colinton but was soon extended out to Juniper Green; it was known as No. 8 and was handled by a single-deck bus which performed two round trips in the morning rush-hour and then ran every twenty minutes during the afternoons and evenings.

The Corporation Motors Department had been set up only the previous year, in 1919, to complement the Tramways Department which had replaced the old Edinburgh District Tramway Company at the expiry of their lease, also in 1919. (It was Edinburgh Corporation Tramways who acquired the virtually defunct Colinton Tramways Company in 1920, and eventually brought trams to Colinton in March 1926.)

On 15th July, 1922 Currie and Balerno received a bus service for the first time. This was operated by the SMT who had agreed a traffic-sharing scheme in 1920 with Edinburgh Corporation whereby all bus services out-with the city would be run by the SMT, who undertook in return not to compete in fare-prices with the Corporation.

From then on local services developed rapidly; and it was to be the success of the bus operators in meeting the needs of the travelling public which eventually resulted in the end of passenger services on the Balerno branch.

While the transport scene changed, so too did the industrial scene. During these early years of the present century many of the old waterside mills had closed – some after surviving for hundreds of years.

Already by 1900 Hailes mill (or Hole mill as it was equally well known) and Upper Spylaw snuff mill had closed. That year the ancient grain mill at East Mills just below Kinleith paper mill (latterly known as Mutter's mill after its owner William Mutter) burnt down; and about the same time Wright's meal mill beside Juniper Green station also closed.

In 1913 the grain mill at Malleny Mills above Balerno burnt down; it was commonly referred to as the "spinning mill" from earlier days. Several years later fire also claimed Spylaw board mill beside Colinton church, in 1917, and Newmills grain mill in 1920. The frequency with which such fires occurred was due to the inherent dustiness of mills and the flammable nature of their products.

The snuff mill at East Mills – which had shared the same lade as Mutter's grain mill and was one of the most picturesque of all – shut in 1920 for economic reasons, for there was no longer much demand for snuff. During the 1920s another two mills were to go in their turn, with Boag's mill at Redhall burning down in 1924 and Leith-head mill closing the same year.

Many mills, however, continued to operate. As well as the four surviving paper mills (Mossy, Woodhall, Kinleith and Balerno Bank) there were two grain mills (West mill making porridge oats, and Inglis' mill at Juniper Green) and the last of the snuff mills at Juniper Green, which had the mill-lade all to itself by now, following the closure of the adjacent Wright's mill. Other mills still open comprised Redhall mill in Colinton Dell, which produced woodflour for linoleum and other products, the tannery at Kinauld, and Harmeny saw mill on the Bavelaw Burn below Balerno Bank paper mill.

Chapter Twelve
Into the LMS

Passengers who used the trains of the Balerno branch during 1923 could see little sign of the railway being under new management, for even after the LMS took full responsibility for the former Caley network on 1st July – after curiously co-existing with the old company for six months – the familiar blue engines continued to appear for some time at the head of carriages still decked out in traditional Caley crimson-lake. Nor was there any change of appearance for the branch stations; and of course the staff remained as before.

The "Balerno Pugs" continued to work the branch passenger service, with the goods service in the charge of several engines of a class built between 1878 and 1881, before the days of Dugald Drummond. These were tender engines, with an 0−4−2 wheel arrangement like that of the original goods engines on the branch. The tenders for both classes were small four-wheeled affairs rather than the normal six-wheelers. Thirty engines of the later class were built: ten in 1878 (Nos. 670−679) and twenty in 1881 (700−719); and most survived into the days of the LMS. Somewhat larger than the 1860s class, they were originally intended exclusively for goods traffic, but in the days of McIntosh had been fitted with Westinghouse brakes and put onto passenger duties as required – before, latterly, returning to goods-only work.

Several of the class were familiar around Edinburgh in the first three decades of this century, such as CR No. 252 (re-numbered thus in 1887 from No. 704), which was withdrawn in 1922; it had become No. 1252 in 1921. Three engines which outlasted her into LMS days were LMS Nos. 17005, 17013 and 17020, all of them used during the 1920s as local goods engines. No. 17013 (ex-CR 711) and 17020 (ex-CR 717) regularly worked the Balerno branch, being withdrawn in November 1931 and December 1932 respectively, by which time the Balerno branch had been in the charge of 0−4−2 engines for freight traffic for nearly 60 years.

It was typical of the LMS in the early years after 1923 that such old ways of doing things should continue; for the new grouping faced an immense task in trying to standardise their fleet of over 10,000 engines inherited from five major companies and some minor ones, and at first the only course was to maintain existing practices and then make gradual changes as time went on.

One ticklish problem was the selection of a standard livery for LMS engines and rolling stock; among the five major constituents of the company there was a strong sense of pride in the old liveries, and any apparent sign of favouritism towards one might offend another! Indeed, the LMS comprised two pairs of strong rivals, not to say enemies, in the LNWR and Midland on one hand, and the Caley and GSWR on the other. And when, in October 1923, the LMS finally chose the red of the Midland Railway as their standard livery, the LNWR supporters were duly piqued. Goods engines were to be painted unlined black. Coaches would also be red, lined in yellow.

Conversion of engines from elegant Caley blue to striking LMS red proceeded slowly, since there were after all hundreds of engines involved. For several years the two liveries occurred frequently side by side. This applied to the "Balerno Pugs", the first of which was turned out in its new colours in early 1924. LMS No. 15151 was the former CR No. 108; it displayed its new number in large numerals along the tank, and the crest of the LMS on the bunker (this crest incorporated the arms of London, the rose of England and the thistle of Scotland). Others of the class would continue in Caley livery for some time yet, though (*see photographic section*). The twelve engines were re-numbered as LMS Nos. 15147–15158, of which eight engines were, as before, based at Dalry Road shed, namely LMS Nos. 15149–15152 and 15155–15158 (formerly CR 106–109 and 167–170).

In the last years of the Caley the "Pugs" had been equipped for the first time with carriage-heating apparatus, and also given new fireboxes. None had as yet received new boilers; but the LMS in due course would set up a "boiler pool" of replacement boilers in 1929, from which most of the class were subsequently supplied. New vacuum brakes were also fitted to five of the "Balerno Pugs" during the 1920s, replacing Westinghouse brakes; these engines were Nos. 15147 (104), 15149 (106), 15150 (107), 15155 (167) and 15158 (170).

If some of these tank engines had to wait their turn to be re-painted, there were more extreme cases of engines still sporting Caley livery in the 1930s! CR No. 1081 was an example.

Ironically, though, having for the most part completed the re-painting programme during the mid-1920s, the LMS then ordered further changes, whereby in 1928 the "Balerno Pugs" along with the standard tanks and other classes were to be turned out in black livery – and this was done, though once again only over a period of time. Some of the tanks remained red into the 1930s.

The demise of the Caley affected the role of the St Rollox works, which under the LMS became largely a repair shop, construction of new engines being concentrated at Derby.

On the Balerno branch in the first year of the LMS two developments affected passenger services. First, fares were reduced in January, in line with a fall in the general cost of living. Special new cheap day return rates were also introduced, valid at first only after mid-day and on Wednesdays and Saturdays (all day) but later extended to every day after 10 am. These gave considerable savings over normal fares.

Then, in June, Sunday services were restored to the branch for the first time since December 1916. Five trains each way ran throughout the summer months, the service being withdrawn in September; thereafter a seasonal Sunday service operated on the line until 1937 apart from a three-year gap between 1930 and 1932. The only year in which trains continued to run on Sundays after September was 1925 (see below).

The decision to restore Sunday working was taken by the LMS Scottish Committee in April 1923 and applied throughout the "Caledonian Section", with the levels of services set at '1914' frequencies; this was evidently a move to return to pre-war normality! Meanwhile the Caley Board were still very much in existence alongside the LMS in early 1923; it was they who took decisions regarding permanent works. Thus in April the Caley autho-rised the installation of electric lighting at Merchiston station; and in June discussed the mundane matter of the water supply (or lack of it) to the gatekeeper's cottage at Curriehill level crossing. The issue was resolved by obtaining permission from the local laird, Sir Henry Gibson-Craig, to take water from a spring on his adjacent estate in return for supplying him with a drinking-trough for his cattle!

The Caley Board at long last wound the company up on 24th July, 1923 after first awarding themselves £14,000 in compensation. Three of their number went on to join the LMS Board.

More developments in road transport took place in 1923, posing an increasing threat to the viability of the Balerno branch train service. In February Edinburgh Corporation Motors began running buses between Juniper Green and Waverley Bridge via Slateford at a frequency of 21 buses on weekdays and 17 on Sundays. The fare all the way, 6d., permitted a return journey to town for 1s., a little more expensive than the cheap day return available on the trains.

This new bus service was known as No. 8, as a result of which the previous service with that number, the bus linking Juniper Green with Craiglockhart tram terminus, was re-numbered 6. In April the tram service itself was converted to overhead wire operation, and in July Edinburgh's last cable trams were withdrawn.

On the established SMT service between Balerno and Edinburgh, frequencies by the end of 1923 had already easily outstripped those of the Balerno branch train service. 34 buses ran each way on weekdays and 29 on Sundays. Ironically, a bus operating on this route was responsible for knocking down and killing two passengers emerging from Balerno railway station early in 1924.

The rapid expansion of bus services shows that road transport had quickly proved its worth to the public. For one thing, it offered greater flexibility than a railway; buses could pass right through Colinton and Balerno, for instance in a way the branch trains could not. And in those days roads were clear of traffic, allowing buses to travel them unhindered. (It was not until 1928 that the first traffic lights were erected in Edinburgh!)

Yet it must be said that railway companies were also unfairly handicapped in their efforts to compete. For example, they were legally bound to accept any and all goods offered to them (road hauliers were not) so that unprofitable running was sometimes incurred. Outdated laws in effect still treated the railways as a monopoly – whereas in reality they were increasingly in competition with road transport.

The General Strike

In 1925 three different sets of carriages were allocated to operate over the Balerno branch, these consisting of seven carriages at most times – two first class, three third class and two brake thirds – but on Saturdays made up to a total of eleven each, with two third class and two brake third coaches added. The three train-sets were Nos. 156, 157 and 158; set 157 worked the Barnton service most afternoons (except Saturday).

In March 1925 the LMS decided that, as an experiment, the seasonal Sunday service which was about to be resumed on various branches including the Balerno branch would be continued beyond September to assess public demand for a winter service. However, in November a review of the situation noted that the response to Sunday trains on two lines – the Balerno and Barnton branches – had been unsatisfactory; the service was abruptly terminated on both lines, to be resumed the following spring.

The 1926 Sunday service operated for just one day, on 2nd May, before an unforeseen development threw all schedules into disarray for much of the rest of the year. This was the General Strike and miners' strike; on Tuesday 4th May the TUC brought workers all over the country out in support of the miners, and for eleven days until 14th May virtually the entire railway system was out of action. After that date the coal strike still dragged on for months.

On the Balerno branch during those eleven days no trains ran, and thereafter throughout the summer and autumn only a skeleton service could be maintained. The intended Sunday service of five trains each way was scrapped, while on weekdays just eight trains ran each way instead of the sixteen scheduled. Among those dropped were the last three in the evening.

Though this was by no means the first time that the Balerno branch service had been disrupted, either by miners' strikes or railwaymen's strikes, the consequences of the 1926 dispute were notable in that railways were now vulnerable to competition from road transport. (Bus and lorry services were not threatened by a coal shortage in the way that train services were.)

Competition was the keener for the recent opening of the tram service to Colinton. On 21st March, 1926 the No. 9 tram-route was extended there from Craiglockhart (its other terminus was at Granton). The No. 10 tram meantime continued to terminate at Craiglockhart, but from 1928 it too ran to Colinton, part-day only. The new tram service incidentally put an end to the No. 6 bus-link between Juniper Green, Colinton and Craiglockhart tram terminus.

The seriousness of the 1926 strike for the railway companies was summed up in a report by Donald Matheson, the LMS deputy general manager for Scotland (and formerly general manager of the Caley) given on 8th June, 1926. He noted that the 50 per cent level of services being operated could not be increased as only nine weeks' supply of coal was available; and outlined the problems posed by a loss of traffic to road competition:

> Immediately following the end of the strike such long distance passenger trains as were run were heavily loaded and continue to be heavily loaded, but short distance local trains were not so well patronised as a result of withdrawal of cheap fares and the intensity of road motor competition.
>
> Restoration in some measure of cheap railway fares, however, has resulted in more passengers travelling by rail. Unfortunately goods traffic as well as passenger traffic was also in some measure driven to the roads, and effort in the direction of ensuring the return of this traffic to the railway is essential.

Matheson also referred to the bitter intensity of the general strike, during which there had been problems with sabotage. At Grangemouth docks, formerly owned by the Caley of course, and in the town of Grangemouth, "for a few days a Soviet government practically existed."

Faster timings, lower fares

Among the trains which did continue to run on the Balerno branch during 1926 were two which represented a curious innovation in services. They travelled in a round trip, from Princes Street station to Balerno along the branch and then westwards to Ravelrig Junction where they stopped at the old Ravelrig Platform to pick up any passengers, before returning to Princes Street via the main line.

The engines of these trains ran round their carriages on the branch close to Ravelrig Junction, before propelling them gently along to the platform on the down (main line) side. Any passengers boarding here would be local cottagers though after 1927 there were also a few golfers from the newly-opened Dalmahoy Golf Course a little to the north.

One train ran daily; another on Saturday afternoons only. The daily service left Princes Street at 5.53 pm on the outward trip, then continued on beyond Balerno at 6.26 pm to arrive back at Princes Street via Ravelrig Junction at 7.07 pm – in other words, the return leg took 41 minutes. The Saturday train, which was to last well into the 1930s, was allowed 46 minutes!

The morale of the LMS men in the Edinburgh area received a boost in 1927 (after the tribulations of 1926) when the first of the 4–6–0 'Royal Scot' class engines began running to the city from Glasgow. The class had been designed by Henry Fowler, chief mechanical engineer on the LMS, and the first fifty were built by the North British Locomotive Company in Glasgow that year. They were to prove excellent engines, helping to establish the LMS in the minds of employees and passengers alike as a company in its own right – not just the Caley under an assumed name. Within several more years, the first LMS-built engines were to appear on the Balerno branch.

Also in 1927 two more local bus services started up. One ran between Balerno, Colinton and Chambers Street, Edinburgh, being operated by White's Motor Hiring Company; the other was a Corporation service (No. 14) which had previously operated between Leith and Slateford and now extended to Juniper Green.

It was in the face of such competition from road services that in 1928 the LMS improved the timings of trains on the Balerno branch – virtually the first change since the line had opened in 1874. The differences were as follows:

Train times (minutes) to/from	Colinton	Juniper Green	Currie	Balerno
1927: (Up/Down):	16/15	21/20	26/26	32/32
1928: (Up/Down):	13	17	21	26/25

The new times were effective from 1928 until the branch closed 15 years later.

Changes were also made to the table of fares in that year, as follows:

	3rd sin.	1st sin.	3rd ret.	1st ret.	3rd (wkly)	1st (wkly)
Colinton–Edinburgh	2d.	4d.	4d.	8d.	2s.	3s.
Juniper Green– Edinburgh	3d.	5d.	6d.	10d.	2s. 6d.	3s. 9d.
Currie–Edinburgh	4d.	7d.	8d.	1s. 1d.	2s. 9d.	4s.
Balerno–Edinburgh	5d.	9d.	11d.	1s. 3d.	3s.	4s. 6d.

These new fares, which lasted until 1937, were in fact the lowest ever charged, a sign of how competitive was the market by this time; they were considerably lower than the 1874 fares.

Again in 1928, an important Act, the Railway Road Powers Act, at last gave railway companies powers to become directly involved in running bus services. The next year the LMS together with the LNER reached a significant agreement with the SMT bus company whereby the two railway concerns each took a quarter share in the re-constituted SMT, which duly became an "associated omnibus company" of the LMS.

The thinking behind this deal, from the LMS point of view, was that it was more practical for them to buy into established bus firms rather than try to compete with them starting from scratch and with no expertise. In effect, they were hedging their bets – this way the LMS, like the LNER, hoped to gain from both bus and rail developments.

Yet the decision did not in fact achieve much for railway services. The opportunity to interlink road and rail services so that buses and trains dovetailed with each other (and with interchangeable tickets) was seldom exploited; and it was the SMT themselves who really benefited from the deal. The company used the injection of capital to finance a huge expansion whereby other firms were acquired and what had been a local company became a national one. SMT mileage rose from 10,500,000 in 1928 to 39,521,635 in 1930!

Incredibly, in October 1931 the LMS lent the SMT a further £400,000 to pay for more expansion. In the same year the LMS also took a half share in the road haulage firm Wordie and Co. – who had been the Caley's old carting agents.

1930 was a year marked by an ominous spate of railway closures in Scotland. Already in 1925 two local branches had closed – the former North British lines to Granton and Macmerry – but now a definite trend was developing. In 1930 the LMS even agreed on a formula with their new bus partners whereby, whenever a railway line closed on the grounds that local bus services gave sufficient cover, compensation should be paid in the form of the increased bus receipts the following year less expenses.

The problem of landslips which had affected the Balerno branch in 1918 and again in 1921 recurred during LMS days. East of Colinton tunnel the line cut across a fairly steep bank, and already (in 1921) a slippage of material had caused problems. In 1927 a flood in the Water of Leith had eroded the bank, leading to an agreement being made – rather belatedly – in January 1930 for a new protective wall to be erected below the railway jointly with Edinburgh Corporation who owned part of the land. The wall cost £700.

However, in December 1934 another landslip occurred, and another wall beside the railway was authorised to support the exposed rock face. In July 1935 it was reported that the rock was in worse condition than first thought and that as "stones and debris continue to slip down the face of the rock, it will be necessary in order to protect passing trains to erect a small parapet wall." The new wall cost £1318 altogether.

In 1931 the local bus network was completed by a new Corporation service between Juniper Green and Tron/Eastfield via Colinton (No. 15). Buses ran every thirty minutes with a top fare of 6d. At this time also the usual maximum fare on Corporation routes was cut from 4d. to 3d., children being allowed to travel for 1d.

So there were now three Corporation services to Juniper Green (two of them via Slateford, Nos. 8 and 14) and also two SMT services to Balerno; for in 1930 the SMT had acquired White's service via Colinton. There were also the trams to and from Colinton. Road services now eclipsed the train services on the Balerno branch completely in terms of frequency.

The end of the "Pugs"

The Balerno branch timetable of 1931 showed 17 trains running each way daily with an additional service up and down on Saturdays as well as a Saturdays-only down train from Balerno via Ravelrig to Princes Street. This train took 43 minutes to reach Edinburgh compared to 25 minutes by the more conventional branch trains!

All except five of the up trains and all except one of the down trains called at Hailes Halt. A market train for farmers still ran to Midcalder via the branch once a week on Wednesday evenings.

The timetable showed some especially fast timings for certain services but only by the device of one or two stops being omitted – a rare tactic down the years. Thus the 8.22 am from Balerno took only 21 minutes to reach Princes Street but did not call at Slateford or Merchiston; it did call at Hailes Halt though. This was clearly of benefit to commuters travelling to work. The 8.33 am from Princes Street to Balerno did the trip in 24 minutes but did not call at Slateford or Hailes Halt or Juniper Green.

In 1931 the LMS vigorously advertised their local Edinburgh passenger services in the following terms (featured in *Murray's Edinburgh Timetable*):

> Suburban travel. Special attention is drawn to the comfort and punctuality of our suburban train services. The trains are the best of modern plant, are all steam heated, and the cheap day fares as well as zone and season tickets are cheaper than any other mode of travel.

The last phrase was a clear reference to the now-abundant local bus and tram services. In their claim to punctuality the LMS were maintaining the traditional boast of the Caley – "The True Line, True to Time". (Zone tickets were weekly tickets.)

Tablet working on the Balerno branch was amended twice during the 1930s. On 17th April, 1934 the LMS Scottish traffic sub-committee noted:

> Balerno Branch. Dispensing with Balerno Goods Junction signal box and provision of three ground frames. Tablet instruments to be transferred to booking office. Also

removal of the disused Kinleith Siding signal box and certain signals on the branch. Cost £251. Net estimated annual savings £317.

The three new ground frames worked the points at the goods junction and at either end of the rounding-loop at Balerno passenger station. They were to be operated by a porter-signalman. The new system came into effect on 10th October, 1934.

The second change in tablet working was to be the closure on 20th March, 1939 of Juniper Green tablet station and the re-introduction of permanent long-section working between Balerno Junction and Currie.

In October 1934 the first of the eight "Balerno Pugs" based in Edinburgh was withdrawn from service and scrapped. No. 15152 (formerly CR 109) was to be followed within just three years by the other seven engines, leaving only one survivor of the class, No. 15153, running after 1937 – and it was in turn withdrawn from duties at Kilbirnie shed (Ayrshire) in 1938. The three others in the class had been withdrawn earlier, between 1929 and 1931, having worked in the Glasgow area, in particular on the Cathcart Circle.

The Edinburgh engines, until their demise, continued to handle the Balerno and Barnton passenger services, and sometimes the Leith service (though usually that was in the charge of 0–6–0 engines), as well as various freight duties, including the Balerno branch goods service on occasion latterly (see below). Most of their goods work involved shunting between Morrison Street yard and various private sidings, though.

The twelve "Balerno Pugs" were withdrawn from service as follows:

March 1929:	No. 15147/CR 104	
July 1930:	No. 15154/CR 111	(Scrapped December 1930)
August 1931:	No. 15148/CR 105	(Scrapped December 1931)
October 1934:	No. 15152/CR 109	
December 1934:	No. 15157/CR 169	
August 1935:	No. 15150/CR 107	
October 1935:	No. 15155/CR 167	
October 1935:	No. 15158/CR 170	
May 1936:	No. 15149/CR 106	
March 1937:	No. 15156/CR 168	
June 1937:	No. 15151/CR 108	
March 1938:	No. 15153/CR 110	

When withdrawn, most of the engines had clocked up close to a million miles in travel; four of them in fact recorded over that total, with No. 15149 achieving 1,202,906 miles.

Yet the class was withdrawn well before most of the other former Caley classes of comparable vintage. For example, the standard passenger tanks remained in use, for the most part, into the 1950s – only two did not last into the British Railways era in 1948, out of 92 – and 55 were still at work in 1960. Similarly, all 138 of McIntosh's standard goods tank-engines survived after 1948, the first not being withdrawn until 1952. Most impressive of all, only six out of 244 0–6–0 'Jumbos', dating from the 1880s and 1890s, did not carry on working after 1948.

However, in pointing out the relatively early demise of the "Balerno Pug" engines set against these classes, like is not really being compared with like.

These small tanks ("the neatest little tanks imaginable", to quote Alan Dunbar, a former fitter at Balornock shed, where he attended to No. 104) were not built to handle traffic in ordinary circumstances, but rather to work on two specific lines where manoeuvrability and compactness were assets. They were thus given a job, namely handling the narrow confines of those two demanding lines (the Balerno branch and the Cathcart circle) and for nearly forty years they continued to give good service. Ultimately the LMS decided that the larger engines of the '439' standard passenger tank class, as well as other 0−4−4 tanks of a McIntosh class built in 1897 and 1900 for low-level working around Glasgow (and formerly fitted with condensers to reduce steam underground), could be allowed onto the territory previously handled by the "Balerno Pugs"; and at that point the latter, with their limited power, had begun to outlive their usefulness.

The decision to open up the Balerno branch to larger engines (and coaches) followed strengthening work being done to the railway in the late 1920s and early 1930s. Thereafter the standard tanks became gradually more frequent visitors to the line. After the last of the Edinburgh-based "Pugs" was withdrawn in June 1937 the standard tanks provided the main motive power until the end of passenger services in 1943; Nos. 15165, 15166, 15169, 15177, 15189, 15204, 15205, 15210 and 15233 were among those involved.

The '439' class, whose dimensions were given earlier along with the "Balerno Pugs", first appeared in 1900 when 17 were built; between 1906 and 1914 McIntosh built a further 51; his successor Pickersgill ordered ten more, in 1915 and 1922 (plus another four to a very similar design in 1915, Nos. 431–434) − making 82 in all. Then in 1925 the LMS constructed a new batch of ten engines, Nos. 15260−15269, on very similar lines, which due to their slight modifications became known as the Naysmith-Wilson tanks. The grand total for the class was therefore 92, a tribute to their efficiency.

When they first appeared in Edinburgh in the early 1930s some were still carrying their initial LMS livery of red, but soon all were converted to unlined black (the "Balerno Pugs" underwent the same change).

The standard tanks were to continue working the Balerno branch in its goods-only years in some cases, along with other engines. LMS 15189 did duty (also as BR 55189) before being preserved in 1963 and restored to her old Caledonian livery; she is today CR 419 on the Bo'ness Railway.

The 0−4−4T engines of the low-level class mentioned above, which came to the Balerno branch in the 1930s, included Nos. 15125, 15139 and 15140. The class totalled 22 in all − Nos. 15125−15146. Ten of them dated from 1897, 12 from 1900.

The Balerno branch goods engines also changed in the 1930s. Following the withdrawal of the last of the old 0−4−2 tender engines in 1932, the goods service was given into the charge of 0−6−0 tank-engines supplemented on occasion by the "Balerno Pugs" themselves, while they survived − though they were not really suited to the work. One of the 0−6−0 tanks employed was No. 11273 (see photo, 1933) which was possibly the first LMS-built engine to work the line. It had been designed for work shunting at docks, on tight, curving tracks, so with its short wheelbase was well-suited to the sinuous Balerno branch. In later years the engine was re-numbered, first as LMS 7103 and then LMS 7163, and then as BR 47163, as which it continued to appear on the Balerno Branch into the 1960s.

One of a class of ten, it was built in 1928 to a design of Henry Fowler, chief mechanical engineer on the LMS.

Peak services

In the mid-1930s passenger train services on the Balerno branch reached what turned out to be their peak frequency. For several years, until World War II, 21 up trains and 20 down trains ran daily. Sunday services were provided in summer only, at the level of nine trains each way, up to September 1937. These Sunday trains did not call at Merchiston, Hailes Halt or Juniper Green.

One train a week continued to run on to Midcalder from Balerno, terminating in fact at Addiewell on the Shotts line, this being a late Wednesday evening service for home-bound farmers after the weekly Edinburgh market.

By then the Balerno branch trains normally consisted of six carriages, increased to eight carriages during morning and evening rush-hours. Rolling stock was provided either in the shape of the Pickersgill four-wheelers or the much longer 57 ft bogie coaches dating from 1921 (also Pickersgill), which had been permitted on the Balerno branch since 1929. An observer in 1935 noted, however, that the bogie stock was largely confined to excursion trains, with the four-wheelers making up most of the trains.

The LMS appendix to working timetables in 1937 noted that the maximum length of train allowed on the branch was 13 four-wheeled carriages or 8 bogie carriages; for purpose of calculation, a 57 ft bogie coach was officially counted as 1½ four-wheelers.

In 1937 fares on the branch were slightly raised – this was the last change.

The summer of 1939 was the last period of "normal" transport activity before the war brought about restrictions in all services due to fuel rationing. The following comparison of local bus, tram and train services shows how keen was the competition to the Balerno branch:

	Balerno	Currie	Juniper Green	Colinton	Frequencies
SMT bus					
via Slateford	x	x	x	. . .	Every 10 mins.
via Colinton	x	x	x	x	Irregular
Corporation bus					
service No. 8	. . .	. . .	x	. . .	Every 30 mins.
service No. 14	. . .	. . .	x	. . .	Every 15 mins.
service No. 15	. . .	. . .	x	x	Every 30 mins.
Tram					
service No. 9	. . .	. . .	. . .	x	Every 10 mins.
service No. 10	. . .	. . .	. . .	x	Every 10 mins.
Train	x	x	x	x	Irregular: 20 per day.

On Sundays the buses and trams had the market to themselves since trains were no longer running on the Balerno branch on that day.

As to fares, each means of transport offered similar value. For instance, from Juniper Green travel by train to Edinburgh cost 3½d. (a cheaper deal was available by purchasing a weekly ticket for 2s. 8d.) while the Corpora-

1936 TIMETABLE

	am	am	am	am	am	am	pm	pm SX	pm	pm SO	pm SX	pm SO	pm SX	pm SO	pm SO	pm SX	pm	pm	pm	pm	pm	pm	pm	pm
Princes Street	6.30	7.12	7.25	8.01	8.31	9.22	12.05	12.32	1.04	1.20	2.03	2.10	2.45	3.22	4.35	4.44	5.13	5.41	6.15	6.48	7.30	8.30	9.33	10.46
Merchiston	6.34	7.16	7.29	8.05	8.35	9.26	12.09	12.36	1.08	1.24	2.07	2.14	2.49	3.26	4.39	4.48	5.17	5.45	6.19	6.52	7.34	8.34	9.37	10.50
Slateford	6.37	7.19	7.33	8.08	8.38	9.29	12.12	12.39	1.11	1.27	2.10	2.17	2.52	3.29	4.42	4.51	5.20	5.48	6.22	6.55	7.37	8.37	9.40	10.53
Hailes Halt	–	–	–	–	–	9.33	12.16	12.43	1.15	1.31	2.14	–	2.56	3.33	4.46	4.55	5.24	5.52	6.26	6.59	7.41	8.41	9.44	–
Colinton	6.42	7.24	7.38	8.13	8.44	9.35	12.18	12.45	1.17	1.33	2.16	2.21	2.58	3.35	4.48	4.57	5.26	5.54	6.28	7.01	7.43	8.43	9.46	10.58
Juniper Green	6.46	7.28	7.42	8.17	–	9.39	12.22	12.49	1.21	1.37	2.20	2.23	3.02	3.39	4.52	5.01	5.30	5.58	6.32	7.05	7.47	8.47	9.50	11.02
Currie	6.50	7.32	7.46	8.21	8.50	9.43	12.26	12.53	1.25	1.41	2.24	2.27	3.06	3.43	4.56	5.05	5.34	6.02	6.36	7.09	7.51	8.51	9.54	11.06
Balerno	6.55	7.37	7.54	8.28	8.57	9.48	12.31	12.58	1.30	1.48	2.29	2.31	–	3.48	5.03	5.10	5.40	6.09	6.43	7.15	7.59	8.56	9.59	11.11

S = Saturdays Only

	am	am	am	am	am	am	am SO	pm SX	pm SO	pm SX	pm SO	pm SX	pm SO	pm SX	pm	pm	pm	pm	pm	pm	pm	pm
Balerno	7.00	7.45	8.18	8.46	9.10	10.13	11.48	12.48	1.38	1.46	2.28	2.34	3.06	4.10	4.33	5.31	6.00	6.34	7.06	7.48	8.15	9.15
Currie	7.04	7.50	8.22	8.51	9.14	10.17	11.52	12.55	1.43	1.50	2.32	2.38	3.10	4.14	4.37	5.35	6.04	6.41	7.10	7.52	8.19	9.19
Juniper Green	7.08	7.54	8.26	8.55	9.18	10.21	11.56	12.59	1.47	1.54	2.36	2.42	3.14	4.18	4.41	5.39	6.08	6.45	7.14	7.56	8.23	9.23
Colinton	7.12	7.58	8.30	8.59	9.22	10.25	12.00	1.03	1.51	1.58	2.40	2.46	3.18	4.22	4.45	5.43	6.12	6.49	7.18	8.00	8.27	9.27
Hailes Halt	7.14	8.00	8.32	9.01	9.24	10.27	12.02	1.05	1.53	2.00	2.42	2.48	3.20	4.24	4.47	5.45	6.14	6.51	–	8.02	8.29	9.29
Slateford	7.18	8.04	–	9.05	–	10.31	12.06	1.09	1.55	2.05	2.46	2.52	3.24	4.28	4.51	5.49	6.19	6.55	7.23	8.06	8.33	9.33
Merchiston	7.21	8.07	8.38	9.08	9.31	10.34	12.09	1.12	1.58	2.08	2.49	2.55	3.27	4.31	4.55	5.52	6.22	6.58	7.26	8.09	8.36	9.36
Princes Street	7.25	8.11	8.42	9.12	9.35	10.38	12.13	1.16	2.02	2.12	2.53	2.59	3.31	4.35	4.59	5.56	6.26	7.02	7.30	8.13	8.40	9.40

Sunday trains:

	am	am	pm	pm	pm	pm	pm	pm
Princes Street	10.15	11.25	2.45	4.35	6.00	7.30	8.55	9.10
Merchiston	10.19	11.29	2.49	4.39	6.04	7.34	8.59	9.14
Slateford	10.22	11.32	2.52	4.42	6.07	7.37	9.02	9.17
Hailes Halt	–	–	–	–	–	–	–	–
Colinton	10.27	11.37	2.57	4.47	6.12	7.42	9.07	9.22
Juniper Green	–	–	–	–	–	–	–	–
Currie	10.35	11.45	3.05	4.55	6.20	7.50	9.15	9.30
Balerno	10.40	11.50	3.10	5.00	6.25	7.55	9.20	9.40

	am	am	pm	pm	pm	pm	pm	pm	pm
Balerno	10.55	11.55	2.07	3.32	5.15	6.47	8.17	9.30	10.00
Currie	10.59	11.59	2.11	3.36	5.19	6.51	8.21	9.34	10.04
Juniper Green	–	–	–	–	–	–	–	–	–
Colinton	11.07	12.07	2.19	3.44	5.27	6.59	8.29	9.42	10.12
Hailes Halt	–	–	–	–	–	–	–	–	–
Slateford	11.12	12.12	2.24	3.49	5.32	7.04	8.34	9.47	10.17
Merchiston	11.15	12.15	2.27	3.52	5.35	7.07	8.37	9.50	10.20
Princes Street	11.19	12.19	2.31	3.56	5.39	7.11	8.41	9.54	10.24

Note: The 10.46 pm up train ran on to Midcalder and stations to Addiewell on Wednesdays only (the only train now running over the Balerno–Ravelrig section).

tion bus fare was 3d. single (maximum) and the SMT fare 3½d.

The outbreak of World War II brought about a return to government control of transport activities, affecting both road and rail services. As in the First War, a Railway Executive Committee took overall charge of the network while the four groups continued to operate within the committee's guidelines.

One of the most pressing needs was the conservation of fuel, which was soon rationed. On 11th September, 1939 an emergency wartime timetable was introduced on the railways.

The Balerno Branch token, as used after 1943 when the line was worked as a single tablet section.   *Courtesy A.J.C. Clark*

Chapter Thirteen

Closure to passengers

On the Balerno branch the new timetable had the effect of reducing services by a third. Only 13 up trains and 12 down trains (13 on Saturdays) remained, whereas during the summer 21 up trains (23 on Saturdays) and 20 down trains (21 on Saturdays) had been running.

One of the casualties of the cuts was the once-a-week train which for many years had run via the Balerno branch to West Calder or, as in 1939, to Addiewell. On days other than Wednesday this train left Edinburgh at 10.46 pm to terminate at Balerno at 11.11 pm, but on Thursdays it carried on along the Ravelrig section and terminated at Addiewell, the next station beyond West Calder. It was run for the benefit of farmers returning from the weekly Edinburgh market. The withdrawal of this train meant the end of passenger services along the Ravelrig section.

The new timetable was to be maintained almost unchanged until the closure of the Balerno branch to passenger traffic in late 1943.

The war had other effects on the railway. Stations were subject to the universal black-out, while station nameboards were removed.

In November 1939 Lothian Road goods station was substantially damaged by fire, the cost being put at £49,000. All but a fragment of the original Caledonian Railway station of 1848 was destroyed.

Though local bus operators were affected by the needs of the war effort – for instance vehicles as well as fuel were in short supply for Edinburgh Corporation Transport after the War Office requisitioned 24 out of their fleet of 215 buses – the district between Colinton and Balerno continued to be fairly well served by its bus and tram routes (and the Corporation did manage to re-purchase its own buses by 1943).

It was in consequence of the adequate cover provided by the buses that in the autumn of 1943 the LMS reviewed the requirement for train services along the Balerno branch and decided to suspend them indefinitely. The news was given out to the public in a short announcement halfway down a column printed in *The Scotsman* newspaper of 15th October, 1943.

> Withdrawal of Balerno passenger train service. The passenger train service on the Balerno branch line will be withdrawn after the passing of the last train on Saturday October 30. Thereafter Hailes Platform, Colinton, Juniper Green, Currie and Balerno stations will be closed for passengers, but parcels and goods train traffic will continue to be dealt with. Beginning on Monday November 1 an augmented passenger train service will be given between Edinburgh (Princes Street) and Kingsknowe.

(The increased service to and from Kingsknowe station would compensate for the branch services withdrawn from Merchiston and Slateford stations.)

Barely two weeks' notice was thus given of the imminent end of passenger services on the Balerno branch. But in that time considerable sentiment and affection for the line was revealed! Several writers reminisced in local newspapers, one recalling pre-war years when

> ... the daily emptying of the 'Balerno Express', as it was affectionately termed, was sufficient to swell the stream of foot traffic in Princes Street into a sudden spate.

The last timetable, October 1943 (Weekdays only)

	am	am	am	pm	pm SX	pm	pm SO	pm	pm	pm	pm	pm SX	pm SO	pm SO	pm
Princes Street	6.30	7.28	8.01	12.05	12.32	1.04	1.58	3.28	4.55	5.12	5.43	6.19	6.30	7.30	8.19
Merchiston	6.34	7.32	8.05	12.09	12.36	1.08	2.02	3.32	4.59	5.16	5.47	6.23	6.34	7.34	8.23
Slateford	6.37	7.35	8.08	12.12	12.39	1.11	2.05	3.35	5.02	5.19	5.50	6.26	6.37	7.37	8.27
Hailes Halt	–	–	–	12.16	12.43	1.15	2.09	3.39	5.06	5.23	5.54	6.30	6.41	7.41	8.31
Colinton	6.42	7.40	8.13	12.18	12.45	1.17	2.11	3.41	5.08	5.25	5.56	6.32	6.43	7.43	8.33
Juniper Green	6.46	7.44	8.17	12.22	12.49	1.21	2.15	3.45	5.12	5.29	5.59	6.36	6.47	7.47	8.37
Currie	6.50	7.48	8.22	12.26	12.53	1.25	2.19	3.49	5.16	5.34	6.04	6.41	6.53	7.51	8.40
Balerno	6.55	7.53	8.28	12.31	–	1.30	2.24	3.54	5.21	5.40	6.10	6.47	6.58	7.56	8.44

	am	am	am	pm	pm SX	pm	pm SO	pm	pm	pm	pm SX	pm SO	pm SX	pm SO	pm
Balerno	7.00	8.18	8.40	12.50	–	1.47	2.34	4.35	5.30	6.00	6.37	6.48	7.09	7.19	8.19
Currie	7.04	8.23	8.44	12.55	1.29	1.51	2.38	4.39	5.34	6.04	6.46	6.52	7.13	7.23	8.23
Juniper Green	7.08	8.27	8.48	12.59	1.32	1.55	2.42	4.43	5.38	6.08	6.50	6.56	7.17	7.27	8.27
Colinton	7.12	8.31	8.52	1.03	1.36	1.59	2.46	4.47	5.42	6.12	6.54	7.00	7.21	7.31	8.31
Hailes Halt	7.14	8.33	8.54	1.05	1.38	2.01	2.48	4.49	5.44	6.14	6.56	7.02	–	–	8.33
Slateford	7.18	8.37	8.58	1.09	1.44	2.06	2.52	4.53	5.48	6.18	7.00	7.06	7.26	7.36	8.37
Merchiston	7.21	8.40	9.01	1.12	1.47	2.09	2.55	4.56	5.52	6.21	7.03	7.09	7.29	7.39	8.40
Princes Street	7.25	8.44	9.05	1.16	1.51	2.13	2.59	5.00	5.56	6.25	7.07	7.13	7.33	7.43	8.44

Now the road has won a long-drawn-out contest, never really in doubt. The road has advantages and pleasures too, but the scenic beauty of this little branch line had a charm of which the road catches only occasional glimpses.

One contributor was even moved to pay tribute in verse to the familiar sight of a Balerno train at work on the line:

No more you'll come puffing by river and wood,
By fields with their gold, waving grain;
This day spells the end; it's like losing a friend,
So, goodbye to you, dear little train.

Such was the attachment which many felt for the branch that the running of the last trains on the evening of Saturday 30th October, 1943 encouraged a substantial turn-out of passengers and onlookers, despite the darkness of the night, which was heightened by the black-out. The final up train pulled out from Princes Street station at 7.30 pm and reached Balerno at 7.56 pm, ready for the last down journey at 8.19 pm.

An *Evening Dispatch* reporter who had boarded the train at Colinton station described the scene:

On arriving at Balerno station the passengers collected in little groups, and old times and personalities were recalled. Several passengers expressed their regret to the guard and the engine-driver that the line was closing.

The final guard signal was given and the train pulled slowly out to the accompaniment of much cheering and the firing of fog-signals, while the engine gave a long-drawn-out whistle as a 'mourning-note' on leaving the station for the last time.

At Currie, Juniper Green and Colinton, fog-signals were set off and the cheering and the long engine whistle repeated.

The last port of call of this last train – on the branch itself – was Hailes Halt in Colinton Dell. Though the four branch stations were to remain open for goods traffic, the halt now fell into disuse.

BRITISH RAILWAYS — SCOTTISH REGION.

TRANSPORT ACT, 1962

WITHDRAWAL OF RAILWAY PASSENGER SERVICES

The British Railways Board HEREBY GIVE NOTICE, in accordance with Section 56(7) of the Transport Act, 1962, that on and from 2nd MARCH 1964 they propose to discontinue all railway passenger train services.

BETWEEN

EDINBURGH (PRINCES STREET)

AND

GLASGOW (CENTRAL)
via HOLYTOWN

and to withdraw all passenger services from the following stations:—

*MERCHISTON	*BREICH	CLELAND
*SLATEFORD	*FAULDHOUSE	*CARFIN HALT
MIDCALDER	NORTH	*HOLYTOWN
WEST CALDER	SHOTTS	*EGLINTON
*ADDIEWELL	HARTWOOD	STREET

* These stations deal with passenger traffic only and would be closed completely.

It appears to the Board that the following alternative services will be available:—

BY RAIL

Through EDINBURGH-GLASGOW PASSENGERS are catered for by the Edinburgh-Glasgow via Polmont fast diesel service.

BELLSHILL, UDDINGSTON, NEWTON, CAMBUSLANG and RUTHERGLEN PASSENGERS are catered for by the Lanarkshire diesel service

NEWTON and UDDINGSTON PASSENGERS are also catered for by the Glasgow-Motherwell electric service.

BY ROAD

SCOTTISH OMNIBUSES LTD.

Table
No 25 —EDINBURGH-GLASGOW, via Midcalder, Blackburn, Whitburn, Shotts, Motherwell, Hamilton and Uddingston.
No 25 —EDINBURGH-GLASGOW, via Midcalder, Blackburn, Whitburn, Chapelhall, Holytown and Bellshill.
No. 25A—EDINBURGH-MIDCALDER (Tor Arms), via Kirknewton.
No. 88 —BATHGATE-SHOTTS, via Fauldhouse.
No. 97 —BATHGATE-FORTH, via Fauldhouse and Breich
No. 99 —BATHGATE-EAST CALDER via Addiewell, West Calder and Midcalder.
No. 100 —EDINBURGH-LOGANLEA, via Midcalder and West Calder.
No. 104 —WEST CALDER-SHOTTS, via Addiewell and Fauldhouse.

CENTRAL S.M.T. CO. LTD.

Service
No. 59 (Table 2)—STRATHAVEN - SHOTTS - WEST CALDER, via Addiewell
No. 44 (Table 9)—WISHAW - GLASGOW, via Cleland, Carfin and Holytown.
No. 56 (Table 24)—SHOTTS - GLASGOW, via Newmains, Wishaw, Motherwell, Hamilton and Uddingston.

EDINBURGH CORPORATION TRANSPORT operate an intensive bus service on several routes between the City Centre, Merchiston and Slateford.

GLASGOW CORPORATION TRANSPORT operate intensive bus services which pass adjacent to Eglinton Street Station.

An assurance has been given that, if required, and subject to the authority of the Traffic Commissioners, the road passenger services can be augmented between Edinburgh and Addiewell, Breich, Fauldhouse and Shotts.

Any user of the rail service at any station from which it is proposed to withdraw ALL passenger services and any body representing such users, desirous of objecting to the proposal, may lodge an objection within six weeks of 6th DECEMBER 1963, i.e., not later than 18th JANUARY 1964, addressing any objection to the Secretary of the Transport Users' Consultative Committee for Scotland at 38 George Street, Edinburgh 2

NOTE:—If any objections are lodged within the period specified above, the closure cannot be proceeded with until the Transport Users' Consultative Committee has reported to the Minister of Transport and the Minister has given his consent (Section 56)

Intimation of proposed closure of the Cleland and Midcalder line. It was reprieved in 1965 (see page 176).

Chapter Fourteen

Goods-only years

The Balerno branch was not the only local line to close during the war. The branch to Dalkeith had already been closed by the LNER in 1942. Just before the war ended, the LMS also withdrew passenger services on their line from Carstairs to Dolphinton on the other side of the Pentlands from the Balerno branch. The LNER line to Dolphinton from Leadburn had closed in 1933; until then it had been possible to emerge from the hills at any point after a day's excursion and catch a train home.

Relatively speaking the Balerno branch was, however, one of the earlier casualties of the Scottish railway network. There was to be a flood of closures in the 1950s and 1960s under British Railways.

On 9th November, 1943 Currie signal box was officially closed. With the ending of passenger services there was now no prospect of more than one train, the morning or afternoon goods, being on the line at any time; in effect the branch was now one block section and no intermediate signal box was needed. The various station sidings and works sidings along the branch were still worked by ground frames (with the section tablets) which was unusual, hand points being more common.

A fatal accident

With the war at last over in 1945 the incoming Labour government turned their attention to a programme of nationalisation, including that of the railways. In 1947 the British Transport Commission was set up to assume ownership of the network and also of canals (and later some road services too), and this came into effect on 1st January, 1948.

The only fatal accident ever to occur on the Balerno branch happened, ironically, not in the days when the line was busy with the activity of dozens of trains daily but in the goods-only era under British Railways.

It involved a train only indirectly; but the actual layout of the Balerno branch was a crucial factor. On 23rd February, 1950, shortly after 10 am, a train comprising several wagons took up position a little way along the branch from Balerno Junction in order to enable a barge to be lowered from the train onto the Union Canal. The barge – an unwieldy flat-bottomed affair – was to be lifted out of its wagon by a crane located in an adjacent wagon. (The boat was to be used in canal maintenance.)

At a critical point in the manoeuvre the crane operator was pulling the barge towards him to bring it within the crane's operating radius when it suddenly came free and, because it had been rubbing against the side of the wagon, exerted sideways pull on the crane which then slewed round at right angles to the track and toppled into the canal.

The crane operator was unfortunately drowned. Vehicles next to the crane-wagon were derailed and ended up hanging over the bridge.

The investigating officer blamed the accident partly on the sharpness of the curve in the line and its superelevation; the other side of the bridge (the west rather than the east side) would have been the better choice for the operation, this being the outer side of the curve in the track, but unfortunately telegraph wires had prevented this. His conclusion was that a completely different location should therefore have been chosen.

Some of the old station buildings were no longer needed, and British Railways began letting them out for commercial and private use. A varied assortment of tenants occupied these premises from then on: in 1958, for example, Currie Youth Club was renting the booking office and waiting rooms at the station there, while Juniper Green booking office and waiting rooms were being used by Woodhall paper mill.

Curriehill station closed to passengers on 31st March, 1951 after 103 years of use. Happily it turns out to have been a temporary closure, for on 5th October, 1987 a new halt opened there.

The Barnton branch also closed to passengers on 7th May, 1951. Goods trains continued to work as far as Davidson's Mains yard for the time being, but beyond there the track was lifted. The section to Davidson's Mains eventually closed in May 1960.

Yet another closure in 1951 was that of the Penicuik branch; the development of this line curiously paralleled the Balerno branch, for both had been authorised in 1865, abandoned and re-authorised in 1870 (each time on the same day, though they belonged to different companies). The Penicuik line lost its passenger service within eight years of the Balerno branch and both were to close to goods traffic in 1967, after serving the two great paper-milling areas of south-eastern Scotland!

Throughout the 1950s the last remaining Caley branch in Edinburgh continued to carry passengers; the Leith line had a monopoly of passenger rail travel to and from the port following the closure in 1952 of the former NB branch to Leith Central. (The former NB line to North Leith had closed in 1947.)

But it was not just trains that were disappearing from the local scene. Between 1950 and 1956 all Edinburgh's trams were withdrawn to be re-placed in nearly all cases by buses operating over the same routes. As a result of new bus services being created the No. 8, No. 14 and No. 15 bus services to Juniper Green were re-numbered 46, 44 and 45 respectively.

On 23rd October, 1955 the tram service to Colinton was withdrawn and the No. 9 and 10 trams were replaced by similarly numbered buses.

Contraction

In 1956 a new siding was provided for the benefit of Woodhall paper mill at Juniper Green station, following the enlargement of the mill by its new owners, Inveresk Paper Company (who also owned Kinleith paper mill).

In 1958 two reports were prepared which analysed the cost-effectiveness of the Balerno branch and its goods service. It was understandable that British Railways management should commission such reports because lines like the Balerno branch – handling just one train for relatively short periods of the day – could run up high costs in maintenance and labour (both on the trains and at stations along the way).

The first report recommended the closure of Juniper Green station, which duly closed on 11th August, 1958. The second, submitted in October 1958, made further closure proposals under the heading "Balerno branch: proposed withdrawal of facilities from certain stations." (As well as being prompted by practical local considerations, this report was also in line with Sir Brian Robertson's modernisation plan of 1955 which envisaged the closure of small goods stations.) The report gave full details of earnings from the goods service in 1957, showing that most traffic had been handled at two of the three remaining sidings, Kinleith paper mill siding and West Mills (porridge oats) siding. The following table gives the complete breakdown for 1957.

	Receipts	Tonnage sent	Tonnage received
Kinleith siding:	£23,289	2477	6299
West Mills siding:	£8448	3825	1045
Balerno station:	£6710	43	2612
Colinton station:	£1844	94	753
Currie station:	£1746	173	891
Juniper Green station:	£894	–	1241
Kinauld siding:	£99	15	36
TOTAL:	£43,030	6627	12,877

There were eight men still employed on the branch, to whom can be added the signalmen at Balerno Junction and Ravelrig Junction. Three staff were based at Colinton – a station master, a clerk and a porter; while four worked at Currie – a station master, a junior clerk, a porter and a checker, the latter in fact employed at Kinleith mill siding. At Balerno there was one porter.

The wage-bill for these eight men in 1957 had come to £3600, with the two station masters receiving £602 each (about £12 a week) and the three porters £406 each (about £8 a week).

The investigating clerk noted that the Currie station master had a large list of responsibilities. As well as looking after Currie station he had charge of Balerno station, Kinleith siding, Kinauld siding, Ravelrig Junction sidings and signal box, Curriehill sidings and signal box (on the main line), Curriehill and Whitelaw level crossings, and even Kaimes quarry siding several miles to the west.

The most striking aspect of the 1957 traffic figures was the value of Kinleith paper mill's trade. From the mill siding 1,252 wagons had been dispatched in 1957 of which all but five contained paper, while in the same period 903 wagons were received at the siding of which 388 contained woodpulp, 371 woodchips, 89 lime, 35 chemicals and 12 sulphuric acid; the raw materials for paper-making.

At West Mills siding A. & R. Scott Ltd. had dispatched 670 wagons of porridge oats of which, however, 130 had been taken only as far as Colinton station before being uplifted by lorry; Scott's had also received 90 wagons containing either coal or building materials.

The same siding was also used occasionally by other customers; the army received 80 wagons of equipment for use at nearby Redford barracks while Alexander Inglis and Son of Woodhall grain mill took delivery there of 32 wagons of damaged wheat and Andrew Scott and Co., paper-makers at Mossy mill, collected just one wagon containing old wrappers.

At Balerno station John Galloway and Co. Ltd had received 162 wagons of lime and 137 wagons of esparto grass; however it was noted with regret that this traffic had now, in 1958, been lost to road transport.

At the other three stations most traffic had been in goods or minerals received; hardly anything had been dispatched. The third siding still in use at Kinauld tannery had seen very little traffic; just eight wagons had been dispatched (all but one containing salted pigskins) while 23 had been received of which 16 contained pigskins and the rest salt or sulphide.

The conclusion reached by the investigating clerk was that the number of staff on the branch should be cut to four and that Colinton and Balerno stations should be downgraded to unstaffed public sidings. A porter would still in fact be based at Colinton but would help out at Currie and Balerno whenever required; the checker at Kinleith mill would be kept on; Currie station alone would have a station master, as well as a clerk. The Kinleith checker would also help out when required at Balerno station.

The investigating clerk anticipated these alterations yielding annual savings in wages of £1700, with the only expense involved being the purchase of a motor-cycle for the use of the Currie station master, who was currently having to cycle 1700 miles a year by push-bike, and was about to have extra mileage imposed on him through taking charge of Colinton station!

Motive power

While the Balerno branch remained open as a goods-only line several different classes of engine appeared on it. One regular visitor was BR No. 47163, formerly LMS 11273, an 0–6–0 tank-engine built to a Fowler design of 1928. One of ten in its class (Nos. 47160–47169), the engine had been originally designed for working in confined dockside locations, with a short wheelbase and small dimensions; others were to be found at places like Birkenhead, Liverpool and Greenock. The class were fitted with outside cylinders.

No. 47162 of the same class also worked for many years in the Edinburgh area, usually around Granton.

No. 47163 worked the Balerno branch goods service into the 1960s. It and the other engines were all withdrawn in the space of five years up to 1964.

Also in charge of the branch goods trains were several of the former standard passenger tanks, the '439' class, of which the majority managed to survive into the 1960s. For these engines, a change of ownership in 1948 had required little alteration in livery: already unlined black, they remained so, with their numbers altered by the addition of 40,000. Thus, LMS No. 15210 became BR 55210, working the branch during the 1950s.

In about 1960 the first diesel shunters appeared on the Balerno branch. At that time the efficiency of diesels was being belatedly recognised – they only began working the Edinburgh–Glasgow service in 1957 and the Edinburgh–Aberdeen service in 1960 – and their introduction to the branch was greeted with interest. Diesel shunter (0–6–0) No. D3891, photographed working the branch goods in December 1960, was a very recent addition to the fleet, having made its debut in July that year.

Diesels were to remain in charge of the branch throughout the few remaining years of its existence, though steam engines made several more appearances.

In 1960, against the general trend, Edinburgh's rail network was actually enlarged when a new section of track was laid between the ex-Caley main line at Slateford and the suburban railway to the south-east, near Craiglockhart. This allowed goods traffic between the coal mines east of Edinburgh and points west of the city to by-pass it on the south (via the suburban line and the new spur) rather than running as before along the foreshore through Granton (via the ex-North British line, then the ex-Caley branch) where the dock commissioners had levied expensive dues.

Balerno Junction signal box closed on 18th December, 1960 as a result of re-signalling work. Ravelrig Junction remained open meantime; the junction sidings there sometimes had an unusual role to play, for the royal train was usually stabled there when the Queen and her family visited Edinburgh.

A passenger train returned to the Balerno branch for the first time in nearly eighteen years when on 30th September, 1961 an enthusiasts' excursion train left Leith North to travel the branch from east to west before continuing to Symington, later returning to Edinburgh by the main line. "The Pentland and Tinto Express" was hauled by engine No. 55124, which was the last survivor of a class of ten locomotives known as the '19' class built by the Caley in 1894; it had recently been withdrawn from regular service on the Ballachulish branch north of Oban and, after doing several tours of duty on excursion trains, was sadly scrapped.

The daily visit to the branch of the diesel-hauled goods train was otherwise the only event to interrupt the almost sleepy atmosphere of the line in these latter years. In February 1962 a feature in the *Evening Dispatch* described the train which performed the branch goods service as a "ghost train". "Anyone seeing it for the first time might well imagine it to be a relic of the past. It looks too peaceful and too forlorn to be part of the rattling, roaring network of gleaming steel that is the modern railway world."

A reporter, Willie Raitt, had travelled on the train one morning from Slateford ensconced in the van with guard Willie Ross. The train that day, hauled by diesel shunter D3742, carried two wagons of chemicals for Kinleith paper mill and several wagons of coal to be deposited at Balerno station. At Currie, station master James Allan, who had just returned from Ravelrig Junction signal box after making his daily visit there by motorcycle, requested the driver to continue on to the junction to drop off a barrel of oil for the signalman. Times had changed from the days when such an improvisation in the schedules would have been unthinkable, what with so many trains coming and going.

The reporter noted that a 20 mph speed limit still applied to the Balerno branch. Both the driver and the fireman of his train, he found, were first and foremost firemen on steam engines who had qualified as diesel drivers after taking a month's course at Leith Central station – by then converted to a depot and training school.

1967 – The End of the Line

After the closure to passengers of the Balerno branch in 1943 and the Barnton branch in 1951, the line to Leith North was the last in the former Caley network around Edinburgh to lose its passenger services, on 28th

April, 1962. Only the former main line remained open, and just fifteen days later, on 13th May, 1962, main line services began to contract when the last Sunday trains to and from Princes Street station ran. From 20th May the services involved were re-routed to Waverley, which for the time being required the use of the suburban line round the south of the city.

On 20th June, 1962 a second excursion train visited the Balerno branch as part of a Scottish tour organised by two societies of enthusiasts. The train, comprising three carriages, was hauled by engine No. 55260, one of the standard passenger tanks familiar on the Balerno branch from the 1930s on; this particular engine, however, had been built not by the Caley but by the LMS in 1925, and was one of a group of ten known as the Naysmith-Wilson engines, all built that year. They differed in only very minor details from the Caley design, being numbered LMS 15260–15269 and then BR 55260–55269.

In 1963 the Ravelrig section of the Balerno branch, between Balerno and Ravelrig Junction, was the first part of the line to close to all traffic. The track was lifted in the course of the year.

In September 1963 British Rail proposed, in the wake of the Beeching report recommending a large programme of closures, to withdraw the service between Princes Street and Kingsknowe stations as from 2nd December. They also announced, with significant implications for Princes Street station's future, that a new connecting line was to be constructed between Slateford and Haymarket to enable trains to and from Carstairs and the south to use Waverley rather than Princes Street as a terminus. The new line would follow the course of the 1853 Haymarket branch built by the Caley, by then just sidings; it became known as the Duff Street spur.

Even more closures were announced on 29th November, 1963. Services between Edinburgh and Glasgow Central were to be withdrawn on 2nd March, 1964, and Princes Street station was to close in April 1964. The end of the Glasgow service was also to entail the closure of Merchiston, Slateford and Midcalder stations.

Considerable opposition was aroused by the proposals. In December 1963 Edinburgh Corporation objected to the closures of Merchiston, Slateford and Kingsknowe stations; and in fact Slateford and Midcalder would eventually be reprieved in 1965, when the Minister of Transport refused to consent to their closure. Kingsknowe station was also to survive in the long run, though it did close in July 1964; it was however re-opened in 1971 after a local campaign.

But Princes Street station and Merchiston station were not to escape. They lost some services on 2nd March, 1964 when trains to and from Stirling, Oban, Perth, and Dundee were re-routed to Waverley. On 7th September, 1964 the new spur from Haymarket to Slateford came into operation, allowing trains to and from Carstairs and Glasgow Central to reach Waverley instead of Princes Street – and after that the end was just a matter of time: twelve months, in fact.

In the meantime the Balerno branch witnessed its last passenger excursion train on 19th April, 1965, when two preserved Caley coaches were conveyed to Balerno and back in the morning and again in the afternoon by 2–6–0 class 2 engine No. 78046. The trips were made as part of an 'Easter Rambler' tour of various lines, and in connection with that day's activities, enthusiasts were taken from Glasgow to Edinburgh and back in a train hauled by CR No. 123, making one of her last trips. She spent the day on shed at Dalry Road, while 78046 (an engine dating only from the mid-1950s, yet scrapped in the mid-1960s) and 78054 of the same class of 65 engines visited Balerno and Leith respectively.

On 2nd August, 1965 the oldest of the ex-Caley local lines in Edinburgh, the Granton branch, was partially closed, between Crewe Junction where the Leith branch diverged and Granton gas works. The gas works continued to be served thereafter from the east, via the old NB line and Granton Square crossing. Granton High goods station closed in 1968, but the line to the gas works was open until the late 1970s and a nearby siding until the early 1980s.

At Princes Street station the end came in the early hours of Sunday morning, 5th September, 1965. The last passenger departure, for Birmingham, was at 11.30 pm on 4th September, with two LMS 'Black Five' engines in charge, while the final arrival was a diesel-hauled service from Glasgow Central which drew in at 12.15 am. The gates shut behind the twenty or so passengers leaving the station to end seventy years of service by an elegant terminus which, with its two fore-runners, had provided the city of Edinburgh with important outlets to west, south and north.

The 90 employees at the station were given alternative work. On the same day Merchiston station also closed; and a month later Dalry Road engine shed (MPD 64C by then) closed in turn.

The theme was continued in 1966. On 15th August Morrison Street depot and the goods station at Lothian Road shut; Edinburgh–Lanark local services ended, resulting in the intermediate stations of Harburn, Cobbinshaw, Auchengray and Carnwath also closing. All except Cobbinshaw dated from the earliest days of the Caley in 1848.

The Balerno branch meantime continued to operate but its fate was effectively sealed in 1966 when Kinleith paper mill closed down. Although a service was maintained into 1967 the loss of the mill's valuable traffic, which had continued to give the railway a lifeline during the previous years, meant that there was no longer enough business in the district to support it.

Amid little publicity the branch was officially closed to all traffic from 4th December, 1967. These being days when goods-only lines were still disappearing ten-a-penny from the landscape, the pro-railway lobby in the Edinburgh area were more concerned with the prospective closure to both passengers and freight of the Corstorphine branch; their opposition was unavailing, and that line closed to passenger traffic on 30th December, 1967.

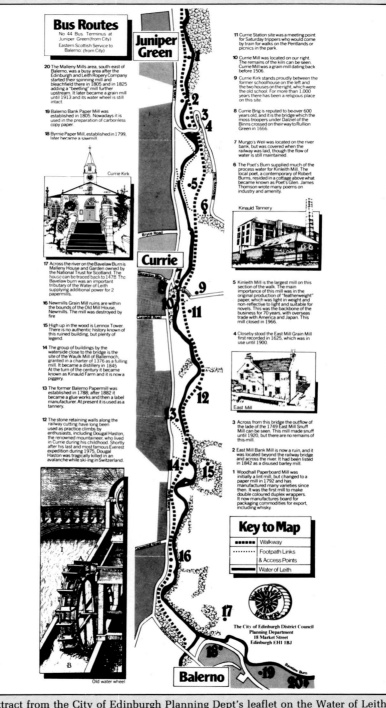

An extract from the City of Edinburgh Planning Dept's leaflet on the Water of Leith Walkway (Juniper Green to Balerno), showing how the old railway line still continues to be of benefit to the community, long after the last train ran.

Chapter Fifteen
From railway to walkway

The demise of the Balerno branch came at the end of a year in which the other surviving branch of the former Caley network around Edinburgh had also largely succumbed. All but the easternmost end of the Leith branch had closed, leaving Leith North station to be reached meantime from south Leith along the line opened by the Caley in 1903. And in 1968 Leith North station, along with that section of track, closed in its turn.

At the time, only one former Caley station, Slateford, remained open in the Edinburgh area where, in peak days, there had been 17 (as far west as Curriehill and Balerno) plus three halts. When Kingsknowe station re-opened in 1971 the total doubled! The old North British network had fared no better, with only the main line stations of Waverley and Haymarket surviving.

The track of the Balerno branch was lifted in 1968. Early that year it was proposed that the trackbed should be preserved and converted into a public footpath, and in May Midlothian County Council backed the suggestion, at least so far as their own Currie-Balerno section was concerned; for the council anticipated a large increase in the local population for whom such an amenity would be a great asset.

The track of the branch has since been incorporated into a walkway stretching from Balerno to Leith, give or take one or two unavoidable gaps, thanks to the efforts of the local councils, Manpower Services and the Walkway Trust.

The Balerno branch thus provides a source of recreation for an increasingly residential area where, during this time, more old mills have gone out of business. In 1967 Redhall mill in Colinton Dell, where woodflour for linoleum and other products had been produced since 1905 and where until then the ancient Colinton barley mill had stood, closed down, as did Spinks' bung mill at Balerno, which had made stoppers for the brewing industry.

When John Galloway and Co. Ltd of Balerno issued a booklet in 1968 to mark a £500,000 investment in new paper-making plant at their mill (and to pay tribute to John Galloway who had died in 1966 after building the mill up very successfully since buying it in 1924) they viewed the future of the local paper-making industry with great confidence. The new plant was "a symbolic act in the company's tradition of technological prowess, for it spans the present and reaches ahead into the future. The new building is a surety that paper-making will go on flourishing beside that mighty stream, the Water of Leith."

Within a short time, however, Galloway's had been taken over by a national producer, DRG (the Dickinson Robinson Group), who now employ the Balerno site as a finishing mill and wrapping plant, linked to a larger works at Markinch in Fife. Far fewer workers are now employed at Balerno. The two other paper mills surviving locally in the 1960s have closed completely: Mossy mill near Colinton, where Andrew Scott and Co. made board for the corrugated case industry, shut in 1972, while Woodhall mill at Juniper Green, where the Inveresk Paper Company and their successors GP Inveresk (part of the American company Georgia Pacific) produced board for cartons, closed in 1984.

With A. & R. Scott Ltd having closed their porridge oats mill in Colinton in 1971 only three of the once-numerous mills of the district are still open; as well as DRG Transcript in Balerno, J. Hewit and Son continue to make dressed light leather for bookbinding and other leather products, while Woodhall grain mill in Juniper Green is also open for grain-drying. On a brighter note, a firm of furniture-makers has taken over part of the old West Mills complex and is thriving.

Transport: the wheel turns full circle

Despite a dramatic increase in the population of the district bounded by Colinton to the east and Balerno to the west during the 1950s, 1960s and 1970s, local bus services scarcely changed in the same period. In fact in the mid-1970s the overall service was poorer than in the early 1950s because Eastern Scottish (formerly the SMT) had actually reduced frequencies on their Balerno–Colinton–Edinburgh route from 25 to 7 buses daily each way, without increasing the number of buses on the Balerno–Slateford–Edinburgh route (52 daily). Furthermore, in the late 1960s Edinburgh Corporation withdrew their No. 46 bus from Juniper Green.

Changes began to be made at last following regional re-organisation in 1975 when the Corporation started extending their buses beyond Juniper Green – particularly after Heriot-Watt University moved to Riccarton in 1976. In the late 1970s Eastern Scottish made the first amendments to their operations for many years, increasing frequencies and co-operating with Lothian Regional Transport to give a new bus service between Balerno, Heriot-Watt and Edinburgh via Calder Road.

In 1985 Balerno had 100 buses daily, of which 68 operated via the Slateford route, just two via the Colinton route, and 30 via the Calder Road route. Currie was served by even more buses (130 in all) thanks to the No. 45 route having been extended from Juniper Green.

Further changes at the end of 1986 followed the de-regulation of bus services with the No. 44 (ex-Corporation) route extending from Juniper Green to Balerno.

Yet, while the level of bus services has been stepped up, their efficiency has not, for in recent years road congestion caused by a growing volume of cars and lorries has become a major problem. In 1985 the fastest buses between Balerno, Currie and Edinburgh took 38 and 30 minutes respectively to cover a distance of some seven miles.

The wheel of progress turned full circle in early 1986 with the decision by British Rail and Lothian Regional Council to re-open the station at Curriehill, closed since 1951, as a halt in October 1987, as well as a new halt at Wester Hailes north of Juniper Green (where a vast housing estate has been built) which opened in May 1987.

With other new stations opening or re-opening around Edinburgh the true worth of rail travel is being seen. It can only be regretted that so few of Edinburgh's formerly numerous local railways are now available for re-opening; the capital has fared far worse than Glasgow in this respect.

Relics of the Balerno branch

Strolling along the track of an old railway can be a poignant experience. Since the last trains ran on the Balerno branch in 1967 there have, inevitably, been changes in the landscape, not all of which have enhanced it. But there is much to enjoy, and for those interested many evocative reminders of the days of the railway. Most obvious are the bridges and retaining walls and, of course, Colinton tunnel; but in fact virtually the whole length of the walkway consists of embankments and cuttings which can be easily overlooked as being the work of nature rather than the pick and shovel of industrious navvies.

Balerno Junction, the easternmost end of the line, is today overgrown with trees and shrubs. It is not easy to visualise any longer the four parallel tracks – two of the branch proper which then merged after 200 yards or so into a single line, and two junction sidings – which once filled up the ground between the Caley main line and the Union Canal.

Where the branch crossed the Lanark Road, the old bridge has been replaced by a high arched footbridge, a result of road widening in the 1970s. Beyond one can follow the track of the branch as it was all the way to Balerno. Passing between two small bridges – the first took the line under Redhall Bank Road, the second over the access lane to Boag's mill – one can see to the right Millbank, a handsome old house where Directors of the Bank of Scotland were entertained in other days while waiting for paper for their bank notes to be produced at the mill below.

Higher up the line in Colinton Dell is the old cobbled track running off on the left towards the river and Kates paper mill; the site of the double siding here is completely overgrown. Just beyond and on the right was Hailes Halt, the only clue to its location being the path which leads off to the Lanark Road nearby. Kingsknowe golf course club house is 100 yards up the road.

From this part of the walkway the views down to the Water of Leith are excellent. In winter, when the trees are bare, one can see the mill-lade which served Redhall mill and Kates mill – or more accurately the tail-race where the water surged down to rejoin the river. There are several paths leading down from the walkway to the riverside in this location.

On the approach to Colinton tunnel one passes the long retaining wall (on the right) built in 1934–35 after a landslip. The mouth of the tunnel is a place to stop and ponder the sheerness of the hillside – the river far below, the track rising at 1 in 50 – and admire the skill and effort involved in gouging a railway out of such terrain. Inside the tunnel the atmosphere is rather moist and gloomy, with part of the left wall adorned by a painting of a Caledonian engine, placed there by some pining enthusiast.

One emerges from the tunnel at the site of Colinton station, of which no trace remains. However the road bridge up ahead is a reminder of the branch in that it was funded by £1500 of Caledonian Railway money (it has since been widened); and, out of sight high above the western tunnel mouth, still stands the little station master's cottage. The connecting steps known as Jacob's Ladder have disappeared, but elsewhere in Colinton village other pathways built in connection with the railway remain, such as The Twirlies which lead down from Woodhall Road to Bridge Road.

Along the walkway beyond the road bridge the station sidings formerly diverged to the right, running back into the station under the two north-ernmost arches of the bridge. Further on the paper mill (and later oat mill) siding ran off to the left; the large building erected here by A. & R. Scott Ltd straddled the siding, with trains passing right through it.

The walkway then crosses the Water of Leith for the first time, over a bridge converted to carry traffic to and from Scott's building – now the offices of the Forth River Purification Board. Running along the south bank of the river for a quarter of a mile, the track then re-crosses it by Upper Spylaw over an elegant bridge, seen to best effect from the road to Mossy mill. A rare straight section is followed by a curve to the left – in imitation of the river – where a striking sight appears ahead.

This is a modern bridge carrying the Edinburgh city by-pass over the river; the road continues north by burrowing under the Lanark Road. What was once one of the more secluded spots on the line has inevitably been over-shadowed by the building of this structure, but it has at least brought peace back to Colinton. One can only wonder what Henry Cockburn would have made of a road thus cutting directly in front of his beloved Bonaly Tower.

Passing Inglis' mill the track hugs the winding river-bank; the retaining walls supporting it are an impressive sight from the south bank of the river. A little way on was Juniper Green station, now marked only by the winding brae which linked it to Lanark Road. The former dispatch shed of Woodhall paper mill stands where the station used to be. Beyond, the track squeezes between a steep bank to the right and the site of the paper mill, now demolished, to the left.

On the bridge which carries the walkway back over to the south bank the old rail timbers are still preserved. No trace remains of the snuff mill which stood so long here, just as at Juniper Green both Watt's snuff mill and Wright's meal mill have vanished.

The track passes on under a bridge which carries the road to the little village of Blinkbonny, built largely for the workers of Kinleith paper mill and of Torphin quarry. The sprawling remains of the mill now provide workshops for small firms but many of the buildings have fallen into ruin. The rails of the complex of mill sidings are still there, so that one can see just how far they penetrated.

The walkway now continues up the long embankment leading to Currie station, where the goods shed still stands, as does much of the station fencing. But trees have obscured the open view across to the village.

Between Currie and Balerno are the retaining walls and bridge on which Dougal Haston, later to be an Everest mountaineer, first practised climbing in the 1950s as a boy.

Of the short siding beyond the fourth and last bridge over the Water of Leith no trace remains. The leather works of Hewit and Son is above to the right. Further along was the distant signal for trains nearing Balerno station; it served as a local point of reference too. The track then crosses the former lade of Newmills mill and, keeping close to the river, skirts Newmills House, immediately beyond which was the goods junction. But modern alterations to the Lanark Road just above have obscured the site of the junction and of the signal box. Off to the left was the goods yard, today the site of a new secondary school for the children of Balerno.

Those road alterations have had the effect of restoring the Lanark Road to the route it followed before 1874, when the needs of the railway caused it to be diverted north. One can cross the road to a private parking area and look over the parapet of the bridge under which branch trains emerged to end their journeys at Balerno station. An attractive garden is now laid out over the course of the track. The station master's and porter's house is along to the left, now used as the office of a firm of chartered surveyors.

The Ravelrig section of the branch is the only part that cannot be walked along without difficulty. There is a narrow path halfway along, which peters out after a time. Approaching Ravelrig Junction the line of the railway becomes obscured by a wood of birches in the midst of which two old loading banks indicate where the quarry tramway abutted on the branch. The tramways themselves have long been pleasant grassy paths but the resumption of quarrying here will soon obliterate them, apart from the easternmost track which led up to Hannahfield quarry (which is to remain disused).

The trains which travelled between Balerno and Edinburgh also ran, of course, along the main line east of Balerno Junction. This is still open from there to Slateford Junction. Further east near Merchiston station the track-bed has become a private roadway giving access to Slateford marshalling yard; while a large part of the line, from Dundee Street to Lothian Road, has been converted to form the Western Approach Road. One can now admire from one's car the mighty archway under Morrison Street and Gardner's Crescent that proved so difficult to construct in 1847.

In retrospect

The Balerno branch, despite its proximity to the city of Edinburgh, en-capsulated all that is best and most appealing about a rural railway. Its trains meandered along discreetly through a sylvan landscape, tucked away in Colinton Dell or half-hidden from view by the riverside in Juniper Green, Currie or Balerno.

Colinton Dell was already a special place before the railway came – a "lost valley" just three miles from the centre of Edinburgh. But it surely gained extra charm by playing host to the Balerno branch, a quaint and unobtrusive guest. Perhaps the Colinton heritors of 1864, worried by the noise and smoke of engines in the narrow valley, would have disagreed! Yet it is surprising how little a railway damages the landscape through which it passes.

Further along the line was the contrasting setting where river and railway ran side by side through a narrow defile between fields rolling down from the Pentlands and on the north the ridge carrying the Lanark Road.

The charm of the railway was enhanced along the way by the many water-driven grain mills and snuff mills – indeed virtually the first build-ings to greet the eye of passengers embarking on a journey from either end of the line were Newmills mill at Balerno and Boag's mill by Redhall – while the paper mills were bustling and impressive centres of industry without which the railway would never have been built.

But it was the Pentland hills, perhaps more than any other feature, which gave the branch its character. The rolling slopes to the south of the line all the way from Colinton to Balerno are a constant reminder of the airy heights above – to be sensed even when not seen. For many passengers the Balerno branch was the road to the hills, a way of getting access to some lovely countryside. And after all it is to the hills that the companion of the railway and now the walkway – the Water of Leith – owes its existence.

The Balerno railway operated through a fascinating period of history. When it opened in 1874 the Ashanti War in West Africa was in the news: a war of empire fought partly with spears. Major Francis Scott of Malleny House was involved in it and was promoted to Lieutenant-Colonel in that year. Two generations on, World War I took a heavy toll of local lives between 1914 and 1918; during the war a number of troop trains left from stations on the Balerno branch. And when the line closed to passengers in 1943 another generation again were involved in fighting a war – one which ended with an atomic bomb.

When the branch opened most local people were employed in the district, chiefly in paper-making, agriculture and domestic service; in those days Lady Dunfermline, the owner of Colinton House, had no fewer than fifteen domestic servants – and they were only the indoors staff! When the railway closed an influx of middle class city commuters with their families had not only swollen the population but altered the social pattern of the district. Their properties had also altered the look of the land; in 1926 the Reverend Marjoribanks of Colinton wrote in the introduction to *Colinton Old and New*:

> Colinton has suffered many changes during the last few years, and is likely to suffer more. Bit by bit the picturesque country village is being transformed into a prosaic 'residential suburb'; slowly but surely are cornfields and pastures giving place to villas and bungalows. One turns with relief to the Pentland Hills and the precipitous banks of the Water of Leith – sanctuaries too steep for the builder to invade.

One wonders what that writer – and even more so the inhabitants of a century ago – would make of today's enlarged community where all four villages run into each other!

In a changing world it is always welcome when some things stay the same and give a sense of continuity. That was part of the appeal of a local railway, which for successive generations came to be a fixture and an integral part of everyday life. Changes might occur, but not often, and when they did they were only minor; after all the scope for change was limited.

Branch railways in fact could be curiously resistant to change. For example the old Caley gas mantles were still in place at Colinton station in the 1960s.

While the appearance in 1899 and again in the 1930s of new engines gave the Balerno branch trains a new look – as did the introduction of Pickersgill's coaches in 1920 – and the gleaming blue of the Caley gave way to LMS red and then black, these were only details to the average passenger. The railway remained the railway.

It was inevitable that passenger services must one day end; yet even after that the branch goods service continued to offer the community the beguiling spectacle of a railway at work, with several mills still reliant on it and a considerable number of men employed on it.

All good things, however, come to an end; suddenly the line was gone and with it a real part of the local heritage. It is fortunate that the foresight of certain people has seen to it that with the railway's demise a new heritage has been created in the form of the walkway, along which a pleasant – if poignant – outing can now be enjoyed in agreeable scenery. The walkway is a suitable memorial to what was in its day not just an efficient and important means of communication but a well-loved institution which, with its charm and character, enhanced the life of the community it served: the Balerno branch railway.

Acknowledgements

For their great help I would like to thank Messrs Barbour, Vasey and Longmore of the Scottish Record Office, the staff of the Edinburgh Room in Central Library, Edinburgh, Mr Nicholson of the Mitchell Library, Glasgow, Mr McMutrie of Blyth and Blyth Partnerships, 135 George Street, Edinburgh (who allowed me to study the original plans and specifications for the Balerno branch), Mr Bunnage of French Kier Construction Ltd, Sandy, Bedfordshire (who sent me papers relating to the contractors Charles Brand and Son), and Mr G. Brown of ScotRail for permission to see and quote from the 1958 report.

Messrs W.S. Sellar, J.L. Stevenson, A.W. Brotchie, W.A.C. Smith, W.E. Boyd, N.R. Ferguson, R. Hamilton, D.L.G. Hunter, D. Stirling, D. Burton and E. Wilson kindly provided me with photos and information, as did the secretaries of Kingsknowe and Torphin Hill golf clubs, H.H. Hoddinott and W.B. Smith. Alan Smaill kindly checked the script. Mr W.D. Stewart kindly allowed the reproduction of his engine drawings.

For permission to quote extracts from books I thank Cork University Press (J.E. Handley: *The Navvy in Scotland*).

Further photos and illustrations were provided by the Royal Commission on the Ancient and Historical Monuments of Scotland; Lens of Sutton; the Historical Model Railway Society; British Rail (Trainlines of Britain); and the Boyd and Mowat Collections. May I particularly thank Mrs Molly Tweedie of Currie for her helpfulness and for allowing me to use material belonging to the late Mr John Tweedie, who did more than anyone to record and preserve the history of the district. As a grandson of the railway I feel he must have been the best person to write the story of the Balerno branch had he chosen to do so. My own account is of necessity mostly factual and second-hand, as I came on the railway much later.

Finally, my thanks to Mr A.J.C. Clark for providing maps and illustrations.

Sources

As the Balerno branch was not an independent line but merely a small part of the Caledonian Railway, it was necessary to delve into the minute books of the company for much of the information about the branch. Many references were frustratingly cryptic. Further details were gleaned from capital accounts, timetables, traffic returns and various other assorted company papers. Unfortunately not as much Caley material has survived as for other railway companies like the North British.

Other material consulted at the Scottish Record Office included the minutes of the LMS Scottish Committee between 1923 and 1943, which unfortunately contain no details of the exact "whys" and "wherefores" of the decision to close the Balerno branch to passenger traffic in 1943; also the papers of A.G. Dunbar (very helpful on engine matters); MOT accident reports; the Langwill papers; the minutes of Colinton Heritors and Kirk Session and of Currie Kirk Session and Parochial Board; minutes of the Midlothian and Slateford Turnpike Trusts; Union Canal minutes; Parliamentary proceedings minutes and Acts; and records of Kates, Balerno and Balerno Bank paper mills.

The records of Kinleith paper mill were consulted at the National Library of Scotland. Board of Trade reports on the Balerno branch were checked at the Public Record Office in London.

Details about engines were drawn from J.F. McEwan's series of articles in *The Locomotive* 1941–1948, from E.L. Ahrons' articles in the same magazine in 1917, from A.B. MacLeod's *The McIntosh Locomotives of the Caley* and from Dr H.J.C. Cornwell's *40 Years of Caledonian Locomotives*.

Newspapers, particularly *The Scotsman*, provided much information.

The following books were consulted:

John Geddie: *The Water of Leith from Source to Sea*
J.E. Handley: *The Navvy in Scotland*
John Tweedie: *Currie in Old Picture Postcards* and *Our Parish*
W.B. Robertson and others: *Portrait of a Parish*
James Hay: *The Call of the Mill*
Jean Lindsay: *The Canals of Scotland*
Duncan McAra: *The Romantic Rationalist* (re James Gowans)
Colinton Tramways inquiry proceedings (held at Central Library, Edinburgh)
Duncan Kennedy: *The Birth and Death of a Highland Railway*
B.H. Blyth's address to the Institute of Civil Engineers, 1914
Robert Louis Stevenson: *Memories and Portraits*
Henry Cockburn: *Journals* and *Circuit Journeys*
The Old and New Statistical Accounts of Scotland.

Chronology

15th February, 1848: Caledonian Railway opened to Edinburgh. Stations at Lothian Road, Kingsknowe, Currie, Midcalder and points west.

January 1853: Slateford station opened.

24th May, 1853: accident at Slateford.

11th November, 1856: second accident at Slateford.

29th August, 1861: Caley branch to Granton opened; goods-only.

1st September, 1864: Leith branch opened; goods-only until 1879.

16th September, 1864: Caley Board to meet deputation proposing a Balerno branch.

6th October, 1864: Balerno branch approved.

29th June, 1865: Balerno branch Act duly passed. The line to terminate by Balerno bridge.

26th July, 1869: Balerno branch Abandonment Act passed – but specifying that a railway must still be made!

2nd May, 1870: a new Edinburgh terminus opened, at Princes Street.

20th June, 1870: Balerno branch re-authorised. This time a link between Balerno and Ravelrig is included in the plan (approved 12.10.1869).

1st August, 1874: BALERNO BRANCH OPENED.

June 1875: Kinleith paper mill siding opened.

4th April, 1877: passenger train derailed near Currie.

March 1879: Kates paper mill siding opened.

1st July, 1879: Leith branch opened to passenger traffic.

24th April, 1880: accident at Ravelrig Junction involving branch train.

1st July, 1882: Merchiston station opened.

4th April, 1884: Ravelrig platform opened.

July/August 1888: railway races to Edinburgh.

January 1889: Balerno branch converted to tablet operation.

January 1889: Colinton paper mill siding opened.

1890: Kates mill siding closed after mill burnt down.

1st May, 1890: temporary Exhibition station opened at Slateford.

16th June, 1890: Princes Street station badly damaged by fire.

1894: new Princes Street station opened.

1st March, 1894: Barnton branch opened.

1899: Balerno engine loop built – allowing engines to run-round their trains at the station rather than run on to Ravelrig Junction to turn.

1899: "Balerno Pug" tank engines built – twelve in all – for the Balerno branch and the Cathcart Circle.

December 1903: Caledonian Hotel opened.

1904: Kinauld glue works siding opened.

16th November, 1908: Hailes Platform opened.

March 1913: first Sunday trains ran on Balerno branch.

1920: a set of 39 carriages specially constructed for the Balerno branch.

4th September, 1920: first motor-bus service provided to Colinton. Later extended to Juniper Green.

15th July, 1922: first motor-buses ran to Currie and Balerno.

1st January, 1923: the London Midland and Scottish Railway came into being. The Caley was not absorbed into the LMS until 1st July, 1923.

1924: "Balerno Pugs" re-painted LMS red.

1928: "Balerno Pugs" re-painted again, this time unlined black.

1929: end of requirement that only four-wheeled carriages operate on Balerno line.

1934: Balerno signal box closed.

1934–1937: the Edinburgh-based "Balerno Pugs" withdrawn, replaced on the Balerno branch mostly by the standard passenger tanks.

September 1937: the last Sunday service operated on the Balerno branch.

11th September, 1939: emergency wartime timetable enforced; branch services cut.

15th October, 1943: end of passenger services on Balerno branch announced.

30th October, 1943: the last passenger train ran; closure of Hailes Halt.

9th November, 1943: Currie signal box officially closed.

1st January, 1948: the LMS succeeded by British Railways.

23rd February, 1950: fatal accident involving Balerno branch train at Union Canal.

31st March, 1951: Curriehill station closed.

7th May, 1951: Barnton branch closed to passenger traffic; goods still handled as far as Davidson's Mains.

11th August, 1958: Juniper Green station closed.

31st May, 1960: closure of remaining section of Barnton branch to goods traffic.

18th December, 1960: Balerno Junction signal box closed.

28th April, 1962: the Leith branch – last of the old local Caley lines – closed to passenger traffic.

9th September, 1963: official closure of Ravelrig section of Balerno branch.

9th March, 1964: Wester Dalry branch closed (linking Princes Street station to the main Edinburgh–Glasgow line); also Dalry Middle Junction to Coltfield Junction section.

6th July, 1964: Kingsknowe station closed.

7th September, 1964: opening of the Duff Street spur, enabling trains to run between Slateford and Haymarket and by-pass Princes Street station.

2nd August, 1965: much of the Granton branch closed (the northern part remained open).

5th September, 1965: Princes Street station and Merchiston station closed.

18th April, 1966: end of Edinburgh–Lanark service; closure of Harburn, Cobbinshaw, Auchengray and Carnwath stations.

4th September, 1967: most of the Leith branch closed; Leith North station remained open, but reached now only from south Leith via the 1903 line.

4th December, 1967: FINAL CLOSURE OF THE BALERNO BRANCH.

5th August, 1968: Leith North station closed.

1st February, 1971: re-opening of Kingsknowe station.

11th May, 1987: new halt at Wester Hailes (north of Juniper Green) opened.

5th October, 1987: new halt at Curriehill opened.

Tables

TABLE OF MILEAGES

(1 mile = 80 chains)

Princes Street–Merchiston:	1m. 11 ch.
Merchiston–Slateford:	0m. 79 ch.
Slateford–Colinton:	1m. 40 ch.
(Slateford–Balerno Junction)	(0m. 15ch.)
(Balerno Junction–Colinton)	(1m. 25ch.)
Colinton–Juniper Green:	1m. 07ch.
Juniper Green–Currie:	1m. 18ch.
Currie–Balerno:	1m. 14ch.

Total, Princes Street–Balerno:	7m. 09ch.	(includes 4m. 64ch. on branch)

Balerno–Ravelrig Junction:	1m. 18ch.

Total, BALERNO LOOP-LINE:	6m. 02ch.

Ravelrig Junction–Midcalder:	2m. 60ch.

Total, Princes Street–Midcalder:	11m. 07ch.	*

*From Princes Street to Midcalder via the MAIN LINE was a distance of 10m. 05ch., just over one mile less than via the Balerno branch.

HOW THE SERVICE IMPROVED

(A comparison of fares and frequencies) (3rd class single/return)

	COLINTON	JUNIPER GREEN	CURRIE	BALERNO	No. of Up/Down trains	Sundays
July 1876	3½d/6d	4½d/8d	6d/10d	7d/1/-	5/5	0
July 1886	3½d/6d	4½d/8d	6d/9d	7d/1/-	8/8	0
July 1896	3½d/6d	4½d/8d	6d/9d	7d/1/-	12/11	0
July 1906	3d/5d	4d/7d	5d/8d	6d/10d	15/14	0
July 1916	3d/5d	4d/7d	5d/8d	6d/10d	17/16	5
July 1926	4½d/9d	6d/1/-	7½d/1/2d	9d/1/5½d	(16/15)*	(7)*
July 1936	2d/4d	3d/6d	4d/8d	5d/9d	21/20	9**
Oct. 1943	2½d/5d	3½d/7d	4d/8d	5d/9½d	12/12	0

Notes
*Services scheduled but curtailed by general strike.
**Summer only.

Index

Ex-Caley standard passenger tank LMS No. 15210, with a train composed of Pickersgill 4-wheelers. The 4.50 pm (ex-Princes Street) seen here at Colinton station on the 30th October, 1943 (the last day of operation of the Balerno Branch).

D.L.G. Hunter